SCENE-BY-SCENE BLUEPRINT

IDENTIFY THE CENTRAL THEME THAT DRIVES YOUR PLOT

HEROES, VILLAINS, AND SUPPORTING CHARACTERS

POINT OF VIEW

THE POWER OF THEME

WINNING READERS' HEARTS

THREE ACTS

SUPERCHARGE YOUR SCENES WITH THEMATIC REVERSALS

PLOT VS. ORGANIZING PRINCIPLE

PLOT PERFECT

HOW TO BUILD
UNFORGETTABLE
STORIES SCENE
BY SCENE

VARIATIONS

LAYERS

TWISTS AND TURNS

FIND YOUR USP

PAULA MUNIER

THE TAPESTRY OF STORY

CATALYST

WEAVE PLOT AND SUBPLOT

BUILD STRONG ARCS FOR YOUR MAIN CHARACTERS

PACING

ACTION IS CHARACTER

PLUS AND MINUS SCENES

WD

WRITER'S DIGEST
BOOKS

WritersDigest.com
Cincinnati, Ohio

For more resources for writers, visit www.writersdigest.com.

18 17 16 15 14 5 4 3 2 1

Distributed in Canada by Fraser Direct
100 Armstrong Avenue
Georgetown, Ontario, Canada L7G 5S4
Tel: (905) 877-4411

Distributed in the U.K. and Europe by F&W Media International
Brunel House, Newton Abbot, Devon, TQ12 4PU, England
Tel: (+44) 1626-323200, Fax: (+44) 1626-323319
E-mail: postmaster@davidandcharles.co.uk

Distributed in Australia by Capricorn Link
P.O. Box 704, Windsor, NSW 2756 Australia
Tel: (02) 4577-3555

ISBN-13: 978-1-59963-814-0

Edited by Rachel Randall
Designed by Bethany Rainbolt
Production coordinated by Debbie Thomas

DEDICATION

For my dear Scribe Tribe,
and plotters everywhere.

ACKNOWLEDGMENTS

First, let me thank my dear fellow writer and colleague, Phil Sexton, publisher of Writer's Digest and all-around swell guy, who encouraged me to write this book. And to all my friends at Writer's Digest, including my editor, Rachel Randall, Alex Rixey, Chuck Sambuchino, Kevin Quinn, Aaron Bauer, and Julie Oblander.

I must also thank all of my sister agents at Talcott Notch Literary, including Jessica Negron, Rachael Dugas, and our fearless leader, Gina Panettieri. Thanks to Scribe Tribers Susan Reynolds, Meera Lester, John Waters, Indi Zeleny, and Mardeene Mitchell, who read the manuscript as I wrote it and offered invaluable advice and support. And a shout-out to the wonderful authors whose plots inspire me every day: not only all of my terrific clients, but also my pals Hank Phillippi Ryan, Hallie Ephron, Jane Cleland, Margaret McLean, Steve Ulfelder, and all of my friends at MWA, SinC, RWA, and SCBAI.

And a final heartfelt thanks to all the writers who've shared their time and work with me over the years. Someone once said that storytelling isn't rocket science—it is more important than that. You are the storytellers the world needs.

ABOUT THE AUTHOR

 Paula Munier, Senior Literary Agent and Content Strategist at Talcott Notch Literary Services, boasts broad experience creating and marketing exceptional content in all formats across all markets for such media giants as WGBH, Disney, Fidelity, Gannett, Greenspun Media Group, F+W Media, and Quayside. She began her career as a journalist, and along the way she added editor, acquisitions specialist, digital content manager, and publishing executive to her repertoire. Her specialties include mystery/thriller, SF/fantasy, romance, YA, memoir, humor, pop culture, health and wellness, cooking, self-help, pop psych, New Age, inspirational, technology, science, and writing. Paula is very involved with the mystery community, having served four terms as President of the New England chapter of Mystery Writers of America as well as on the MWA board. (She's currently vice president of that organization.)

Paula has also served as both co-chair and Agents and Editors chair on the New England Crime Bake committee for seven years and counting, and she's an active member of Sisters in Crime. A well-published journalist, author, copywriter, and ghostwriter, Paula has penned countless news stories, articles, essays, collateral, and blogs, and has authored or co-authored more than a dozen books, including *Fixing Freddie*, *5-Minute Mindfulness*, and *A Miscellany of Murder*.

TABLE OF CONTENTS

INTRODUCTION

This is narrative: The king died, and then the queen died.

This is plot: The king died—and then the queen died of grief.

This definition of plot comes from the great E.M. Forster, author of *A Passage to India, Room with a View, Howards End*, and many other wonderful novels whose plots were as rich in theme as they were in twists and turns. The way he wove theme through his stories gave his work a dimension and depth that earned him a place on bestseller lists, in the ranks of English literature, and—most important—in readers' hearts.

Just like Forster, you want your stories to be page-turners with dimension and depth that earn a place in the world of literature and in readers' hearts. As a writer, I know how hard it can be to create great thematic storylines. But as an editor and a writing teacher, I also know that you can learn to create compelling plots with themes that resonate with readers. And as an agent, I know that what makes the difference between a sale and no sale is often theme.

In a time when more and more stories read like video games, theme is often given short shrift—if it's given any thought at all. Now, as in Forster's time, the most successful stories are the ones with multilayered plots rich in theme, character, and nuance. These are the stories that stand out—and find a devoted readership. In this book, you'll learn how to devise such a compelling plot.

I've based my system on the one I developed for my online course for Writer's Digest, the Plot Perfect Boot Camp. It's a plotting system that anyone can use to create a story structure that works—no matter what your genre. Whether you're writing a novel, short story, memoir, stage play, or screenplay, you'll learn the strategies you need to build your own scene-by-scene blueprint in record time, including how to:

- identify the central theme that drives your plot
- devise powerful master plots and subplots based on theme and variations on theme
- build strong character arcs for your main characters
- develop engaging secondary characters to drive your subplots
- brainstorm scenes to bring your theme-driven plot to life
- supercharge your scenes with thematic reversals
- create a scene list for maximum impact
- use dialogue, setting, tone, and voice to enhance your plot
- learn tips and tricks to speed up your pacing

I designed *Plot Perfect* as an interactive plotting primer, with templates you can use to help you identify your themes and variations on themes, structure your plot and subplots, and build out your plot scene by scene. Please take the time to complete the templates and do the exercises. They are the tools you need to create the kind of story guaranteed to keep readers turning the pages. And don't forget to reward yourself with the fun activities sprinkled throughout the book. These "edutainment breaks" are designed to be fun, sure, but they will also give your writer's brain a creativity boost. Finally, you'll find suggested reading lists in every chapter; these are books that have proven invaluable to me and remain on my bookshelf today, ready to inspire me again, as I hope they might inspire you.

Let's get started.

PART I

WHAT IS PLOT?

"Throughout the ages, stories with certain basic themes have recurred over and over, in widely disparate cultures; emerging like the goddess Venus from the sea of our unconscious."

—Joan D. Vinge

CHAPTER ONE
THE POWER OF THEME

> *"Get your character in trouble in the first sentence and out of trouble in the last sentence."*
>
> —Barthe DeClements

THE THEME'S THE THING!

Whether we're talking about *A Passage to India* or *Gone Girl*, *The Perks of Being a Wallflower* or *Unbroken*, a great story embodies a great theme. Every work has a theme; in other words, what the story is really about, and what the writer is trying to say in writing it. (That's why scholars can spend hundreds of years debating a writer's themes!)

Theme-driven plots are the ones that resonate most with readers—because they strike close to home. Themes run the gamut of human emotion and experience, and are as numerous as the stories they appear in. Here are just a few.

- love
- power
- sex
- loyalty
- truth
- revenge
- family
- courage
- resiliency
- sacrifice
- greed
- friendship
- self-actualization
- coming of age
- man's relationship to God
- man's relationship to nature
- man's relationship to technology
- and many more!

In this chapter, you'll learn how to recognize the themes in your work and create theme statements that (1) resonate with readers and (2) are unique enough to stand out in a tough marketplace. You'll use your theme statements to create plots that are fresh and meaningful as well as clever and commercial.

> *"All stories interest me, and some haunt me until I end up writing them. Certain themes keep coming up: justice, loyalty, violence, death, political and social issues, freedom."*
>
> —Isabel Allende

FIND YOUR THEME

Theme is not nearly as complicated as you may have been led to believe in your high school or college English classes. Theme is simply what your story is really all about.

Is it a love story (*One Day*)?

Or a story about revenge (*Death Wish*)?

Or a story about love and revenge (*Wuthering Heights*)?

If you're not sure, ask yourself what motivates your protagonist. Is it jealousy or magnanimity? Greed or generosity? The search for truth or a desire to see justice done?

If you're not sure what your themes are, look to other stories in your genre for hints. If it's a romance, your themes will be related to romance—true love, soul mates, broken hearts. If you're writing erotica, the themes will revolve around the nature of lust, domination, submission, and so on. Crime stories explore the nature of good and evil; science fiction often examines man's relationship to technology. Examine the themes of your favorite stories in the genre in which you're writing, and you'll often find that those same themes can be applied to your story—or can at least suggest related themes that may be a better fit or that fuel your brainstorming efforts.

THEME BY TITLE

Sometimes the themes are right there in the title.

- *Wicked* by Gregory Maguire
- *Eat Pray Love* by Elizabeth Gilbert
- *Pride and Prejudice* by Jane Austen
- *War and Peace* by Leo Tolstoy
- *Fear of Flying* by Erica Jong
- *Heart of Darkness* by Joseph Conrad

The Thematic Power of Proverbs

Themes in stories are, in effect, the themes of our lives. That's why proverbs, sayings, and common phrases often embody theme.

These adages also provide a point of view—that is, they say something about the theme that reveals a particular attitude about that theme. You can use these various points of view to good advantage in your plotting.

Here are some common proverbs that speak to theme.

- "Beauty is in the eye of the beholder."
- "Honesty is the best policy."
- "Two wrongs don't make a right."
- "Curiosity killed the cat."
- "You reap what you sow."
- "Love is blind."
- "Birds of a feather flock together."
- "When you lie down with dogs, you will get up with fleas."
- "All that glitters is not gold."

When it comes to theme, proverbs are a great resource. Think of the proverbs that might apply to your story. Not only can proverbs help you identify your themes, they can help you pinpoint particular nuances of the larger themes—such as love or evil or power.

Let's say that you know your story is about power. Well, that's a pretty broad term covering a lot of ground. There are many kinds and aspects and levels of power, good, bad, and otherwise. Try to nail it down to a more specific type of power. You can use proverbs to help you do this.

For example, two of the most successful novels on the bestseller list today are *A Game of Thrones* and *The Hunger Games*. Both stories are about the game of power—and each names the game in its title. That said, each explores different aspects of power. We can look at these different aspects of power in terms of the proverbs that apply to the plots of each story.

A GAME OF THRONES

A Game of Thrones is all about power: How you get it, how you keep it, how it changes you and those you wield power over. The series explores themes of power, including:

- "Might is right."

- "Live by the sword, die by the sword."
- "Power corrupts; absolute power corrupts absolutely."

THE HUNGER GAMES

The Hunger Games is all about power, too. The power themes explored here are more about government control, Big Brother, and independence (personal power):

- "Never trust the Man."
- "Big Brother is watching you."
- "Live free or die."

WRITER AT WORK

Make a list of the proverbs, quotes, and sayings that may apply to the themes of your work. Here are a few to get you started:

- **LOVE:** "It takes two to tango."
- **TRUTH:** "Dying men speak true."
- **FORGIVENESS:** "Let bygones be bygones."
- **CORRUPTION:** "One bad apple can spoil the whole bunch."
- **FAMILY:** "Blood is thicker than water."
- **DEATH:** "Let the dead bury the dead."
- **REVENGE:** "Revenge is best served cold."
- **COURAGE:** "Fortune favors the bold."
- **WAR:** "The best defense is a good offense."
- **FRIENDSHIP:** "A friend in need is a friend indeed."
- **CRIME:** "Crime does not pay."
- **MONEY:** "Money talks."
- **SELF-ACTUALIZATION:** "To thine own self be true."
- **LIFE:** "It's not how long, but how well we live."

STATE YOUR THEME(S)

The more complex your story, the more themes you may have. Once you figure out what your themes are, you can use them to engage your reader. Themes speak to the universal; they address the human condition. The best writers know this—and milk it, starting from page 1. Put a fresh face on a classic theme—and in so doing, you can create a classic of your own.

WRITER AT PLAY

Most writers find that certain themes appear and reappear in their work. If you aren't sure what your themes are, try this brainstorming exercise. Using the bubble chart below as your guide, pick a bubble— say, "Things You Love"—and make a list of things you love. Do this quickly—don't think about it too much. When you're finished, think about the themes that have surfaced during this exercise. These are your preoccupations, the themes of your life—and you can use them in your work. You can do this with every bubble on the chart—and learn a lot about yourself and your themes in the process!

NOTE: You can also do this with your writer's group as a group activity.

> *"I think artists in general make a statement—and for the rest of their lives—every album, every book—are variations on a theme."*
>
> —Mark Mothersbaugh

POSITION YOUR THEME

There's an old journalism saying about structure that goes:

1. Tell 'em what you're going to tell 'em.
2. Tell 'em.
3. Tell 'em what you've told 'em.

The best writers do something like this with theme in their novels. In many of our favorite stories, the authors "tell 'em" what their themes are in the very first lines.

"Be careful what you wish for." (from Alice Hoffman's *The Ice Queen*)

"Happy families are all alike; every unhappy family is unhappy in its own way." (from Leo Tolstoy's *Anna Karenina*)

"People do not give it credence that a fourteen-year-old girl could leave home and go off in the wintertime to avenge her father's blood but it did not seem so strange then, although I will say that it did not happen every day." (from Charles Portis's *True Grit*)

"It was the best of times, it was the worst of times, it was the age of wisdom, it was the age of foolishness, it was the epoch of belief, it was the epoch of incredulity, it was the season of Light, it was the season of Darkness, it was the spring of hope, it was the winter of despair." (from Charles Dickens's *A Tale of Two Cities*)

"Once upon a time, there was a woman who discovered she had turned into the wrong person." (from Anne Tyler's *Back When We Were Grownups*)

"The past is a foreign country; they do things differently there."
(from L.P. Hartley's *The Go-Between*)

"Justice?—You get justice in the next world, in this world you
have the law." (from William Gaddis's *A Frolic of His Own*)

By stating your theme right at the beginning, you tell your readers—
and remind yourself—what your story is really about.

Other writers write their last lines first. This last line is often
an embodiment of theme. Then these writers write their stories—
always aiming for that last line. Doing so keeps them focused and
on track.

John Irving is famous for this. He insists that he can't begin the
process of telling a story until he knows the ending and can write the
last sentence—which is probably why his last sentences are so splendid.

> *"I can't imagine what the first sentence is, I can't imagine
> where I want the reader to enter the story, if I don't know
> where the reader is going to leave the story. So once I know
> what the last thing the reader hears is, I can work my way
> backward, like following a road map in reverse."*
>
> —John Irving

And he's not alone. Look at the theme-related last lines of some of the
best novels ever written.

"In the world according to Garp, we are all terminal cases." (from
John Irving's *The World According to Garp*)

"So we beat on, boats against the current, borne back ceaselessly
into the past." (from F. Scott Fitzgerald's *The Great Gatsby*)

"For everything to be consummated, for me to feel less alone, I
had only to wish that there be a large crowd of spectators the
day of my execution and that they greet me with cries of hate."
(from Albert Camus's *The Stranger*)

"It is a far, far better thing that I do, than I have ever done; it is
a far, far better rest that I go to than I have ever known." (from
Charles Dickens's *A Tale of Two Cities*)

"I never saw any of them again—except the cops. No way has yet been invented to say goodbye to them." (from Raymond Chandler's *The Long Goodbye*)

"He loved Big Brother." (from George Orwell's *Nineteen Eighty-Four*)

"Tomorrow, I'll think of some way to get him back. After all, tomorrow is another day." (from Margaret Mitchell's *Gone with the Wind*)

You can do the same thing as you think about your plot, using thematic first lines and last lines to create your own structure.

- **FIRST LINE:** Tell 'em what you're going to tell 'em.
- **BODY OF THE STORY:** Tell 'em.
- **LAST LINE:** Tell 'em what you've told 'em.

How might your first and last lines serve your plot? How might they reflect your theme? How might you set up your plot with your first line and then clinch it with your last line?

WRITER AT WORK

Try writing your first and last lines now, whether you've finished your story or not, and make sure they embody your theme.

In creating first and last lines that speak to theme, these writers have gone a long way toward defining the parameters of their stories. They've rewritten the proverbs, sayings, or quotes that embody their themes within the context of their individual stories and have made them their own. They have reimagined the old themes, giving them their own unique twists, and have adapted them to fit within their distinct stories. They are *the same, but different.*

"I write the ending first. Nobody reads a book to get to the middle."

—Mickey Spillane

THE SAME, BUT DIFFERENT

The same, but different is what publishing is all about in today's challenging marketplace. Publishers are looking for something *the same as [insert your favorite bestseller here], but different.* "Just like a bestselling XYZ," because this proves there is a market for this kind of book. But it should also be different enough to set it apart from the bestseller and to distinguish itself in a marketplace full of similar stories. *The same, but different.*

Here are some examples of *the same, but different.*

> "Just like J.R.R. Tolkien's *The Lord of the Rings*, only based on the War of the Roses." (George R.R. Martin's *A Game of Thrones*)

> "Just like Jane Austen's *Emma*, only set in Beverly Hills." (Amy Heckerling's *Clueless*)

> "Just like Margaret Mitchell's *Gone with the Wind*, only the slaves are the main characters." (Alice Randall's *The Wind Done Gone*)

In marketing parlance, the "same, but different" statement is known as a unique selling proposition (USP). This term refers to the qualities that differentiate a product in the marketplace.

A USP is the marketing angle to your theme. It's what you need to pitch the book to publishers, producers, booksellers, and, ultimately, readers. There's no point in trying to sell a story that has no USP, that is just "same old, same old," that cannot find its place in today's competitive market.

Consider what you've come up with so far. Ask yourself these questions.

- What is your story really about?
- What are you trying to say?
- How is your story different from all the others on the same shelf?
- Why would readers choose to read this story instead of [insert bestseller here]?

Now describe your own story in terms of "the same, but different." Consider the plot of the work you are comparing your own story to—and how yours differs from it. Now do the same for the theme of that work, and compare it to the theme of yours. Not only will this help you come up with a strong USP, it should also deepen your understanding of your plot and your theme.

KILL YOUR CATEGORY

A "category killer" is a story that outsells all the other stories in its genre. Here's a list of the stories that have "killed their categories."

- **ROMANCE:** *River Road* by Jayne Ann Krentz
- **PARANORMAL:** *Dark Witch* by Nora Roberts
- **EROTICA:** *Fifty Shades of Grey* by E.L. James
- **CRIME FICTION:** *Sycamore Row* by John Grisham
- **INSPIRATIONAL:** *The First Phone Call from Heaven* by Mitch Albom
- **HORROR:** *Doctor Sleep* by Stephen King
- **SCIENCE FICTION/FANTASY:** *A Game of Thrones* by George R.R. Martin
- **YOUNG ADULT:** *Divergent* by Veronica Roth
- **MIDDLE-GRADE:** *Wonder* by R.J. Palacio
- **PICTURE BOOK:** *The Day the Crayons Quit* by Drew Daywalt, illustrated by Oliver Jeffers
- **WOMEN'S FICTION:** *Beautiful Ruins* by Jess Walter
- **UPMARKET FICTION:** *The Goldfinch* by Donna Tartt
- **MEMOIR:** *Wild* by Cheryl Strayed

Compare your story to the best-selling stories in your genre. What makes yours different? How do those differences relate to your themes?

X MEETS Y = USP

Another way to think of USPs is to borrow from the classic Hollywood high-concept formula: *X meets Y*. This works well when your story is a new twist on an old favorite or a mash-up of two genres, ideas, or characters.

Abraham Lincoln meets Vampires (Seth Grahame-Smith's *Abraham Lincoln: Vampire Hunter*)

The Handmaid's Tale meets *The Hunger Games* (Shannon Stoker's *The Registry*)

Prizzi's Honor meets *True Lies* (Simon Kinberg's *Mr. and Mrs. Smith*)

Try coming up with an *X meets Y* formula for your story. Once you've got it, ask yourself how the respective themes of X and Y relate to your story—and perhaps create a new theme.

THE ONLY TROUBLE IS . . .

If you're still stuck trying to find a USP for your story, identify the main conflict and rework your USP so that it highlights your hero or heroine's problem. This is another way of looking at plot, as in the following examples.

"A young man meets the girl of his dreams. The only trouble is, she's a fish." (Lowell Ganz, Babaloo Mandel, and Bruce Jay Friedman's *Splash*)

"A playboy joins a single parents' group to hit on single moms. The only trouble is, he doesn't have a kid." (Nick Hornby's *About a Boy*)

"A newly crowned king must comfort his people during troubling times. The only trouble is, he stutters very badly." (David Seidler's *The King's Speech*)

What's the trouble in your story? What's the main obstacle your protagonist must overcome—and how does that obstacle relate to your theme?

> *"The secret of good writing is to say an old thing in a new way or to say a new thing in an old way."*
>
> —Richard Harding Davis

THE THEME STATEMENT

We've looked at a number of ways to think of your story in terms of plot, theme, and USP. Now let's combine them all into a theme statement, one that can serve as the core driver of your story, the vision that you will strive to realize, the light in the window that will guide you as you make your way through the writing process. You'll want to be sure to include the main action of the story (plot), the emotional impact (theme), and what sets it apart (USP).

Let's take a look at some sample theme statements.

GONE GIRL BY GILLIAN FLYNN

Gone Girl is a thriller about a wife gone missing and the husband held responsible for her disappearance. Is she dead—or just pretending? Is he a murderer—or just a cuckold? **[plot]**

Told from alternating "his" and "her" points of view **[USP]**, this twisted love story reveals the terrible truths about an ordinary marriage—the tie that binds, for better or worse. **[theme]**

EAT PRAY LOVE BY ELIZABETH GILBERT

Eat Pray Love is a memoir about an unhappy divorced woman who sets out on a journey of self-discovery—and learns to feed her body in Italy (Eat), her soul in India (Pray), and her heart in Bali (Love). **[plot and theme]**

Its perfect three-act structure—revealed right there in the title— gives this endearing story of self-actualization a solid foundation that resonates with readers. **[USP]**

THE ART OF RACING IN THE RAIN BY GARTH STEIN

The Art of Racing in the Rain is a mainstream novel about a dog that watches over his human race car driver Denny and his family with great care—even more so when tragedy strikes. **[plot]**

Told from the point of view of the dying dog Enzo **[USP]**, this heartwarming and heartbreaking story shows us that life, like racing, is not just about going fast. **[theme]**

CREATE YOUR THEME STATEMENT

The theme statement will serve as your guiding light as you outline the structure of your work, sort out the details of your plot, and make your way through the writing process. (You'll also find it useful later when you are ready to market your work.)

Now that you've developed your theme statement, you have the foundation you need to proceed with your work. In the next chapter, you'll build upon your plot and themes, brainstorming the subplots and variations on themes that will mold your work into an intricately plotted and multilayered story, rich in theme, character, and nuance.

CHAPTER TWO

SUBPLOTS AND VARIATIONS ON THEMES

> "I lost the plot for a while then. And I lost the subplot, the script, the soundtrack, the intermission, my popcorn, the credits, and the exit sign."
>
> —Nick Hornby

The best stories do not strike just one note—they are symphonies whose main themes are mirrored by variations on those themes and whose plots are layered with melodies and harmonies and rhythms. The stories we remember are as big in scale and emotional range as a work by Beethoven. They are masterful constructions of main plots and subplots, theme and variations on theme. The works of literary heavyweights like Shakespeare and Dickens and modern bestsellers like George R.R. Martin and J.K. Rowling demonstrate that subplots and variations on theme are what make the difference between a story that works and a story that doesn't. (And they also help you plot your way through that most dangerous morass known as the middle.)

As plots are related to theme, so are subplots related to variations on theme. In this chapter, we'll build on your theme statements by exploring possible subplots and variations on theme—and use them to create a main plot and subplots that you can knit together into a gripping storyline.

THEME A BEGETS THEMES B, C, D . . .

Variations on theme are the inspirations for your subplots. They are the consonances and dissonances, harmonies and rhythms of your main melody. By creating subplots that illuminate variations on your theme, you invariably illuminate your theme as well.

When you sit down to brainstorm subplots for your story, you can use a bubble chart, just as you did in chapter one. Let's say you are writing a love story. After writing the general term *love* in the big bubble in the middle of the diagram, you would add bubbles for all of the different aspects of love, good and bad, positive and negative, old and new.

Here's a sample of what that bubble chart might look like for the theme of love.

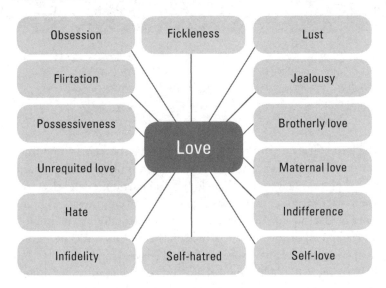

Of course, you can come up with many more types, qualities, and facets of love. But this gives you an idea of the wealth of options you have when developing your stories.

NOTE: Whenever you need inspiration while you're plotting, listen to a symphony—and let your subconscious do the work for you. Here's a list to get you started.

- Beethoven's Fifth Symphony
- Dvorak's Ninth Symphony
- Tchaikovsky's Sixth Symphony
- Brahms's Fourth Symphony
- Mozart's Fortieth Symphony
- Sibelius's Second Symphony
- Berlioz's Symphonie Fantastique
- Mahler's Fifth Symphony
- Haydn's Eighty-Eighth Symphony
- Schubert's Ninth Symphony

"The moment at which music reveals its true nature is contained in the ancient exercise of the theme with variations. The complete mystery of music is explained right there."

—Pierre Schaeffer

TRANSLATING VARIATIONS ON THEME INTO SUBPLOTS

Sticking with the theme of love, let's analyze the classic *Pride and Prejudice* and compare it to our bubble chart. This wonderful love story is as popular as ever, cherished by readers and viewers alike in its original form as well as in many TV and film adaptations, not to mention the countless imitative novels, stories, and films written by modern authors. Perhaps most startling of all is the fact that one of the most popular and perceptive stories ever written about love and marriage was penned by a spinster at the turn of the nineteenth century and first published in 1813. Two hundred years later, Jane Austen remains the queen of love stories, and her work illustrates how subplots and variations on theme can be used to help plot a compelling story.

For those of you who have never read *Pride and Prejudice* (seriously?), here's the main plot of this love story.

When the lively and quick-witted Elizabeth Bennet, second of five unmarried sisters, meets the rich and handsome Mr. Fitzwilliam Darcy, sparks fly. But falling in love with a woman beneath his class appalls Mr. Darcy, and the judgmental Elizabeth regards his aristocratic hauteur as pride. When crises strike the Bennet family and Mr. Darcy intervenes for better and worse, misunderstandings drive the couple apart. Only when Elizabeth overcomes her prejudice and Mr. Darcy overcomes his pride can the two find their way to happiness together.

Let's go through the bubble chart on love, bubble by bubble, and see how they relate to the many subplots in *Pride and Prejudice*. Remember that Elizabeth has four single sisters—and their respective searches for husbands provide lots of fodder for subplots.

I originally created the bubble chart above for my Plot Perfect Boot Camp presentation. Only months later, when I sat down to write this book and decided to analyze the bubble chart in the context of *Pride and Prejudice* did I realize that the novel is so rich in plot, subplot, theme, and variations on theme that virtually every bubble on the chart applied to the story in one way or another.

FICKLENESS: The theme of fickle behavior runs through the subplot involving Elizabeth's younger sister Lydia, who crushes on every soldier she meets, and George Wickham, whose attentions to Elizabeth are replaced by his attentions to her sister Lydia. Similarly, in another subplot, when Elizabeth refuses Mr. William Collins's proposal of marriage, he quickly transfers his affection for her to her best friend, Charlotte Lucas.

LUST: George Wickham's history of bedding—or at least trying to bed—and then abandoning young women is a critical subplot in *Pride and Prejudice*. When he persuades Elizabeth's younger sister Lydia to run off with him, he has no intention of marrying her, even though he has essentially ruined her reputation—and possibly the reputations of her sisters as well, which would destroy their ability to make good marriages.

JEALOUSY: Lady Caroline Bingley is Mr. Charles Bingley's haughty sister, who has designs of her own on her brother's wealthy best friend, Mr. Fitzwilliam Darcy. Her jealousy drives her to make fun of the Darcy family in front of Mr. Darcy, thereby highlighting the difference in class that troubles Mr. Darcy. She also tries to sabotage Jane Bennet's attachment to her brother, Mr. Bingley.

BROTHERLY LOVE: Mr. Darcy and Mr. Bingley's friendship is the subplot that drives much of the main plot. Their friendship is what brings Mr. Darcy to visit Mr. Bingley when he rents Netherfield Park, thereby setting the stage for Mr. Darcy to meet Elizabeth. Later, in the name of this friendship, Mr. Darcy warns Mr. Bingley against marrying Jane. Mr. Bingley takes his friend's advice to heart—and cuts his courting of Jane short. This breaks Jane's heart. Infuriated on her sister's behalf, Elizabeth rejects Mr. Darcy's proposal of marriage.

MATERNAL LOVE: Mrs. Bennet loves her daughters, but she also understands that if they don't marry, they'll have no future. Their father's estate must be handed down to a male heir, and there is none—which means she has five daughters to marry off. Her obvious scheming alienates the aristocracy, encourages her girls to pursue liaisons good and bad, and often sabotages her girls' burgeoning relationships—most notably Jane and Mr. Bingley's and Elizabeth and Mr. Darcy's.

INDIFFERENCE: Jane, the eldest Bennet daughter, is in love with the rich and amiable Mr. Bingley. But her reserve is perceived as indifference toward her suitor, and both Mr. Darcy and Lady Caroline Bingley use that seeming indifference (as well as her status) to dissuade Mr. Bingley of his affections for her.

SELF-LOVE: The theme of self-love may not be, at first glance, one that you'd expect in a nineteenth-century comedy of manners like *Pride and Prejudice*. And yet it is ultimately self-love that drives the actions of Jane Bennet and Charlotte Lucas. Each values herself enough to choose what is best for her. In the Jane and Mr. Bingley subplot, Jane knows she loves Mr. Bingley, and when he suddenly ceases his courting of her, she is distraught. But she resolves to get over the loss in time. When Mr. Bingley resumes his visits to the Bennet household, Jane welcomes him warmly, but without expectation. She knows her own heart, however, and promptly accepts his proposal when it finally comes.

On the other hand, in the Charlotte and Mr. Collins subplot, Charlotte respects herself enough to acknowledge that the best option for her and her family is for her to marry Mr. Collins, whom she may not love in the "true love" sense that Jane and Elizabeth long for, but would give her a secure and content life.

SELF-HATRED: This bubble is perhaps the one most likely to burst upon close examination. That said, a case can be made that George Wickham's many faults are at their core a form of self-hatred. He longs to be one of the landed gentry, but he is born the son of a steward on the Darcy estate. Wickham is Mr. Darcy's father's godson and is raised alongside Mr. Darcy, but despite the Darcys' kind treatment, he is ultimately not one of them, and he hates himself and the Darcys for it. For more on Wickham's misadventures (a.k.a. subplots) see "Lust," "Infidelity," and "Hate" in this list.

INFIDELITY: The grossest incidences of infidelity are committed by George Wickham, and given his selfish, amoral nature, they play a role in all the subplots that concern him. He's disloyal to the memory of his father by blowing all of his money. He's disloyal to Mr. Darcy, whom he's known since childhood, when he attempts to seduce Mr. Darcy's young sister. He's also disloyal to Elizabeth Bennet's younger sister Lydia, whom he convinces to run off with him, promising a wedding he has no intention of attending.

HATE: This subplot is borne of George Wickham's resentment toward Mr. Darcy, which goes back to Wickham's childhood resentments. After wasting his father's money, he attempted to elope with Mr. Darcy's fifteen-year-old sister, Georgiana Darcy, in the hope of securing a quick marriage and access to her large dowry.

So it's safe to say that Wickham and Mr. Darcy hate each other, and this animosity only grows when Wickham rewrites his own history, casting Mr. Darcy as the villain and spreading rumors to that effect around town. He tells Elizabeth that Mr. Darcy has wronged him, and she believes him, creating one of the many rifts between the two would-be lovers.

UNREQUITED LOVE: Mr. Collins's affections for Elizabeth are not returned, which is just the beginning of the unrequited love running through this subplot. After Elizabeth denies him, Mr. Collins's search for a proper vicar's wife leads him to Elizabeth's best friend, the amenable if plain Charlotte Lucas, who agrees to marry him even though she is not in love with him. His feelings for her are not returned, but the sensible Charlotte makes him happy anyway, as he is easy to please and she appreciates the security he provides her.

POSSESSIVENESS: The theme of possessiveness shows up in the subplots concerning the upper classes and their attempts to keep their men, their daughters, and their money safe at home among the aristocrats, where they believe they all belong. Lady Caroline Bingley believes that Mr. Darcy belongs to her, and that the lowly Elizabeth Bennet is not worthy of an attachment to him; she feels the same way about her brother, Mr. Bingley, whom she believes should marry Mr. Darcy's sister rather than Jane Bennet. She conspires against what she considers to be inappropriate alliances, as does Lady Catherine de Bourgh, Mr. Darcy's aunt, who wants her nephew to marry her own daughter, Anne. Lady Catherine de Bourgh pays a visit to the Bennet home in an attempt to bully Elizabeth into refusing Mr. Darcy—and is aghast when the outspoken Elizabeth refuses to be cowed by the overbearing matriarch.

FLIRTATION: In the aforementioned Lydia and Wickham subplot, it is Elizabeth's younger sister Lydia's heedless flirtatious nature that lands the silly fifteen-year-old girl in such trouble. She's a sitting duck for the wily and wicked Wickham, who thinks nothing of ruining her and her family. It is only the intervention of Mr. Darcy that saves Lydia, forcing Wickham to marry her, thereby restoring the reputation of the Bennet family, not to mention endearing the once-rejected Darcy to his true beloved, Elizabeth Bennet.

OBSESSION: You could make the case that the entire underlying premise of *Pride and Prejudice* is obsession—that is, the obsession of nineteenth-century society to marry off all the single young women of good family as neatly and expediently as possible. Certainly Mrs. Bennet is obsessed with seeing her daughters all married, the sooner the better, with little regard for their future happiness. But it is equally true that her daughters are preoccupied with their search for good husbands—and given the economic realities faced by single females at the time, it's an understandable preoccupation.

> *"My novels tend to come about from a fusion of two big ideas, creating a critical mass that then fissions, throwing off hundreds of other particles, riffs, tropes, and characters."*
>
> —Will Self

WEAVING A TAPESTRY OF PLOT AND SUBPLOT

Jane Austen was a master at weaving subplots and variations on theme through her main plot and theme. Even more impressive was the way she interrelated the subplots and variations on theme, which are as meaningful in relation to each other as they are to the main plot and theme. Her work is a carefully woven tapestry, connecting the various storylines as artfully as her prose weaves all of the elements of fiction—character, setting, dialogue, action, description, narrative, backstory, and plot.

As you make your way through this book, you'll learn how to create a rich and variegated tapestry of your own, weaving plot and subplots, theme and variations on theme throughout your narrative. As you can see from this analysis of the subplots and variation on themes in *Pride and Prejudice*, the sky's the limit when it comes to finding subplots and variations on theme for your story.

> *"Beginning writers are often advised to 'write what you know,' and since I knew about quilters—their quirks, their inside jokes, their disputes and their generosity, their quarrels and their kindnesses—the lives of quilters became a natural subject for me. Quilting wove together my two themes as completely and effortlessly as I could have hoped."*
>
> —Jennifer Chiaverini

No matter what kind of story you're writing, create a bubble chart like the one earlier in this chapter for your main themes. It will help you identify and exploit variations on theme to create subplots that will give your story depth and dimension.

Sometimes the first bubble chart you create is just the beginning. Feel free to play and experiment by delving deeper into the variations you come up with. In the case of my "love" bubble chart, each variation on theme could be expanded into its own chart.

FICKLENESS: *A Midsummer Night's Dream* by William Shakespeare
In one of his most popular comedies, Shakespeare explores the fickle nature of love. As Puck arranges for everyone to fall in love with everyone else, this main theme is intertwined with themes of mischief, attraction, intoxication, foolhardiness, and expediency.

LUST: *Fifty Shades of Grey* by E.L. James
This breakout bestseller tapped into the closeted desires of middle-aged women—and created a new subgenre of mainstream erotica—by exploring the theme of lust and such variations as sexual attraction, sexual power, domination, submission, and male/female roles.

JEALOUSY: *Othello* by William Shakespeare
In this tragedy, Othello's jealousy drives the main plot—and is inextricably bound up with subplots exploring the themes of prejudice, self-hatred, loyalty, betrayal, and revenge.

BROTHERLY LOVE: *Band of Brothers* by Stephen E. Ambrose
Ambrose's bestseller recounting of the Easy Company of the U.S. Army 101st Airborne division and its mission in WWII Europe from Operation Overlord through V-J Day inspired the TV miniseries of the same name. Its themes (and variations on theme) of brotherly love, comradeship, loyalty, heroism, and sacrifice for the greater good are evident in every mission they face—from parachuting into France on D-Day to capturing Hitler's Eagle's Nest.

MATERNAL LOVE: *The Joy Luck Club* by Amy Tan
In this moving novel about four Asian immigrants and their Asian-American daughters, the theme of maternal love is illuminated by the many ways in which this theme is explored, raising questions about the cultural and generational gaps between them, as well as the sacrifices and sorrows, rivalries and rebellions, misguided hopes and misunderstandings that can complicate mother/daughter relationships.

INDIFFERENCE: "The Open Boat" by Stephen Crane
This sad story centers around four men adrift in a dinghy after their ship goes down. As they attempt to row to the distant shore to safety, Nature's indifference weighs heavily upon them, as does the variations on theme, such as existential angst, the nature of the human condition, man's losing battle against Mother Nature, and the ultimate realization that man is alone in an uncaring universe.

SELF-LOVE: *Eat Pray Love* by Elizabeth Gilbert
In this perfectly structured memoir, the neurotic heroine must learn to love herself—body, heart, and soul—before she can find and keep her true love. The variations on the theme of self-love—self-nurtur-

ance, forgiveness, integrity, truth, and more—are all lessons she must learn to live a love-filled life.

SELF-HATRED: *The Bluest Eye* by Toni Morrison
This masterpiece explores the devastating effect that self-hatred wields on one little girl, Pecola, as well as on her friends, family, and the society that names blue eyes beautiful. It's a story that weaves the themes of self-hatred, prejudice, race, class, conformity, and beauty into a splendid and terrible tapestry of tragedy.

INFIDELITY: *Anna Karenina* by Leo Tolstoy
In this classic tale of forbidden love, the plot of the married Anna's illicit affair with Count Vronsky is illuminated by the many subplots and variations on this theme—including passion, love, marriage, loyalty, conformity, and what it means to live a fulfilled life.

HATE: *Schindler's List* by Thomas Keneally
Hitler's irrational hatred of the Jews serves as the catalyst for this true story about German playboy Oskar Schindler, who employs Jews at his factory in Cracow during the war in an attempt to save them from the Nazis' concentration camps. The story highlights the contrasting themes of heroism, sacrifice, love, and humanism.

UNREQUITED LOVE: *Jezebel* by Owen Davis Sr.
This popular play was the basis for the William Wyler film about the selfish and headstrong New Orleans heiress, played by Oscar winner Bette Davis, who loses the man she loves to another—only to redeem her envious and spoiled self and her unrequited love in the name of generosity, devotion, and sacrifice.

POSSESSIVENESS: *Misery* by Stephen King
When his "number-one fan" Annie Wilkes rescues romance novelist Paul Sheldon from a car accident, she takes him home and forces him to rewrite the latest manuscript in his Misery Chastain series, the better to her liking. Her possessiveness of both Sheldon and his character Misery is the main theme here, but in true Stephen King fashion, this main theme is driven home by variations on theme that include loyalty, obsession, and addiction.

FLIRTATION: *Fatal Attraction* by James Dearden

James Dearden wrote the original short film for British television and adapted it for the blockbuster feature film about a married man's one-night stand gone very, very wrong. For Dan Gallagher (played by Michael Douglas), his affair with Alex Forrest (played by Glenn Close) is just a fleeting flirtation—but for Alex, it's true love, obsession, and psychosis all rolled into one. When he rejects her, he realizes to his horror that he's really flirting with betrayal, violence, and death—for himself and his family. In this psychological thriller, the main theme of flirtation is the flame that sets these variations on theme on fire. Can we say "bunny boiler?"

OBSESSION: *Damage* by Josephine Hart
In this relatively short but harrowing novel, a middle-aged man finds himself obsessed with his son's enigmatic fiancé—and the damage he does to himself and his family in the name of such variations on theme as passion, infidelity, and betrayal threatens to destroy everything and everyone he loves.

No matter what your theme, you can use a bubble chart to help identify the variations on theme that will allow you to create subplots you can weave throughout your main plot.

> *"The way that Dickens structured his books has a form that we most readily recognize now from, say, the great TV series, like* The Wire *or* The Sopranos. *There's one central plotline, but then from that spin off all kinds of subplots."*
>
> —Jennifer Egan

THE THEMATIC POWER OF PROVERBS, PART II

You can also use the proverbs you identified in chapter one to brainstorm variations on theme. Let's say that your theme is love, and the proverb that best reflects your main theme is "Love conquers all." Your main plot is the typical romantic comedy—*boy meets girl, boy loses girl, boy gets girl back*—and as such is driven by the "Love conquers all" theme. Your subplots will be driven by variations on that theme, which could include:

- Love sucks.
- Love is commitment.
- Love is sex.

- You have to love yourself before you can love anyone else.
- 'Tis better to have loved and lost than to never have loved at all.
- Love is fidelity.
- Once burned, twice shy.
- Love is a warm puppy.

Make a list of the proverbs related to your theme. Brainstorm subplots for your story that embody these variations on theme. A quick Internet search on proverbs, adages, and sayings can help if you get stuck.

These theme-related proverbs can help you develop the subplots you need. Returning to our *Pride and Prejudice* example, the subplots we talked about earlier might be summed up by the following proverbs, building on the main theme of "Love conquers all."

- **FICKLENESS**: "Love the one you're with."
- **LUST**: "Lust and love are two different things."
- **JEALOUSY**: "O! beware, my lord, of jealousy; It is the green-eyed monster …"
- **BROTHERLY LOVE**: "Be kindly affectioned one to another with brotherly love."
- **MATERNAL LOVE**: "An ounce of mother is worth a pound of clergy."
- **INDIFFERENCE**: "Love is a verb."
- **SELF-LOVE**: "To thine own self be true."
- **SELF-HATRED**: "What you hate in others is what you hate in yourself."
- **INFIDELITY**: "But the man who commits adultery is an utter fool, for he destroys himself."
- **HATE**: "The wicked envy and hate; it is their way of admiring."
- **UNREQUITED LOVE**: "'Tis better to have loved and lost than never to have loved at all."
- **POSSESSIVENESS**: "Possession is nine-tenths of the law."
- **FLIRTATION**: "You are flirting with disaster."
- **OBSESSION**: "Love is as much of an object as an obsession."

PLAN YOUR SUBPLOTS AND VARIATIONS ON THEME

Now that you've explored the ways in which you might create subplots to support your main plot and variations on theme to mirror your main theme, you can plan these out on paper using the Plot Your Themes Chart that follows. Have fun with it!

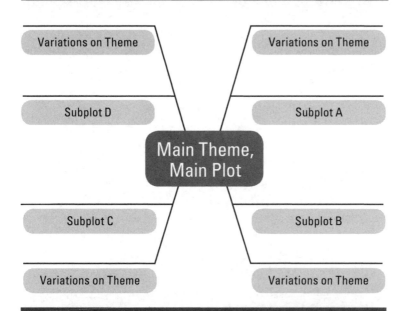

PLOT YOUR THEMES CHART

Variations on Theme

Variations on Theme

Subplot D

Subplot A

Main Theme, Main Plot

Subplot C

Subplot B

Variations on Theme

Variations on Theme

READING FOR WRITERS

Getting your head around theme and its critical interrelationship to plot can be challenging. The best way to do it is to read, read, read. Here is a sampling of stories whose titles reflect the themes that define them—and us.

- *The Grapes of Wrath* by John Steinbeck
- *Sense and Sensibility* by Jane Austen
- *Othello* by William Shakespeare
- *To Kill a Mockingbird* by Harper Lee
- *Angels in America* by Tony Kushner

NOTE: The film versions of all of these stories are spectacular as well.

Plan a movie night—and watch movies with lots of subplots and variations on theme—so you can see the way a carefully plotted story works in action on the screen. Here's a list of films to get you started.

- *The Maltese Falcon*, starring Humphrey Bogart and Mary Astor
- *Casablanca*, starring Humphrey Bogart and Ingrid Bergman
- *Sense and Sensibility*, starring Emma Thompson and Kate Winslet
- *Titanic*, starring Leonardo DiCaprio and Kate Winslet
- *Moonstruck*, starring Cher and Nicolas Cage
- *Beautiful Girls*, starring Matt Dillon and Timothy Hutton
- *The Great Escape*, starring Steve McQueen and James Garner
- *Crazy Stupid Love*, starring Steve Carell and Ryan Gosling
- *Crash*, starring Don Cheadle and Sandra Bullock
- *Love Actually*, starring Colin Firth and Liam Neeson

PEOPLE YOUR PLOTS—AND SUBPLOTS

The same bubble charts and proverbs you use to develop subplots and variations on themes can be used to develop the secondary characters that will drive the subplots you've just mapped out in the Plot Your Themes Chart. In the next chapter, we'll take a look at how you can ensure that both your hero and your villain are complex characters, and that your secondary characters serve as true mirrors to both your protagonist and antagonist. The secret to creating such multidimensional characters lies in their actions as well as their psyches—in your plots as well as your themes.

> *"A symphony is a stage play with the parts written for instruments instead of for actors."*
>
> —Colin Wilson

CHAPTER THREE
ACTION IS CHARACTER:
Heroes, Villains, and Supporting Characters

> *"Action is character."*
>
> —F. Scott Fitzgerald

In the words of Daisy Buchanan, the woman for whom Fitzgerald's great Gatsby reinvents himself, "What'll we do with ourselves this afternoon ... and the day after that, and the next thirty years?"

This is the question that all writers face as we plot our stories: What'll we do with our own Gatsbys and Caulfields and Eyres? What obstacles will we place in their paths, what hoops will we make them jump through—and to what end? What motivations will we give them; what will propel them to act and cause them to react? Why will they act in certain ways—and how can you make that clear to readers?

If action is character, then we need to make our characters *do* something. This is where plot comes in. Plot is what your characters do—what they make happen and what happens to them in return. That's why themes and variations on theme apply to characters as well as to plot. Your protagonist embodies the theme of your story and drives the main plot; secondary characters serve as mirrors to the protagonist, embodying the variations on theme and driving the subplots. In this chapter, you'll learn how to enrich your plot and subplots by developing characters who reflect your theme and variations on themes.

WHATEVER HAPPENED TO CHARACTER-DRIVEN STORIES?

I can hear it now. You're saying, "I don't plot my stories before I write them. For me, it's all about the character. I write character-driven stories."

You may even be thinking that all of this emphasis on plot is, well, a little crass. That I'm, well, a little crass.

I have a client who's a great writer—and he has received four prestigious Pushcart Prize nominations to prove it. But despite those heady credentials and his newly minted Master of Fine Arts, he's having trouble with plot.

"I'm not really about plot," he told me.

Not really about plot? Really? Seriously?

As I said to him, and as I'm saying to you: If you want to write commercial fiction, you *need* to be about plot. Really. Seriously. (To his credit, my client went on to learn a lot about plot and to sign a two-book deal with Random House, thereby proving two things: (1) your agent is always right, and (2) plot pays.)

Even if your aim is to write literary fiction, ask yourself this: Am I content teaching literature and composition at the college level and publishing short stories in literary journals? If so, fine. Forget about plot.

But if you want to write literary fiction that's successful—à la John Irving and Joyce Carol Oates and Alice Hoffman and Neil Gaiman and David Sedaris and Zadie Smith and Dennis Lehane and Kazuo Ishiguro and Annie Proulx—you need plot as well as style. Something needs to happen—and that something is plot.

> *"All fiction is about people, unless it's about rabbits pretending to be people. It's all essentially characters in action, which means characters moving through time and changes taking place, and that's what we call 'the plot.'"*
>
> —Margaret Atwood

TO DO OR NOT TO DO

The most obvious example of a brilliant writer whose themes are as rich as his language is one whose works have endured longer than those of most any other writer in the English language: William Shakespeare. His gift for language is topped only by his gift for drama—from swordplay to suicide, love to lunacy, murder to mayhem, Shakespeare's plays are plotted to perfection. What's more, his plays always tap into something critical to the human experience, which is why his themes still resonate with readers four hundred years later. Most important, Shakespeare created wonderful characters to embody his themes and enact his plots.

Shakespeare knew that action is character, and he gave his characters plenty to do. His motives may have been driven by the desire to please the actors and the audience as well as by a superior literary wisdom. But either way, the man knew how to bring his characters to life within the context of compelling plots.

Shakespeare's characters embody the themes of their stories even as they drive the action of their respective plots. Perhaps the most telling example is the enigmatic and melancholy Hamlet, whose notorious indecision does not slow the plot (as it might have in the hands of lesser authors), but rather propels the story. Shakespeare puts Hamlet through the wringer in this dark existential tragedy: Hamlet sees ghosts, vows to avenge his father's death, breaks a girl's heart, hires a troupe of actors to reenact his father's murder at the hands of his uncle, berates his mother, kills an innocent man, gets banished by the king, evades assassins, is attacked by pirates, engages in deadly swordplay, watches his mother drink poison meant for him, stabs his opponent, kills a king, and dies, only to be lauded as a fallen soldier.

That's a lot of action for an indecisive, guilt-ridden protagonist who believes that "conscience does make cowards of us all," and deliberates endlessly on "what a piece of work is man!" And yet, Shakespeare makes it work. We fall in love with this tortured, suicidal young man who speaks so eloquently of the bewildering mess that is his life—and ours.

Hamlet personifies "action is character," even as his complex and contradictory nature allows him to maintain a measure of mystery that bemuses critics to this day. Creating such well-rounded characters to drive the stories we tell is every writer's challenge. But as we'll see, using theme and variations on theme can help us do just that.

> *"When I'm writing a book, sentence by sentence, I'm not thinking theoretically. I'm just trying to work out the story from inside the characters I've got."*
>
> —Salman Rushdie

CREATING COMPLEX CHARACTERS

Hamlet is not only a complex character, he's the best of all complex characters: He's a walking contradiction. Walking contradictions make the most compelling characters, because they are the most like real people. We human beings are all walking contradictions—it's what makes us human. We are kind and cruel, happy and sad, gracious and gross, sweet and sour. We have our good days and our bad days, our strengths and our weaknesses, our virtues and our vices. Shakespeare knew this, which is why Hamlet is who he is—and why we still love him all these years later. The chart below illustrates Hamlet's status as a walking contradiction.

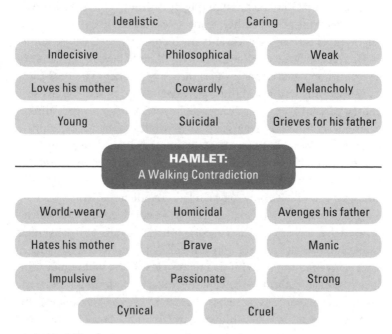

In this bubble chart, we can see the contradictions that make up Hamlet's character. Above the lines we see one aspect, and below the line we see its opposite.

Idealistic	Cynical
Indecisive	Impulsive
Loves his mother	Hates his mother
Cowardly	Brave

Philosophical	Passionate
Caring	Cruel
Young	World-weary
Melancholy	Manic
Weak	Strong
Suicidal	Homicidal
Grieves for his father	Avenges his father

These pairs of opposites compete for dominance within Hamlet—and they're the fodder for conflict. His contradictory impulses propel the plot.

- He believes in the human virtues of honor and loyalty; he thinks man is "a piece of work."
- He can't make up his mind whether to kill the king or not; he impulsively stabs the curtain, where he thinks the king is hiding. (Oops! Wrong guy.)
- He loves his mother; he hates his mother for marrying the king so soon after his father dies.
- He feigns madness to avoid his fate; he risks his own life to avenge his father's death.
- He intellectualizes everything; he reacts emotionally, acts out, and rages.
- He cares for Ophelia; he breaks her heart.
- He's young and proactive; he's world-weary and passive.
- He's too depressed to act; he's scheming to prove the king's guilt.
- He wimps out the first time he tries to kill the king; in the end he succeeds.
- He wants to kill himself; he wants to kill the king.
- He grieves for his father; he plans to avenge his father's death.

> *"When writing a novel a writer should create living people; people, not characters. A character is a caricature."*
>
> —Ernest Hemingway

CREATE A PROTAGONIST WORTHY OF READERS

When you develop your characters, start with your protagonist. This is the character who will embody your theme and drive your plot. Most important, this is the character your readers will identify with—and fall in love with. He's the hero they'll root for from the first page to the last—and all the pages in between. She's the heroine they'll follow to hell and back—and all the purgatories you produce along the way.

Fail to create a strong protagonist, and you shoot your story in the foot before the race has even begun. As a storyteller you have a lot riding on this character. So you need to bring your protagonist to life as fully as possible. Make him real. Make her 3-D. Make them walking contradictions.

To aid in this, try creating a bubble chart for your protagonist, as I did for Hamlet. List the contradictory aspects of your hero or heroine's personality and psyche. Go for broke—the more qualities, quirks, traits, and tendencies you can come up with, the better.

Once you've listed several pairs of opposites, think about how they might relate to your main theme and plot, as well as your variations on theme and subplots. And consider how you can play to those opposing forces when you plot your story.

For example, say you're writing a love story about a girl named Alice. Your heroine is a thirty-two-year-old sculptor in Venice Beach whose actor fiancé left her at the altar. Your theme is "Love conquers all," and your variations on theme include "Once burned, twice shy" and "'Tis better to have loved and lost …".

Alice's list of contradictions might look something like this.

- She's heartbroken, but she still believes in love.
- She's attractive, but she's lost whatever confidence she had in her looks.
- She's brave about getting on with her life, but she's scared to fall in love again.
- She's bold in her work, but she's shy in her dealings with men.
- She's a romantic, but she's cynical about men, especially actors.
- She loves her father, but she hates him for his philandering.
- She loves her mother, but she hates her for her bitterness.
- She's an unconventional artist, but she's very conventional in her approach to love.
- She's part of a supportive community of artists, but she feels very alone.
- She loves the Travel Channel, but she's never been anywhere.
- She's obsessed with 1890s Art Nouveau style, but she lives in the twenty-first century.

Plot Perfect

- She's kind to others, but she's hard on herself.
- She's a fun-loving person, but she works all the time.
- She creates works of harmony and beauty, but she feels broken and ugly.

These pairs of opposites suggest a number of themes and plots, variations on theme and subplots, some of which you've considered, and some of which you have not. Let's imagine some scenarios together.

SHE'S HEARTBROKEN, BUT SHE STILL BELIEVES IN LOVE. This suggests Alice's backstory, which includes being left at the altar by an actor. It also suggests that she is a romantic who believes in love and who eventually will risk loving again, provided that she—and here's where more potential plotting comes in—learns to tell the good guys from the bad guys (subplot with another Mr. Wrong), meets the right guy (main plot with Mr. Right), and listens to her clear-eyed best friend (subplot built around her BFF's secure and happy love life). Or she *doesn't* listen to her *cynical* best friend (subplot built around her BFF's lack of a love life due to her mistrust of men). You choose.

SHE'S ATTRACTIVE, BUT SHE'S LOST WHATEVER CONFIDENCE SHE HAD IN HER LOOKS. This contradiction conjures up visions of our heroine hard at work in her studio, dressed in paint-splattered dungarees, her hands covered in dust as she works the clay. She avoids all contact with eligible men and neglects her hair, makeup, and wardrobe. And here's a possible subplot: Her big sister (now she has a sister!) is a Melrose Avenue *fashionista* who deplores her little sister's neglectful ways and is dying to make her over.

SHE'S BRAVE ABOUT GETTING ON WITH HER LIFE, BUT SHE'S SCARED OF FALLING IN LOVE AGAIN. Being left at the altar prompts Alice to focus on her work life rather than her love life—and that opens up all manner of possibilities. How about this: She's offered a part-time gig teaching sculpture classes to adults, which leads her to hire artist models, most of whom are out-of-work actors—just like the guy who left her at the altar. That's just one way we could build a subplot around this contradiction in Alice's character.

SHE'S BOLD IN HER WORK, BUT SHE'S SHY IN HER DEALINGS WITH MEN. How might this manifest itself in our plot? Maybe Alice sublimates her sex drive now by creating a new body of work, one that is inspired by the male nude form—bold! But when she finds herself attracted to one of her sculpture students, she holds back, hiding behind her role as a teacher, even though it's obvious that the attraction is mutual.

SHE'S A ROMANTIC, BUT SHE'S CYNICAL ABOUT MEN, ESPECIALLY ACTORS. Alice may still believe in love, but she no longer believes in actors. And yet … when one of those out-of-work actors shows up to model for her sculpture classes, she dismisses him when he flirts with her. But guess who her next nude male sculpture clearly resembles?

SHE LOVES HER FATHER, BUT SHE HATES HIM FOR HIS PHILANDERING. A philandering father can contribute to any story's plot and subplots, themes, and variations on theme in myriad ways. Alice's backstory can include when her father left her mother (and her) when she was little, and you can force her to reexamine that past event when he shows up to see her twenty years later. Or he can be an active part of Alice's life—and camp out in her studio when wife no. 4 kicks him out of the house. You get the idea.

SHE LOVES HER MOTHER, BUT SHE HATES HER FOR HER BITTERNESS. Psychologists like to say that there are six people in every couple's bed: him, her, and both sets of parents. (That's why parents and in-laws make such great secondary characters—they're great mirrors for our heroes and heroines!) Like Alice's father, her mother is a gold mine of plotting ideas. Maybe Mom is as rich as she is bitter—and Alice learns that she hired a private detective to check out her fiancé and then used what she found out to blackmail him into leaving town, breaking her daughter's heart but sparing her a life with a loser. Or maybe her mom married again right away and is always preaching that boring is better when it comes to husbands—even if it's obvious that she still loves Alice's dad. Again, the possibilities are endless here.

SHE'S AN UNCONVENTIONAL ARTIST, BUT SHE'S VERY CONVENTIONAL IN HER APPROACH TO LOVE. Maybe what Alice needs is to modernize her love life—and modify her old-fashioned sensibilities when it comes to love. At least that's what her gay artist friend Jake is always telling her. And he gives her a little push in that direction, à la *Amelie*, unbeknownst to Alice. Or maybe the man who wins her heart in the end is the one who challenges her conventional approach to love.

SHE'S PART OF A SUPPORTIVE COMMUNITY OF ARTISTS, BUT SHE FEELS VERY ALONE. Alice is isolating herself post-jilting, but we can count on her friends and family (she has so many now!) to lure her out of her shell. A surprise party for her birthday, an exhibition of her bold new work at a local gallery, a wedding or a christening or a funeral she must attend … you name it.

SHE LOVES THE TRAVEL CHANNEL, BUT SHE'S NEVER BEEN ANYWHERE. An artist who's never seen Paris? Now that's a trip waiting to happen. Maybe that's where Alice was supposed to go on her honeymoon or her dream vacation, but she couldn't bear to go without her fiancé. Or maybe she goes alone on her honeymoon—and that changes everything.

SHE'S OBSESSED WITH 1890s ART NOUVEAU STYLE, BUT SHE LIVES IN THE TWENTY-FIRST CENTURY. Well, luckily, we just sent her to Paris, didn't we? Paris—where Art Nouveau is everywhere, starting with the Metro stations, where our heroine can ride to her destiny from one *arrondissement* to another. And just imagine the men she might meet in Paris. Or not. If you're determined to keep Alice stateside, then maybe she could time travel back to the 1890s, where she meets a mysterious Parisian artist and hobnobs with Klimt and Toulouse-Lautrec and Mucha, which would make this a time travel romance.

SHE'S KIND TO OTHERS, BUT SHE'S HARD ON HERSELF. How can we use Alice's generosity of spirit to benefit our plot? Maybe she has an elderly neighbor she watches out for—and who's always trying to fix Alice up with her many grandsons, grand-nephews, and other assorted single male relatives. This would make a fun running subplot throughout the story—until the right grandson comes along. Or maybe Alice's elderly neighbor is a widower who appreciates the soup Alice brings him and tells her stories about his late wife and their sixty-five-year-long marriage.

SHE'S A FUN-LOVING GIRL, BUT SHE WORKS ALL THE TIME. How about this: Alice babysits for her *fashionista* sister, and we see how much fun they have with their Auntie Alice. But we also see that she spends most of her Saturday nights this way. Or maybe we see her alone in her studio, dancing around as she gets to work. Or maybe it's the work itself that reveals Alice's playful side. Discouraged by her dealings with people, she turns to sculpting animals—penguins and puppies—and wins a big commission for the Boston Children's Museum.

SHE CREATES WORKS OF HARMONY AND BEAUTY, BUT SHE FEELS BROKEN AND UGLY. This theme of self-worth should play into the main plot, because Mr. Right should be the one who values Alice for herself—and honors both the genius and the vulnerability in her. And she must heal her broken heart before she can love another man the way Mr. Right deserves to be loved, too. How can we dramatize this? This calls for a grand, selfless romantic gesture like the one in O. Henry's "The Gift of the Magi." What grand gestures can Alice and Mr. Right make to prove their worth? Maybe he's an artist who secretly forfeits his place in an exhibition to make room for her work. Maybe she creates a lovely sculpture of herself as a present for him, one that reflects the way he sees her—and the way she comes to see herself.

> *"A lot of my characters in all of my books have a self-destructive urge. They'll do precisely the thing that they know is wrong, take a perverse delight in doing the wrong thing."*
>
> —Richard Russo

This simple brainstorming exercise with Alice demonstrates how useful it can be to list contradictions for your character, which can then be used to build your plot, subplots, theme, and variations on theme. What's more, you can also see how thinking of your protagonist as a walking contradiction can help you populate your story with secondary characters who serve as mirrors for your hero or heroine and help drive the subplots of your story as well.

WRITER AT WORK

Once you've completed your Walking Contradiction bubble chart for your protagonist, create a list of scenarios outlining the possible subplots and secondary characters that these contradictions suggest. Brainstorm as many scenarios as you can, just as we did for Alice. The more you come up with, the more you'll prime your pump for plotting ideas—and the more deeply you'll understand your protagonist.

SPEAKING OF SECONDARY CHARACTERS

Your protagonist is the fulcrum of the wheel of your cast of players—just as Hamlet was at the center of the events that rocked the rotten state of Denmark. Once you've brainstormed the walking contradictions that characterize your protagonist, create a bubble chart of the secondary characters that your brainstorming suggested to you. Build this bubble chart around your protagonist as we have done with Alice in the sample that follows.

> *"My characters surprise me constantly. My characters are like my friends—I can give them advice, but they don't have to take it. If your characters are real, then they surprise you, just like real people."*
>
> —Laurell K. Hamilton

> *"Sometimes even when the book is over, I don't know who's good and who's bad. It's really more interesting, I think, to write about gray characters than it is to write about black and white."*
>
> —Harlan Coben

KNOW YOUR ANTAGONIST

Your protagonist deserves a worthy antagonist. Too many writers give their antagonists short shrift—and their stories suffer as a result. The best way to ensure that your hero has a foil clever and challenging enough to bring out the best—and worst—in him is to spend as much time developing your villain as you do your hero.

The most satisfying antagonists are those we love to hate.

- Hannibal Lecter (from *Red Dragon* by Thomas Harris)
- Claudius (from *Hamlet* by William Shakespeare)
- Voldemort (from the Harry Potter series by J.K. Rowling)
- Nurse Ratched (from *One Flew Over the Cuckoo's Nest* by Ken Kesey)
- Javert (from *Les Misérables* by Victor Hugo)
- Cruella de Vil (from *The Hundred and One Dalmatians* by Dodie Smith)
- Mrs. Danvers (from *Rebecca* by Daphne du Maurier)
- The Shark (from *Jaws* by Peter Benchley)
- The Wicked Stepmother (from *Cinderella* by Charles Perrault)
- Annie Wilkes (from *Misery* by Stephen King)
- Professor Moriarty (from the Sherlock Holmes stories by Arthur Conan Doyle)
- Hilly Holbrook (from *The Help* by Kathryn Stockett)
- Sauron (from *The Lord of the Rings* by J.R.R. Tolkien)

These antagonists really put their respective protagonists through their paces. They're clever and cruel, ruthless and resourceful, strong and spiteful. They give our heroes and our heroines hell and force them to bring their "A game" to every encounter. It's a fight to the finish every step of the way. This makes for great conflict, and great drama. In other words, great plot!

The best antagonists are walking contradictions, just as the best protagonists are. Often villains are drawn in black and white—completely dark and evil, without the slightest hint of redeeming qualities—and therefore they become caricatures rather than well-rounded characters. Check out this bubble chart for one of the most memorable villains in fiction, Hannibal Lecter.

Psychiatrist	Well-mannered	Charming
Cultured	Cool	Gourmet
Protects Clarice	Calm	Grieves for his sister

HANNIBAL LECTER:
A Walking Contradiction

Taunts Clarice	Violent	Avenges his sister
Barbaric	Passionate	Cannibal
Psychopath	Kills rude people	Brutal

Making a bubble chart can help you develop well-rounded villains who will earn the reader's respect even as they rile up your heroes and heroines. *Remember:* Your hero is only as good as his foil.

> "I've always preferred writing about gray characters and human characters. Whether they are giants or elves or dwarves, or whatever they are, they're still human, and the human heart is still in conflict with the self."
>
> —George R.R. Martin

THE DEEP DIVE FOR YOUR CHARACTERS

Now that you've outlined the contradictions of your protagonist(s), your antagonist(s), and your secondary characters, and you have considered how these contradictions might influence your plot and subplots and reflect your theme and variations on theme, it's time to go deep. Going deep means knowing as much as you can about your characters—everything from their hair color and body type to their favorite movies and their darkest secrets.

The best way to learn about your characters is to create a profile for each of them. The character profile is a common means of developing characters, and—just as important—keeping track of them as you begin to write your story.

But these profiles are far more than simple tracking devices. They can be used to shape characters with enough depth to capture the hearts of readers everywhere. The trick here is to go beyond the superficial when creating these profiles.

Here are the data and questions that should inform your character profiles. You can use this template for all of your characters. Don't worry if you can't complete the entire template right away; it takes time for characters to grow into your story. You can add material as you discover—and uncover—it. Your characters will reveal more and more of themselves as your story unfolds.

> "I have a cheat sheet for each one of my characters about their personality, the way they look, etc. So there is no possible way that I could have writer's block."
>
> —R.L. Stine

CHARACTER PROFILE

Name _____

Age_____

Marital status _____

Sexual preference _____

Hair _____

Eyes _____

Height _____

Body type _____

Date of birth _____

Place of birth _____

Mother's name _____

Father's name _____

Siblings _____

Birth order _____

Best childhood memory _____

Worst childhood memory _____

High school _____

GPA _____

Voted "Most Likely to" _____

College major and minor _____

Favorite book _____

Favorite film _____

Heroes/heroines _____

Drug of choice _____

Virtues _____

Vices _____

Guilty pleasures _____

Things worth fighting for _____

Things worth dying for _____

Biggest lesson learned _____

Biggest lesson yet to learn _____

Relationship with mother _____

Relationship with father _____

Relationship with siblings _____

Biggest secret kept about someone else _____

Biggest secret kept about self _____

Biggest lie told in childhood _____

Biggest lie told in adulthood _____

Favorite place on earth _____

Most embarrassing moment in childhood _____

Most embarrassing moment in adulthood _____

Most humiliating failure in childhood _____

Most humiliating failure in adulthood _____

Biggest fear in childhood _____

Biggest fear in adulthood _____

Best coping mechanism _____

Worst coping mechanism _____

First love _____

Most recent love _____

Pets _____

Favorite meal _____

Favorite sport _____

Best childhood friend _____

Best friend now _____

Enemies _____

Frenemies _____

Obstacles overcome _____

Obstacles yet to overcome _____

Actual profession _____

Dream profession _____

Greatest ambition _____

Bank balance_____

Credit score _____

Religious affiliation _____

Relationship with boss/co-workers _____

Relationship with lover _____

Relationship with God _____

How s/he met significant other_____

First sex ever had _____

Best sex ever had _____

Best vacation ever _____

Worst vacation ever _____

Best job _____

Worst job _____

If s/he won the lottery_____

Proverb _____

Words to live by_____

To access a printable version of this worksheet, visit www.
writersdigest.com/plot-perfect-worksheets.

"So when I write characters and situations and relationships, I try to sort of utilize what I know about the world, limited as it is, and what I hear from my friends and see with my relatives."
—Charlie Kaufman

WORDS TO LIVE BY ...

Perhaps the last entry on the character profile template is the most important: *Words to live by*. What does your protagonist believe—and how will that belief be challenged in your story? What code does he live by, and can he stay the course no matter what happens? How does her personal mantra inform her relationships—and influence her behavior?

We all have a preferred way of being in the world, a sometimes subconscious motivation that defines our deepest desires and governs our decisions.

I just want to be happy.
I just want to be loved.
I just want to be in charge.
I just want to be left alone.
I just want to create.
I just want to explore.
I just want to help.

Who does your hero just want to be? What does your heroine just want to do? How do these desires conflict with those of your antagonist and your secondary characters? How might these motivations drive the plot and subplots?

> *"I live intimately with my characters before starting a book. I cut out pictures of them for my wall. I do time lines for each major character and a time line for the entire novel: What is going on in the world as my characters struggle with their problems?"*
> —Walter Dean Myers

THE PERSONALITY TYPOLOGIES OF STORY CHARACTERS

You may find that creating characters from scratch is difficult for you. This may especially be true if you consider yourself good with plot but lousy with character development. But even if you consider character development your strength, you need to make sure that your characters are compelling enough to engage readers for the duration of your story—and beyond. One of the most common complaints editors make about stories is "I just didn't fall in love with the characters." One way to avoid this pitfall is to explore personality typologies.

Explore the different personality typologies that exist to determine which resonates with you as a storyteller. Are you a fan of the Myers-Briggs Type Indicator assessment? Then designate your lively heroine an ENFP and your strong, laconic hero an INTJ, and plot accordingly. If you're a student of the Enneagram, you may see your poetic heroine as a 4 (the artiste), and your politician villain as a 3 (the leader). Or maybe you're into astrology, and you see your fiery heroine as an Aries and her stalwart steady as a Taurus. You can think of your career woman heroine as a classic Type A and her laid-back musician Mr. Right as a Type B. Or model your hero after one of the classic Greek heroes, complete with the hamartia (tragic flaw) that may spell his doom.

There are many ways in which you can think of your characters; use whatever works for you. But whatever you do, do your due diligence. Your characters will thank you for it—and so will your readers.

READING FOR WRITERS

Here are a number of resources that may help you create great characters.

- *The Birth Order Book: Why You Are the Way You Are* by Dr. Kevin Leman
- *The Birth Order Effect* by Clifford E. Isaacson
- *Gifts Differing: Understanding Personality Type* by Isabel Briggs Myers and Peter B. Myers
- *Linda Goodman's Sun Signs* by Linda Goodman
- *The Book of Questions* by Gregory Stock, Ph.D.
- *Personality Types: Using the Enneagram for Self-Discovery* by Don Richard Riso and Russ Hudson
- *The Everything Enneagram Book* by Susan Reynolds
- *Poetics* by Aristotle
- *Psychological Types (The Collected Works of C.G. Jung, Vol. 6)* by C.G. Jung

At the beginning of this chapter, we recalled Daisy Buchanan's lament in *The Great Gatsby*: "What'll we do with ourselves this afternoon … and the day after that, and the next thirty years?" Now that you have a deeper understanding of just who your characters really are, you'll be able to figure out what they'll do with themselves—if not for the next thirty years, then at least for the next scene … and the next … and the next.

Which brings us to the scene, the building block of plot. In the following chapter, we'll discuss the ingredients of strong scenes that you can use to build up your plot, brick by brick.

"I suppose all fictional characters, especially in adventure or heroic fiction, at the end of the day, are our dreams about ourselves. And sometimes they can be really revealing."

—Alan Moore

CHAPTER FOUR
SCENE:
The Basic Unit of Plot

"Show the readers everything, tell them nothing."
—Ernest Hemingway

No matter how rich your theme, selling in today's market means writing in scenes. No matter how clever your plot, selling in today's market means writing in scenes. Once more, with emphasis: *Selling in today's market means writing in scenes.*

If you're writing a stage play or a film script or a teleplay, you're thinking: *Duh.* But if you're writing a short story or a memoir or a novel, you may be thinking: *Wait a minute … .* You know that the one thing fiction and creative nonfiction can give people that film, television, and theater cannot is a glimpse into the characters' inner lives. Only in these forms can you as the writer directly reveal what your characters are thinking and feeling. Readers appreciate this, and that's why even with fierce, visually compelling competition from television, film, and theater, they still turn to short stories, novels, and memoirs. They want that glimpse into the inner lives of their favorite characters—from Holden Caulfield and Humbert Humbert to David Sedaris and Elizabeth Gilbert.

That said, the great advantage of fiction and creative nonfiction can also prove its weakness. For inner life without outer conflict is death. There's nothing worse than being stuck in the head of someone who spends all of her time deliberating and none of it *doing*. (We all know people like that, and we don't want to go to lunch with them, much less read a book about them.)

Without dramatization, the story dies on the page, never to be seen or read or published, much less find its place in the world of literature. One of the most common reasons manuscripts are rejected is that the writer has failed to dramatize the story. It's all talk—and no walk. Nothing happens, or if it does, the reader hears about it secondhand, rather than experiencing it right along with the characters. Which is about as admissible in the court of storytelling as hearsay is in a court of law.

You can blame television, film, Hemingway, or Aristotle for the classic writer's idiom "Show, don't tell." But even if you resent this advice, you still need to write your story primarily in scenes if you ever want your story to sell.

> "If you give me a typewriter and I'm having a good day, I can write a scene that will astonish its readers. That will perhaps make them laugh, perhaps make them cry—that will have some emotional clout to it. It doesn't cost much to do that."
>
> —Alan Moore

Scenes are the building blocks of plot. Writing in scenes can help you ensure that something is actually happening on every page of your story. In this chapter, you'll learn what makes a good scene and how writing in scenes will keep your plot engine running smoothly—from page 1 to the end.

WHAT'S A SCENE?

A scene is defined by its *continuous action*. This is what writing cinematically really means: telling your story through snippets of continuous action. We're not necessarily talking about explosions or car chases—although that kind of action may come into play if you're writing a thriller or an action adventure story. Action comes in all sizes, shapes, and intensities, from a shy teenager's awkward first kiss to an elderly widow's eulogy for her deceased husband's funeral.

Here are some of literature's most moving scenes, ones that we remember—and that have been immortalized on film as well as in print. These scenes are units of continuous action that move the story forward—and pack an emotional punch. What's more, they don't *tell us* about the characters; they *show us* very clearly what they're thinking and feeling.

- The balcony scene, from *Romeo and Juliet* by William Shakespeare ("O Romeo, Romeo, wherefore art thou Romeo?"). We watch a young couple fall into a forbidden love—and we remember what it was like to fall in love for the first time ourselves.

- The dinner scene in which Tom's mother serves her belligerent husband doctored-up dog food, from *The Prince of Tides* by Pat Conroy ("Now this is food, Lila. Simple food, but good."). When Lila serves her husband dog food, we watch in shock and approval right along with her children—and we pray he doesn't figure out what he's really eating.

- The scene at the ball in which Elizabeth Bennet overhears Mr. Darcy insulting her behind her back, from *Pride and Prejudice* by Jane Austen ("She is tolerable; but not handsome enough to tempt me …"). We feel Elizabeth's indignation when she's insulted by the proud Mr. Darcy—and we suffer the petty indignities of our own youth all over again.

- The scene at the hospital in which Garp's mother conceives her son, from *The World According to Garp* by John Irving (She felt more receptive than prepared soil—the nourished earth—and she had felt Garp shoot up inside her as generously as a hose in summer [as if he could water a lawn]). When Jennie Fields decides that Garp would make the perfect sperm donor for the child she so badly wants to bear, we marvel at her ingenuity and her resourcefulness—even as we squirm at her arguably ruthless behavior.

- The scene in which Katniss Everdeen insists on taking her little sister Prim's place when her name is called in the lottery, from *The Hunger Games* by Suzanne Collins ("I volunteer as tribute!"). We fall in love with Katniss when she volunteers to take her little sister's place for what she—and we—know is a one-way ticket to almost certain death. We're rooting for her all the way through *The Hunger Games*—and we wonder if we'd have the courage to do what she did if we were in her shoes.

- The scene in which Daenerys walks into her dead husband's funeral pyre, from *A Game of Thrones* by George R.R. Martin ("I am Daenerys Stormborn, daughter of dragons, bride of dragons, mother of dragons, don't you see?"). Watching Daenerys march into the fire to unite with her dead husband is one of the most powerful scenes in the novel. As we watch it happen, we're marching with her, seduced by her belief in her own destiny—and hoping that we can face our destiny with as much confidence.

- The scene in which Lisbeth Salander turns the table on her abuser, from *The Girl with the Dragon Tattoo* by Stieg Larsson ("I am a sadistic pig, a pervert, and a rapist."). Lisbeth's carefully plotted and executed revenge on her tormentor is terrifying and satisfying at the same time—and we are with her every step of the way, in the name of every girl who was ever abused by a man.

Not all scenes are as memorable or momentous as the ones mentioned above. But you can create every scene in your story to speak to readers and to move them in ways only fiction and memoir can.

> *"Don't tell me the moon is shining; show me the glint of light on broken glass."*
>
> —Anton Chekhov

WRITING IN STORY QUESTIONS

If writing an entire story as a series of continuous actions is your idea of a plotting nightmare, welcome to the world of the screenwriter. Seriously, writing in scenes can be a challenge, especially if you've been relying on backstory and exposition to tell much of your story, as many writers mistakenly do.

But once you get the hang of it, you'll see that not only is writing in scenes an effective means of dramatizing your story, it's *fun*. The trick is not to drive yourself crazy trying to think of clever action sequences, but rather to think in terms of *story questions*.

Story questions are those questions that readers will ask themselves as they read a story. It's your job as a storyteller to pose these questions throughout your story in such a way that you encourage the reader to keep reading to discover the answers.

There are three basic kinds of story questions: the leading question, the big story questions, and the little story questions. The most riveting stories are those that mix big and little story questions throughout the narrative and are driven by the leading question.

Leading questions are the ones you don't answer until the end of the story. I've organized some classic leading questions by genre.

- **MYSTERY:** Whodunnit?
- **THRILLER:** Whydunnit?
- **LOVE STORY:** Will they get married and live happily ever after?
- **SCIENCE FICTION:** How can we defeat the aliens and save Earth?
- **WESTERN:** Will the new sheriff clean up the town?
- **WAR STORY:** Will they complete their mission—and at what cost?
- **FAMILY DRAMA:** Will the family survive their ordeal *as a family* or fall apart?
- **SPORTS STORY:** Who will win the game?
- **ROMANCE:** Will she find Mr. Right?
- **SPY STORY:** Who's the mole?
- **CAPER:** How will they pull it off?

Leading questions like these will drive the main plot, but it's a long way from page 1 to the end—and that's why you need to pepper your prose with big and little story questions every step of the way. Just as every main plot has a leading story question, every subplot has a big story question as well. Similarly, every big scene has a big story question, every smaller scene has smaller story questions, and every page has multiple little story questions.

> "Anytime you get two people in a room who disagree about anything, the time of day, there is a scene to be written. That's what I look for."
>
> —Aaron Sorkin

Think of it this way: The best stories are, in effect, long Q&A sessions—that is, a dialogue of questions and answers between you and your reader. The challenge is to write a story that plants questions in the reader's mind, questions critical enough to propel the reader to keep reading until you answer them.

The most successful stories combine the leading story question, big story questions, and little story questions to create a compelling narrative. You build your plot around these story questions.

- **MAIN PLOT:** Leading story question
- **BIG SCENES:** Big story questions
- **SCENES:** Big and little story questions

Let's take a look at this story question hierarchy in the classic film *Star Wars*. As its title implies, at some level *Star Wars* is a war story. Its leading plot question matches the one from our list above: *Will they complete their mission—and at what cost?*

Every mission has parts, a procession of interim goals that, when well met, result in a successful mission. These interim goals become *the big scenes* in the plot, driven by the big story questions.

For *Star Wars*, the hierarchy looks like this.

- **LEADING QUESTION:** *Will they complete their mission—and at what cost?*
- **BIG STORY QUESTION 1:** *Will the droids R2-D2 and C-3PO find someone to rescue Princess Leia?*
- **BIG STORY QUESTION 2:** *Will Luke join Obi-Wan now that his family has been killed?*
- **BIG STORY QUESTION 3:** *Will Luke, Han, and their team be able to rescue Princess Leia without getting caught?*
- **BIG STORY QUESTION 4:** *Will Obi-Wan have to sacrifice himself so that Luke and company can escape?*
- **BIG STORY QUESTION 5:** *Will Luke learn to trust the Force and bring down the Death Star?*
- **BIG STORY QUESTION 6:** *The Death Star battle is won, but will the Empire strike back?*

Note: These big scenes also correspond to the big plot points, which we'll discuss at greater length in chapter five.

To break down the story question hierarchy even further, let's take a deeper look at Big Story Question 1 and the scenes in the story that are part of the answer to that question. Notice how each scene includes its own set of little story questions.

BIG STORY QUESTION 1: *Will the droids R2-D2 and C-3PO find someone to rescue Princess Leia?*

SCENE 1
- Princess Leia heads for home with the Death Star plans. (*Will she make it?*)
- Darth Vader and his goons take over the ship. (*Will they find her?*)
- They capture Princess Leia. (*What will they do to her? Will they find the plans?*)

- Princess Leia hides the plans along with a message in her droid R2-D2. (*Who will find the message?*)

SCENE 2
- R2-D2 and C-3PO flee in an escape pod and land on a planet called Tatooine—where they are captured by Jawas and sold to Owen Lars. (*What will happen to them there? Will the plans fall into the wrong hands?*)

SCENE 3
- Lars's nephew Luke Skywalker works on R2-D2. (*Will he find the message?*) Luke discovers Princess Leia's message. (*What will he do about it?*)

SCENE 4
- R2-D2 takes off to find Obi-Wan, for whom the message is meant. (*Will he find him? Who is this Obi-Wan?*)
- Luke and C-3PO go after the droid. (*Will they find the droid before Obi-Wan does?*)
- They are all attacked by the Sand People. (*Will the Sand People kill them? How can they get away?*)
- Obi-Wan rescues them. (*Who is this guy? How did he defeat the Sand People?*)

SCENE 5
- Obi-Wan invites them inside his home, where he tells Luke that he's a Jedi Knight. (*What is a Jedi Knight, really?*) He also tells him about the Force. (*What is this Force, really?*)
- Obi-Wan reveals that Luke's father was a Jedi Knight who was murdered by Darth Vader. (*Why did Darth Vader kill him? How did he defeat him? What does that mean for Luke?*)
- Obi-Wan gives Luke his father's lightsaber. (*Will Luke learn to use the lightsaber? Will he become a Jedi Knight like his father?*)
- They play the message from Princess Leia, in which she asks Obi-Wan to bring R2-D2 and the Death Star plans to the planet Alderaan. Obi-Wan asks Luke to join them. (*Can they make it to Alderaan? Will Luke go along? Will Darth Vader find them? Is Princess Leia still alive?*)
- Luke refuses. (*What is wrong with him? Isn't he bored and longing for adventure?*)

SCENE 6

- Luke returns home, only to find his aunt and uncle murdered by stormtroopers. (*What will Luke do now?*)
- Luke joins Obi-Wan, and they embark on the quest to rescue Princess Leia and destroy the Death Star. (*Will they succeed in rescuing Princess Leia? Will they be able to destroy the Death Star? What lies in store for them?*)

You can see how each scene raises certain questions that pull readers along from one scene to the next, from big scene to big scene, from the beginning of the story to the end. A fully developed plot is like a set of those charming Russian *matryoshka* nesting dolls, with small scenes within bigger scenes within the overall structure, and small story questions within bigger story questions within the leading question.

> *"The writer must be a participant in the scene ... like a film director who writes his own scripts, does his own camera work, and somehow manages to film himself in action, as the protagonist or at least the main character."*
>
> —Hunter S. Thompson

WRITER AT PLAY

Watch the original 1977 *Star Wars* again. (This is the one now known as *Star Wars Episode IV: A New Hope*.) Make note of the story questions as you view the film. See how tightly plotted it is—and how its themes of good and evil, love and war, identity and self-mastery are closely related to the plot and subplots. This is a particularly good story to watch for structure, not just because it is so tightly plotted but also because George Lucas used the hero's journey as his structural model. It's a model that works for many stories—maybe yours. For more on the hero's journey, see chapter five.

WORD BY WORD

We've explored how story questions work within the framework of the main plot, the big scenes, and the smaller scenes—and how you can pose story questions for each of these. But how do you pose story questions within the prose itself? This requires an attention to detail within the actual text. To do this effectively, you need to anticipate the questions readers may ask as they read your words, answer the ones that must be answered, and postpone the answering of the ones that can wait. This is a delicate balancing act. You need to answer the questions that, if left unanswered, will frustrate and distract the reader, and you must delay answering the questions that, if left unanswered, will keep them reading late into the night.

POSING LITTLE STORY QUESTIONS

Once you've plotted your story questions for your big scenes, make sure that you pose little story questions between the big questions. Aim for at least one story question every page (or around every 250–500 words).

You may be surprised at how many story questions appear in the typical scene. In the following excerpt from my memoir *Fixing Freddie*, I've underlined all the prose that poses questions for the reader. As you read the excerpt, note these underlined passages and consider what story questions are raised, which ones are answered—and which are not.

Note: This excerpt is the opening scene of the story.

FIXING FREDDIE: A TRUE STORY ABOUT A BOY, A MOM, AND A VERY, VERY BAD BEAGLE
By Paula Munier

CHAPTER ONE

"Meaning what you say is just as important as saying what you mean."
—Jennifer Bridwell, *Everything Dog Obedience Book*

We didn't need a dog. [**Why not? What's wrong with getting a dog?**] We had a perfectly nice dog, a big, loveable, huggable shaggy black mutt from the pound we called Shakespeare. And a cat, a beautiful tabby named Isis. We were a family, me and the dog and the cat and Mikey, my youngest child and the only one left at home. His siblings were grown and gone. His father was just gone. [**What happened? Where'd he go? Why? What about Mikey?**]

It was moving day. [**Why are they moving? Did they lose the house in the divorce? Did Mikey want to move?**] We'd had many moving days since the divorce a few years before—too many. [**Why so many?**] From Las Vegas to Massachusetts to California and back to Massachusetts once again. [**All the way across the country? What's up with that?**] But now, after years of financial struggle, I'd finally scraped up the money to buy us a home of our own. [**Did she get a better job? How poor are they?**] It was a small house, to be sure, just a converted summer cottage really, but the fact that it sat on a lovely lake blinded us to all its failings. [**What failings? Is this going to be a money pit?**] On this beautiful, crisp, sunny autumn day, lost in the rustle of scarlet leaves and the gentle lapping of the waves and the clean scent of pine, we were finally at home—and happy.

"Let's go get the puppy," said Mikey, as we stood on the front deck and watched the moving truck pull out of the driveway.

"What puppy?" [**What puppy?**] I considered the prospect of opening the hundreds of boxes crowding the 900 square feet of living space behind us.

"*Our* puppy." [**Why does Mikey think he's getting a puppy?**]

"We don't have a puppy." I wondered how I could squeeze a hundred pairs of shoes into my locker-size closet. [**A hundred pairs of shoes? Seriously?**] Not to mention my clothes.

"But it's time to get one."

"I don't know what you're talking about, son." I didn't do puppies. [**Why doesn't she do puppies? Doesn't she know**

every kid wants a puppy?] Mikey knew that. I calculated the cost of putting in a dishwasher once we got settled.

"'When we get a home of our own,' you said," insisted Mikey. "Remember?"

Mikey was twelve now, tall for his age, all legs and arms and attitude. **[What attitude?]** But underneath that bravado was a sad little boy who missed his father—and pulled at my mother's guilt like a champion milker. **[Why does she feel guilty? Was the divorce her fault?]**

Mikey turned to face me, placing his hands on my shoulders. At twelve, he was already nearly as tall as I was. "We have a home now, Mom," he said slowly and solemnly, as if he were explaining the nature of the universe to a three-year-old. "It is time to go get the puppy." **[Why does he think this?]**

Uh-oh. Buried deep in my parental memory I vaguely recalled was one of those rationales we serve up when our children want something very badly and we can't—or won't—give it to them. Like cake for breakfast and trips to Disney World and Daddy home for good.

Now, every kid wants a puppy, sooner or later. But puppies were too much trouble—not to mention politically incorrect. Why get a puppy when there were millions of abandoned dogs who needed a home? That's what I'd always told Mikey, and when that failed to convince him, I would always add, "You can't have a puppy in an apartment. Maybe someday when we get our own house...," **[Why did she ever make that promise?]** never dreaming given our unfortunate circumstances at the time that such a day would actually come to pass. **[Better think again?]**

"You promised," persisted Mikey. **[Is she going to honor that promise?]**

"But, honey, we have Shakespeare." At the sound of his name, Shakespeare bounded up to us, tail wagging. Shakespeare, the perfect dog, whom I'd adopted and brought home to ease the pain of that first terrible Christmas Mikey and I had spent alone. **[What makes Shakespeare the perfect dog?]**

Mikey removed his hands from my shoulders, abandoning me for the more loyal Shakespeare. "Shakespeare's great, but he's not a puppy, Mom. When we got him, he was already a *grown-up* dog."

"*And* we have a cat." I searched the yard for our intrepid tabby Isis. "<u>Have you seen her?</u> **[She's already lost the cat?]** She must be around here somewhere." Every time we moved I worried that she'd stray too far too soon and never make it back home again. One moving day a couple of years back, she'd been chased into a nearby wood by a runaway Rottweiler and didn't find her way home for two weeks.

"She's up that tree." Mikey let Shakespeare go and pointed to a tall maple across the yard. Isis was perched on a low limb, ready to pounce on a squirrel nearly as big as she.

"Puppies can't climb trees," I said, joking. "What use are they, anyway?"

"That's not funny, Mom."

"I know." I paused, and tried another tack. "We just moved in. Maybe later—"

"<u>But *you promised*.</u>" **[Doesn't she know that she must honor that promise?]**

You promised—the two words in the English language most likely to bring a single mother to her knees.

"But," I started, knowing even as I spoke it was <u>another lost cause in a string of lost causes</u> in *My Life as Supermom*. **[What lost causes? What other mistakes has she made as a Mom?]**

Mikey stuck his hands in the pockets of his jeans. He kicked at the <u>loose boards on the porch.</u> **[Loose boards? Is this house a dump?]** I made a mental note to nail them down later.

"We have a house of our own now," Mikey said in a small voice, "so we can get the puppy now."

"We'll see," I said. As soon as the <u>words were out of my mouth I regretted them</u>. **[Why does she regret them?]** <u>In our familial vernacular, "we'll see" was MommySpeak for "no way."</u> **[Is she copping out?]**

Mikey looked up at me with <u>a mild disgust I knew would soon enough morph into an active adolescent scorn</u>. **[What does she know about teenagers?]** <u>"So you didn't mean it. You never really meant it."</u> **[Has she failed him before? Does she always say things she doesn't mean?]**

I looked up at the cloudless blue sky and sighed. We'd moved for my work; I'd taken a great new higher-paying job on the South Shore. The good news was we could afford (just barely) a house now, the bad news was we had to relocate some 45 miles south. Mikey had left behind his friends, his school, his soccer team—life as he knew it. He was in a new school in a new town, lonely and friendless, as all new kids inevitably were. I was an Army brat, so I knew just *how* lonely. I thought about the poodle puppy my dad had brought home to me when I was not much younger than Mikey was now. That little dog—we named him Rogue—had been my one constant friend through a dozen new schools. *God*, how I'd loved that dog.

We didn't need a puppy. We certainly didn't need a beagle. <u>And we most certainly didn't need Freddie.</u> **[Who's Freddie?]**

But as all children teach you sooner or later, a promise *is* a promise. <u>And as I was going to learn very shortly, if you don't mean what you say and say what you mean, you've lost the battle before you've even begun.</u> **[Will she lose the battle? What battle? So she's caving and getting Mikey the puppy? When will they get the puppy?]**

READING FOR WRITERS

To get a sense of what makes a scene a scene, I recommend reading plays, starting with the Bard. Also useful is reading collections of scenes that actors use when preparing for auditions. These are scenes rife with the kind of drama and theme that allow actors to show off what they can do—and who they can become.

- *The Globe Illustrated Shakespeare* by William Shakespeare
- *The Actor's Scenebook* by Michael Schulman
- *99 Film Scenes for Actors* by Angela Nicholas

ASK YOUR OWN STORY QUESTIONS

Modest as the *Fixing Freddie* excerpt is, it proves that story questions don't all have to be life or death decisions any more than scenes all have to feature car chases and explosions. Examine one of your own scenes and find the story questions within it. Identify the story question hierarchy in your scene, and ask yourself where and how you could pose additional questions.

WRITER AT WORK

Make a list of your favorite scenes from your favorite novels. Choose one (preferably one from this century). Now copy that scene *word for word* into a notebook or onto your computer. Put yourself in the author's place as you type, and imagine the scene that lies ahead as the author might have done while writing the original. Consider what actually happens in the scene—and how that affects the rest of the story. Think about the prose and the story questions, big and small, that are posed within the text. Also note the balance of elements—action, dialogue, narrative, description, and so on—and how the writer achieved that balance. Ask yourself why you love this scene so much and how emotion factors into that admiration.

NOTE: You might be tempted to skip this exercise, as it may seem like a waste of time. Don't. You'll be surprised at how constructive the act of copying out a scene can be. It's a visceral learning experience with benefits that may not register with you consciously, or at once. Trust the process.

Now that you've examined the hierarchy of story questions, you can consider how to build your story question hierarchy—and what it might look like. What is your leading question? What are your big scenes and your big story questions? What are your smaller scenes and your smaller story questions? How do you put it all together in a cohesive storyline?

In Part II, we'll take a look at the overall structure of your story—and how you can create a scene-by-scene outline of your plot.

"The scene is dull. Tell him to put more life into his dying."
—Samuel Goldwyn

PART II

THE THEME-BASED THREE-ACT STRUCTURE

"Every great magic trick consists of three parts or acts."

—Christopher Priest

CHAPTER FIVE
YOUR PLOT IN THREE ACTS

> *"A plot is just one thing after another, a what and a what and a what."*
>
> —Margaret Atwood

All stories are made up of three parts: beginning, middle, and end. Whether you're entertaining your friends at the water cooler with a story about the bachelorette party you attended in Las Vegas or amusing your child with a bedtime fairy tale, the story will naturally be comprised of these three parts. It's the classic storytelling structure: from "Once upon a time …" to "… happily ever after," and all the good stuff in between.

The beginning, middle, and end constitute the *de facto* three-act structure: Act One is the beginning, Act Two is the middle, and Act Three is the end. In this chapter, we'll explore how the three-act structure works and how theme informs that structure. You'll learn how to apply the three-act structure to your work and how to create a scene list you can organize into three acts to best advantage.

> *"The three-act structure is intrinsic to the human brain's model of the world; it matches a blueprint that is hard-wired in the human brain, which is constantly attempting to rationalize the world and resolve it into patterns. It is therefore an inevitable property of almost any successful drama, whether the writer is aware of it or not."*
>
> —Edoardo Nolfo

THE THREE-ACT STRUCTURE

Breaking a story down into three acts—beginning, middle, and end—is the first step in plotting. These are terms we've heard and used all our lives, but defining them in regard to storytelling is not as easy as you might think.

THE BEGINNING: Where to begin? That's the decision every writer faces—and the first place many writers go wrong. The beginning of your story is the point at which everything is about to change. It's the first step of the journey, the first fork in the road, the first turn in the right (or wrong) direction. Think of lonely, single Bridget Jones snubbing Mark Darcy at her parents' holiday party in Helen Fielding's *Bridget Jones's Diary*; ambitious law school grad Mitchell McDeere interviewing for his first job in John Grisham's *The Firm*; or the shark attacking its first victim in Peter Benchley's *Jaws*. The beginning is "Once upon a time there was protagonist X—and then Y happens, changing everything for X."

THE MIDDLE: And after Y happens, you're not in Kansas anymore; you're in the middle. The cyclone has hit, and Dorothy wakes up surrounded by Munchkins in Frank L. Baum's *The Wonderful Wizard of Oz*. Sherlock Holmes is on a baffling new case, and the game is afoot in Sir Arthur Conan Doyle's *The Hound of the Baskervilles*. Beauty has swapped her life for her father's and must now live with the Beast in Gabrielle-Suzanne Barbot de Villeneuve's *Beauty and the Beast*. The middle is where X must deal with all of the complications resulting from Y. Dorothy needs to deal with Oz and the Wicked Witch of the West and those creepy flying monkeys to get home to Kansas. Sherlock must use his detecting genius to solve the case and preserve his reputation as the world's greatest detective. Beauty must learn to love the Beast as he is before she can win the love of her Prince. In the middle, X must overcome the obstacles, master the skills, and learn the lessons needed to brave the ultimate test: Y Squared, the climax of the story. The middle is the meat of the story, in which all the twists and turns and detours on the journey home to The End challenge X to be his best—or worst—self.

THE END: Survive the middle, and you're ready for the end. It's as if your protagonist X has trained for the Olympics, and now all those obstacles overcome and skills mastered and lessons learned have armed her for the final contest, which is the mother of all trials and tribulations: Y Squared. Ben Braddock crashes Elaine Robinson's wedding to run off with her in Charles Webb's *The Graduate* (yes, it was a novel first). Andy Sachs tells monster boss Miranda Priestly where to stuff her fashion magazine in Lauren Weisberger's *The Devil Wears Prada* (yes, this, too, was a novel first). Mattie Ross, Rooster Cogburn, and LeBoeuf wrangle with Mattie's father's killers—not to mention deadly snakes—in the final showdown of Charles Portis's *True Grit* (yes, there's a pattern here). Y Squared is X's worst nightmare—and to survive, X needs to become that best self, once and for all. If X succeeds, we call it a happy ending. If X fails, we call it *The Godfather* or *No Country for Old Men* or *Anna Karenina*. Either way, from the writer's perspective, all's well that ends well.

Let's take a look at how that breakdown works in three archetypal stories that are very different from one another—in length, genre, origin, audience, and so on—and yet structurally have much in common.

CINDERELLA

This classic fairy tale remains one of the most popular stories of all time. From its tightly plotted storyline to its timeless themes, it gives us a likable heroine in Cinderella, a determined and cruel villain in the wicked stepmother, and perfectly mirrored secondary characters in the ugly stepsisters.

ACT ONE (BEGINNING): Cinderella finds out about the ball, but her wicked stepmother won't let her go.
ACT TWO (MIDDLE): The Fairy Godmother helps Cinderella get to the ball in style, where she meets Prince Charming, falls in love, and loses the glass slipper.
ACT THREE (END): Prince Charming shows up with the glass slipper, slips it on Cinderella's foot for a perfect fit—and they get married and live happily ever after.

STAR WARS

One of the most successful film franchises in history, *Star Wars* is an epic tale of grand scope that redefined the space opera. But at its heart, it's a coming-of-age story about a young man looking for adventure—and finding himself.

ACT ONE (BEGINNING): When Princess Leia is captured, she sends out a plea for help. After his aunt and uncle are murdered, Luke Skywalker answers her call—and joins Obi-Wan to rescue the Princess and destroy the Death Star.

ACT TWO (MIDDLE): Luke becomes a Jedi knight under Obi-Wan's tutelage. Together they enlist the help of Han Solo and Chewbacca to rescue Princess Leia.

ACT THREE (END): The rebel forces plan their attack on the Death Star. During the conflict, Luke must trust The Force to destroy the Death Star.

EAT PRAY LOVE

The brilliant conceit of *Eat Pray Love* is its structure, which is neatly divided into three acts, just as its title implies. What's more, each act has a complete dramatic arc, with its own beginning, middle, and end. The larger story is the heroine's complete self-actualization—body, soul, and heart—while each act tells the story of how she learns to nurture herself within each component.

ACT ONE (BEGINNING): Eat in Italy. Elizabeth leaves New York City and her ex-husband for Italy, where she makes good friends; sleeps alone for the first time in her adult life; masters the art of gesticulation, ordering in Italian, and doing nothing; indulges in the fine food and drink of Italy; and finally learns to feed herself. She regains her appetite for life.

ACT TWO (MIDDLE): Pray in India. Elizabeth leaves Italy for India, where she must journey within and learn to listen to her true self. She struggles with the mosquitoes, the heat, the chanting, the endless hours of meditation. She meets Richard, who challenges her to confront her inner demons, forgive herself, and let the past go. She regains her confidence and self-respect.

ACT THREE (END): Love in Bali. Elizabeth leaves India for Bali, where she reconnects with her mentor Ketut. She makes friends with a single mother and raises money to help her get a home for her and her daughter. She helps Ketut compile his memoirs. She meets another man who isn't right for her—and, realizing it, she walks away. She meets another man who's right for her—and, realizing it, she walks away. But then Elizabeth returns—right into his arms. She regains her capacity to love, truly and deeply.

YOUR BEGINNING, MIDDLE, AND END

Breaking down your story into the beginning, the middle, and the end is the first step in building your plot. For many genres, the broad strokes of your story are somewhat preordained. Let's take a look.

LOVE STORY
- **BEGINNING:** Boy meets girl.
- **MIDDLE:** Boy loses girl.
- **END:** Boy gets girl back.

MURDER MYSTERY
- **BEGINNING:** Someone gets murdered.
- **MIDDLE:** The cops, detective, or amateur sleuth investigates the murder.
- **END:** The murderer is brought to justice.

COMING-OF-AGE STORY
- **BEGINNING:** A young person longs for adventure—and new acquaintances and events conspire to make that happen.
- **MIDDLE:** With the help of the new friends and mentor, the young person undergoes a series of transformative experiences.
- **END:** Armed with this newfound knowledge and experience, the young person triumphs against overwhelming odds—and comes of age.

WAR STORY
- **BEGINNING:** Our hero (or heroes) learns of the mission.
- **MIDDLE:** Our hero (or heroes) plan out, train for, and undertake the mission.
- **END:** Our hero (or heroes) must go above and beyond to overcome the enemy—and the mission is won.

Consider the preordained beginning, middle, and end that characterize your particular genre. Write them out. Now write a two- to three-sentence synopsis (as in the examples of *Cinderella*, *Star Wars*, and *Eat, Pray, Love*) of the beginning, middle, and end of your own story. How does the genre-based structure compare to your synopsis-based structure? How can you play with these forms to make the best three-act structure for your story?

Can you change the preordained templates for your genre? Sure, if it works for your story. For example, most love stories do end with "happily ever after" (boy gets girl back). But in others, "happily ever after" is not in the cards for the couple, who part ways rather than remaining together. In fact, some argue that the most poignant love stories end this way. Think of Margaret Mitchell's *Gone with the Wind*, Charles Frazier's *Cold Mountain*, Woody Allen's *Annie Hall*, and Arthur Laurents's *The Way We Were*.

Similarly not all murderers go to jail in every murder mystery. Justice takes many forms—and sometimes is not served at all. Such twists on the nature of justice happen in stories such as Robert B. Parker's *Mortal Stakes*, Patricia Highsmith's *The Talented Mr. Ripley*, Thomas Harris's *Hannibal*, and even Agatha Christie's *Murder on the Orient Express*.

WRITER AT WORK

Now that you have identified the conventional beginning, middle, and end for your genre as well for your own story, play with these conventions. Brainstorm ways in which you, too, can twist and tweak these conventions for your own purposes as a storyteller. Change the structure, the chronology, the setting, the point of view, and so on. Make a list of the popular stories in your genre that do the same, and see if you can adapt any of their strategies to your own story.

Say you are writing a war story. Your list of war stories that play with the standard "take that hill" structure discussed above could include:

- Joseph Heller's *Catch-22*, which uses the storylines of several U.S. airmen in World War II, told in and out of chronological sequence, to drive home the horror of war.
- Kurt Vonnegut's *Slaughterhouse-Five*, in which an American POW who survived the bombing of Dresden travels back and forth in time—past, present, and future.

- J.G. Ballard's *Empire of the Sun*, told from the point of view of an English boy in Shanghai caught up in the Japanese invasion of China.
- Lothar-Günther Buchheim's *Das Boot*, which follows a World War II German submarine as it hunts down British supply ships—but soon the hunter becomes the hunted.
- Ernest Hemingway's *A Farewell to Arms*, the story of a disillusioned American ambulance driver in World War I who becomes a deserter.
- Pierre Boulle's *The Bridge over the River Kwai*, in which British POWs are forced to build a bridge for their Japanese captors.
- Bette Greene's *The Summer of My German Soldier*, a young adult novel in which a young Jewish girl in Arkansas befriends a German POW.
- Marge Piercy's *Gone to Soldiers*, an epic tale that interweaves the storylines of ten women actively serving the war effort as spies, pilots, war correspondents, and more.

As these writers played with their genre's traditional story structures, so can you. What changes might you make? How would that change your plot? Your characters? Your theme? Your USP?

> *"What we call the beginning is often the end. And to make an end is to make a beginning. The end is where we start from."*
> —T.S. Eliot

REFINING THE THREE-ACT STRUCTURE

Once you've determined the basic beginning, middle, and end of your story, you can begin to build your plot by breaking each of those three acts into smaller units. There are two main ways to approach this refinement: plot points and the hero's journey. The plot points approach is events-driven and applies to virtually every story. The hero's journey approach is character-driven and applies to stories in which the main protagonist undergoes a series of experiences that transforms him forever (which is the case for most of our stories, but not all, as you'll see.)

Plot Perfect

Which approach you use is up to you and the story you want to tell. If you are writing a political thriller about a group of terrorists targeting the President and the various law enforcement agencies trying to stop the assassination, thinking of your story in terms of plot points might work best for you. But if you were writing a political thriller about a disgraced Secret Service agent who uncovers a plot to assassinate the President and foils that attempt, thereby redeeming himself, you might prefer the hero's journey approach.

Let's take a look at both approaches, each in turn.

THE PLOT POINTS APPROACH

With the plot points approach, you break your beginning, middle, and end into the six major events of the story. If you're writing a traditionally structured love story—boy meets girl, boy loses girl, boy gets girl back—then your major events might look like this.

BEGINNING/ACT ONE/BOY MEETS GIRL
> 1. Meet-cute
> 2. First kiss

MIDDLE/ACT TWO/BOY LOSES GIRL
> 3. First fight
> 4. Breakup

END/ACT THREE/BOY GETS GIRL BACK
> 5. Reconciliation
> 6. Wedding

We've described these events in very general terms here. But they translate to the big scenes of your story, so the more specific you can be, the better. One way to do this is to think of these six main events as the *answers* to the big story questions that we talked about earlier. Those big story questions relate to the plot points of the story. Remember in the last chapter when we talked about the big story questions in *Star Wars*? Let's look at those story questions once more with this in mind, only this time we will focus on the answers.

INCITING INCIDENT: This is the ACT ONE event that jump-starts the action of your story—and prompts the reader to ask Big Story Question 1. In *Star Wars*, the inciting incident is when Princess Leia is captured and places the message and plans in R2-D2—the event tied to the question: *Will R2-D2 and C-3PO find someone to rescue Princess Leia?*

PLOT POINT 1: Plot Point 1 is the event that takes the story in a different direction and propels the reader into ACT TWO. In *Star Wars*, Plot Point 1 is the murder of Luke's aunt and uncle, which changes everything for him. You can see how this directly relates to Big Story Question 2: *Will Luke join Obi-Wan now that his family has been killed?*

MIDPOINT: This event occurs right in the middle of the story, thereby making sure that your readers are still engrossed in the plot—and avoiding what the Hollywood folks call that awful rustling in their seats that strikes moviegoers who grow bored halfway through a film. In *Star Wars*, the midpoint comes as Luke, Obi-Wan, Han Solo, and Chewbacca attempt to rescue Princess Leia. Which is what Big Story Question 3 is all about: *Will Luke, Han, and their team be able to rescue Princess Leia without getting caught?*

PLOT POINT 2: This is the second event that takes the story in a different direction (just as Plot Point 1 does), propelling us into ACT THREE. Obi-Wan takes on Darth Vader in a fight to the death, which allows Luke and the team to escape unharmed. This has huge ramifications for everyone, but especially for Luke, and it answers Big Story Question 4 in an unforgettable way: *Will Obi-Wan have to sacrifice himself so that Luke and company can escape?*

CLIMAX: The climax is the biggest event in the story, the one that answers the Leading Question as well as Big Story Question 5. In *Star Wars*, Luke must use what his mentor Obi-Wan has taught him to destroy the Death Star. This is related to both the Leading Question (*Will they complete their mission—and at what cost?*) and to Big Story Question 5 (*Will Luke learn to trust the Force and bring down the Death Star?*).

DENOUEMENT: This is the wrap-up that ties together all the loose ends of the story—and sets the scene for the sequel, should there be one in the works. In *Star Wars*, Luke comes home to a hero's welcome—but we know that however sweet this victory, there will be more challenges ahead. This is linked to Big Story Question 6: *The Death Star battle is won, but will the Empire strike back?*

> *"All stories are about transformation. In every story a caterpillar becomes a butterfly."*
>
> —Blake Snyder

Start with Your Big Scenes

We've taken a look at the big story questions; the beginning, middle, and end; and the plot points that correspond to your big scenes. You've been mulling over the big story questions, the main events, and the three acts of your own story. You recognize that breaking down the three-act structure into plot points can help you visualize the big scenes you need to build a compelling plot. Now it's time for you to integrate those deliberations and identify your own big scenes.

```
Inciting Incident: _____

Plot Point 1: _____

Midpoint: _____

Plot Point 2: _____

Climax: _____

Denouement: _____
```

Once you've determined your big scenes, you're ready to refine your storyline even more—and build it out, scene by scene. But before you do, let's take a look at the character-driven approach to the three-act structure.

THE HERO'S JOURNEY APPROACH

> *"The usual hero adventure begins with someone from whom something has been taken, or who feels there is something lacking in the normal experience available or permitted to the members of society. The person then takes off on a series of adventures beyond the ordinary, either to recover what has been lost or to discover some life-giving elixir. It's usually a cycle, a coming and a returning."*
>
> —Joseph Campbell

The hero's journey approach is a character-driven way of breaking down the three-act structure that describes the transformation the protagonist must experience over the course of the story. If you prefer reading and writing character-driven stories, the hero's journey approach may resonate with you. That said, if your story is plot-driven and you know your characters could use some development, looking at your story as a hero's journey may help you create more well-rounded characters. Regardless, a familiarity with the hero's journey will benefit you and your storytelling, independent of the approach you use.

Famed mythologist Joseph Campbell introduced the journey of the archetypal hero in his seminal work, *The Hero with a Thousand Faces*—a book that should be on every writer's shelf. In this classic work, Campbell defines the hero's journey as a story in which the protagonist embarks on an adventure and faces trials and revelations that demand everything of him. He rises to the challenge and is transformed in the process. Campbell also shows us that the hero's journey is the most popular story type known to man, common to mythologies of every culture. Countless modern writers have since adopted the hero's journey, notably the Wachowskis, who wrote *The Matrix*. Even (or especially) if you write memoir, you are in effect writing your own hero's journey, because *you* are the hero of your own life.

HERO ... OR TRICKSTER?

Not all stories can be told as a hero's journey. Some protagonists do not change over the course of the story, but rather serve as catalysts who come to town and change everyone around them. These trickster heroes are the James Bonds, Bart Simpsons, and Pippi Longstockings of the story world.

Stories with multiple points of view or multiple protagonists can also be challenging to break down using the hero's journey. For these, as well as for trickster stories, consider using the plot points approach instead.

The Hero's Journey, Step by Step

As we have seen, all stories have beginnings, middles, and ends—and the hero's journey is no exception. The hero's journey—like the journey of life itself—is made up of three acts, and each act is made up of the steps of the journey the hero must make—a journey that will change him irrevocably and bring him to wholeness.

The six plot points we discussed earlier may—or may not—compare to these steps. That's because the steps of the hero's journey represent the stages of the hero's transformation. Let's examine this transformation step by step. (*Note:* There are various terminologies for the steps of the hero's journey. In this book, I use a simple, updated transformational terminology for modern stories.)

ACT ONE (BEGINNING)

THE STATUS QUO: When we meet our hero, we see him in his everyday world, before he undertakes the journey that will change his life. This is Dorothy before the cyclone hits in *The Wonderful Wizard of Oz*; Harry Potter with the Dursleys before he receives an admissions letter to Hogwarts in *Harry Potter and the Sorcerer's Stone*; and Katniss before her sister's name is called in the lottery in *The Hunger Games*.

THE CATALYST: This is the event that calls for our hero to act, leave his everyday world behind, and embark upon a journey into the unknown. Think of Clarice Starling given the opportunity to interview Hannibal Lecter in *The Silence of the Lambs*; Scarlett O'Hara meeting Rhett Butler for the first time in *Gone with the Wind*; and Hamlet visited by the ghost of his murdered father in *Hamlet*.

DENIAL: Typically our hero balks at this call to adventure and rejects the opportunity outright—often out of fear or hesitation or pride. Here we have such reluctant protagonists as war hero Michael Corleone, who refuses to join the family business in *The Godfather*; Marianne Dashwood, who rebuffs Colonel Brandon in *Sense and Sensibility*; and Aibileen, who turns down Skeeter's request for an interview in *The Help*.

ENCOUNTER WITH THE GURU: Every hero needs a mentor, someone whose knowledge and wisdom is vital to the hero's transformation. This sage advisor can help him navigate the twists and turns of life, and, most important, of the hazardous journey ahead. Think of Luke Skywalker and Yoda in *The Empire Strikes Back (Episode V)*; King Arthur and Merlin in the Arthurian legends; and Conrad Jarrett and Dr. Berger in *Ordinary People*.

ACCEPTANCE AND ACTION: This is the event that prompts the hero to change his mind and accept the new reality of his life. He decides to act, which means leaving his everyday world behind and crossing the physical and psychological threshold into a new world. Picture Civil War hero Lt. John Dunbar going West to the frontier in *Dances with Wolves*; Beauty entering the castle of the Beast in *Beauty and the Beast*; and Bertie going to locution lessons at Lionel Logue's house in *The King's Speech*.

ACT TWO (MIDDLE)

TRIALS AND TRIBULATIONS, FRIENDS AND FOES: In this new world, our hero encounters the people who will help him along his journey—and those who will thwart him. The tests that challenge him will help him determine friend from foe. Think of Dorothy meeting the Tin Man, the Scarecrow, and the Lion—and the Wicked Witch of the West—on the yellow brick road; Harry Potter making friends and enemies at Hogwarts; and Katniss figuring out which of her fellow *Hunger Games* contestants are the least deadly.

THE EDGE OF THE ABYSS: Now our hero is poised at the edge of the second threshold, but before he crosses it, he must regroup, rest, and plan his next course of action. Here we find Percy preparing to journey to the underworld in *The Lightning Thief*; John Book dancing with Rachel Lapp in the barn in *Witness*; and Kevin setting up booby traps to thwart the burglars in *Home Alone*.

THE PLUNGE: The hero takes the plunge into the abyss, facing his greatest fear in a confrontation with death—literal or metaphorical. Indiana Jones finds himself stuck at the bottom of the pyramid surrounded by snakes in *Raiders of the Lost Ark*; Drill Sergeant Foley breaks Mayo down ("I got nowhere else to go") in *An Officer and a Gentleman*; and Logue tells a terrified Bertie that he'd make a better king than his brother David in *The King's Speech*.

THE PAYOFF: Having survived the abyss, the hero earns his prize. This reward can take many forms: the ruby slippers and broomstick Dorothy takes with her after she douses the Wicked Witch of the West, the Holy Grail found by the Knights of the Round Table in the Arthurian legends; or the kiss that seals Rick and Ilsa's reconciliation ("Here's looking at you, kid") in *Casablanca*.

ACT THREE (END)

THE WAY THROUGH: At this point in the story, the hero is on the road back to prepare for the biggest test of all. He may be running from the forces unleashed in Act Two—which is why the way out is often a chase scene. Shrek (and Donkey) race back to Duloc on a dragon to stop Fiona's wedding in *Shrek*; Elliot and E.T. escape from Keys on a magical bicycle ride in *E.T.*; and Westley comes back to life thanks to Miracle Max in *The Princess Bride*.

THE TRUE TEST: This is the final test, the one in which the hero must prove that he has truly learned his lesson. This is Harry telling Sally that "when you realize you want to spend the rest of your life with somebody, you want the rest of your life to start as soon as possible" in *When Harry Met Sally*; Jane refusing St. John Rivers's proposal and returning to Thornfield in *Jane Eyre*; and Simba defeating Scar and taking his rightful place as king in *The Lion King*.

RETURN TO THE NEW NORMAL: Our hero comes home, transformed by his journey, his reward—physical and metaphorical—in hand. This is the part where Ennis finds the shirt in Jack's closet in *Brokeback Mountain*; where Red and Andy meet again on the beach in Zihuatanejo in *The Shawshank Redemption*; and where Snow White and the Prince get married and live happily ever after in *Snow White and the Huntsman*.

Before we discuss how to apply the hero's journey to the writing of your story, let's deconstruct the stories *Cinderella*, *Star Wars*, and *Eat Pray Love*.

ACT ONE (BEGINNING)
THE STATUS QUO

- Cinderella is miserable, living with her wicked stepmother and ugly stepsisters.
- Luke Skywalker is bored at home on the farm with his aunt and uncle.
- Elizabeth Gilbert is unhappily married in the suburbs.

THE CATALYST

- Cinderella learns about the ball.
- Luke finds a message from the kidnapped Princess Leia.
- Elizabeth gets divorced.

DENIAL

- Cinderella's stepsisters prevent her from going to the ball.
- Elizabeth falls into another bad relationship.

ENCOUNTER WITH THE GURU

- Cinderella meets her fairy godmother.
- Luke meets Ben, a.k.a. Obi-Wan [**Encounter with the Guru**], but refuses his offer to train as a Jedi knight [**Denial**].
- Elizabeth goes to Italy and meets Europeans who challenge her American way of thinking, eating, and living.

ACCEPTANCE AND ACTION

- Cinderella goes off to the ball in the pumpkin coach.
- Stormtroopers kill Luke's family, and he begins his training as a Jedi knight.
- Elizabeth makes friends, eats pasta, and learns to love her body.

ACT TWO (MIDDLE)
TRIALS AND TRIBULATIONS, FRIENDS AND FOES

- Cinderella goes to the ball and meets the prince.
- Luke travels with Obi-Wan, C-3PO, and R2-D2 to the cantina and meets Han Solo and Chewbacca.
- Elizabeth leaves lovely Italy for the chaos of India.

THE EDGE OF THE ABYSS

- Cinderella dances with the Prince, and they fall in love.
- Luke and the team board the Death Star to save the princess.
- Elizabeth goes to India to pray, but she resists the surrender meditation requires as well as the wisdom of her fellow seekers, most notably Richard.

THE PLUNGE

- The clock strikes twelve, and Cinderella loses the glass slipper as she runs away.
- Luke encounters a series of ordeals including the monster in the sewage, the collapsing trash room, attacking stormtroopers, and so on.
- Elizabeth befriends Richard and benefits from his wisdom and that of her fellow seekers.

THE PAYOFF

- The prince issues a proclamation announcing that he will marry whomever the glass slipper fits.
- Luke saves the princess.
- Elizabeth learns to forgive herself, let go of the past, and surrender to the moment.

ACT THREE (END)
THE WAY THROUGH

- Cinderella's prince arrives with the glass slipper.
- Luke et al evade Darth Vader and go home to prepare for the attack on the Death Star.
- Elizabeth goes to Bali.

THE TRUE TEST

- The ugly stepsisters try to keep Cinderella from trying on the shoe when the prince comes to their house. She perseveres and stands up to the sisters.
- Luke uses the Force to destroy the Death Star.
- Elizabeth meets a good man—and, despite her fear of making another mistake, learns to love again.

RETURN TO THE NEW NORMAL

- Cinderella marries the prince and lives happily ever after.
- Luke comes home to a hero's welcome.
- Elizabeth sails off into the sunset with her beloved.

READING FOR WRITERS

Studying the hero's journey is a great way to study structure. Here are the books that will help illuminate this monomyth for you.

- *The Hero with a Thousand Faces* by Joseph Campbell
- *The Hero's Journey: Joseph Campbell on His Life and Work* by Joseph Campbell
- *The Writer's Journey* by Christopher Vogler
- *The Heroine's Journey* by Maureen Murdock
- *The Power of Myth* by Joseph Campbell, with Bill Moyers
- *Myth and the Movies* by Stuart Voytilla

NOTE: *The Power of Myth* is also available on DVD as a six-part video series.

"Madame, all stories, if continued far enough, end in death, and he is no true storyteller who would keep that from you."
—Ernest Hemingway

Plot Perfect

The Hero's Journey, Moment by Moment

If you're thinking that this hero's journey structure only applies to epic hero stories like *Star Wars* and *Dances with Wolves* and *The Wonderful Wizard of Oz*, think again. You may be surprised at how this structure applies to more domestic stories built out of smaller moments. In the following story "God Bless Dad ... Again," you'll see how you can use the hero's journey to inform modest stories of family life well.

GOD BLESS DAD ... AGAIN
By Paula Munier

THE STATUS QUO

Every night when I put Joey to bed, I prompted him to say his prayers. He was only eight, so his prayers were typically short.

"God bless my Dad," he always began, "and Mom and Grandma and Grandpa and Mrs. Harper my teacher and Charlie my best friend and, uh, amen."

"Amen." I would hug him tight and tuck him in. He'd be out in minutes and sleep soundly until I roused him in the morning.

But tonight was different.

"Time for prayers," I told Joey as I did each evening when he scampered into bed.

"Do we have to?" Joey turned away from me and tucked his arm over his head so I couldn't see his face.

I laughed. "Yes, we have to."

"Can't we skip it, just this once?" Joey's voice was muffled.

"There's no skipping God," I said. I sat down on the edge of the bed to wait him out. After a couple of minutes, Joey sat up.

"All right, but I'm not praying for Dad anymore."

"I see," I said, which was how I tried to answer every comment regarding my ex-husband. We had divorced nearly a year ago. For me, it meant that I could finally feel at peace again, and for Joey it meant that he could love his father without worrying about his mother. He stayed at home with me during the week and visited his dad on the weekends. I prided myself on saying as little as possible about Joe Sr., since I didn't have much good to say. I didn't blame Joey; I wasn't praying for his dad, either, but I was praying about not praying for him. That was the best I could do, at least for now. Apparently it was the best Joey could do, too.

THE CATALYST

Joey folded his stubby little fingers into each other. "God bless Mom and Grandma and Grandpa and Mrs. Harper my teacher and Charlie my best friend and, uh, amen."

"Amen." I hugged Joey, and he burst into tears. I took him onto my lap and rocked him until his sobs subsided. Finally I asked. "What happened?"

"I can't be a Scout anymore." He looked at me with sad, reddened eyes.

"What? What do you mean?"

"Dad says that since Nathan and Tyler aren't in the Scouts, I can't be either."

The month before Joe Sr. had moved in with his girlfriend Jennifer. She had twin boys Joey's age, Nathan and Tyler. Joe Sr. cut his weekly visits with Joey to every other weekend—the same weekends the twins were home. On the alternate weekends when the twins visited with their father, Joey stayed home with me. Joe Sr. and Jennifer liked their time alone. So when he was with his dad, Joey found himself competing for his attention with Nathan and Tyler—and he didn't like it.

"I have to do what they do." He frowned. "Basketball."

DENIAL

Apparently the twins were grammar school giants. They towered over Joey—and every other kid in the third grade.

"So? I can take you if your father can't do it." *Or won't*, I thought.

"I need *Dad*." Joey wiped his tears with the back of his hand and sniffed. "He's supposed to help me with the Pinewood Derby."

I had no idea what the Pinewood Derby was. I had never been a Boy Scout. "Anything he can do I can do better."

Joey giggled. "Yeah, right." He giggled again. "You have to take a block of wood and carve it into a race car, Mom."

Carve. I thought for a moment. "I can carve a turkey. I can carve a pumpkin. I can carve a heart out of ice."

"No way."

"I did it once—for a prom back in high school. I think I can handle a little car."

"I don't know, Mom. You need tools and stuff. Like Dad's." Joey's voice broke. "Last year, Dad helped me carve this really cool car. We painted it blue."

Joe Sr. was a weekend carpenter, with lots of tools he'd charged on my Sears card while we were married. I was still paying it off—while the tools languished in Jennifer's three-car garage.

"We'll get whatever we need at the hardware store." I gave him a hug. "It'll be fun! Now go to sleep."

"You're dreaming, Mom," Joey said.

"Quiet now." I sat by my son until he fell asleep, praying for the Pinewood Derby.

ENCOUNTER WITH THE GURU

The next day was Saturday. I drove Joey down to the official Boy Scout store to pick up the official Pinewood Derby block of wood, which was heavy as a brick and just as inspired. The official Boy Scout who waited on us greeted my trepidation with a wise tranquility.

"No worries," he said. "All you need to know is in the package. Just follow the instructions."

I'd always been very good at following directions. Feeling better, I escorted Joey to the hardware store, where I spent all my mad money on handsaws, glue, carving knives, sandpaper, whittling books, paint, and stickers.

But back home, the official Boy Scout instructions proved too Zen for me to implement. So Joey and I searched the Internet for directions, reading up on aerodynamics, preferred weights and shapes, and the best way to build the fastest cars. We printed out pictures of previous Pinewood Derby winners from across the country. These sleek race cars bore no resemblance to the block of wood before us.

ACCEPTANCE AND ACTION

"I told you it wasn't going to be easy, Mom." Joey sat in the kitchen with a carving knife in one hand and the block in another. He looked at the design we'd decided upon—a gleaming silver bullet on four wheels—then looked back at the wooden block. "Here goes." He took the knife and shaved a miniscule sliver off one side of the block. And another. And another. Twenty minutes and barely an eighteenth of an inch later, he put down the block and said, "Your turn, Mom. I'm going to watch TV."

How long could this take? I thought, and took over the whittling.

It was hard work, and my fingers ached. Then my thumb slipped—and the knife sliced into the palm of my hand. "Ouch!" I dropped the block, grabbed a paper towel, and ran for the Band-aids. Joey came running after me. "Are you all right?"

"I'm fine."

"I told you we couldn't do it, Mom. We need Dad."

I held my breath, then let it out slowly. *We do not need that man,* I thought, but aloud I said, "We're not through yet."

TRIALS AND TRIBULATIONS, FRIENDS AND FOES

"Mom, we have to take it in to get weighed tomorrow. The race is the day after that." He regarded me with a disdain I'd come to recognize while I was married to Joe Sr. "It'll take forever to carve it. And you're bleeding, Mom."

"I'm fine." I wrapped my hand in gauze and, with Joey's help, secured it with several Band-aids. "See? Good as new. Come on, we've got work to do."

Back in the kitchen, Joey and I stared at the block.

"What we lack in craft we'll make up for in imagination," I said.

"What?"

"We need an idea." I shuffled through their printouts of past Pinewood Derby winners. "Some of these aren't carved much at all. Look, here's one cut to look like a vampire's coffin."

Joey giggled. "That's funny. They painted it black and everything."

"Okay, so what else is shaped like this? What else comes in blocks?"

Joey thought about it. "Bricks."

"Concrete."

"Ice."

"Ice! That's brilliant!" I kissed Joey. "You're my little genius!"

"What did I say?"

"Go get that diorama you made for your book report."

"The one with the penguins?"

"Yes." I grinned. "Go on, go get it!"

While Joey fetched the diorama, I said a quick prayer. *Please let this work, God. I'm no Boy Scout.*

The diorama was half a cardboard box lined with aluminum foil "ice." The sides were painted blue. Around the bottom and on top of the silver "glacier" were wind-up plastic penguins from the toy store. A scene from a children's book called *Penguins on Ice*.

"I don't get it, Mom."

"Sure you do." I placed one of the little plastic penguins on the block of wood. "Paint the block white and what do you have?"

Joey grinned. "An iceberg!"

"Exactly!" I pointed to the box of model paints. "Start painting!"

THE EDGE OF THE ABYSS

By the next morning, we were finished. Joey had painted the block and attached the wheels. Together we glued on five of the little penguins.

"It looks stupid." Joey frowned.

"It looks great!"

"It's stupid!" Joey shook his head. "I'm going outside to wait for Dad. See you tomorrow."

After Joe Sr. picked up Joey, I drove over to the Boy Scout leader's house. There were several dads there, waiting in line outside the garage for the official weigh-in. They were discussing the tools they'd used, the strategies they'd employed, the models they'd designed. They were as excited as children—

but there wasn't a kid in sight. All of their rocket race cars were as sleek as the ones we'd seen on the Internet. Once inside the garage, I found myself in a handyman's heaven. The Boy Scout leader laughed when he saw the little iceberg.

"Cute," he said. "And it falls within the weight specifications. You're good to go." He handed it back to me. "See you tomorrow night."

THE PLUNGE

The school cafeteria was overflowing with Boy Scouts, dads, and their friends and family. Joey was excited, even though he told me that he still thought the iceberg car looked stupid. We'd glued a couple of quarters to the underside of the block, as I had seen one of the fathers do at the weigh-in, hoping to speed up the little car's descent down the long curved track. Shaped like a ski ramp, the racetrack was equipped with an electric timer that clocked each race car's time to a hundredth of a second. *Boys and their toys*, I thought.

The races began, and each troop lined up their cars. Joey's troop had a dozen cars, all sleek and shiny; only Joey's was shaped like an iceberg. Only Joey's had plastic penguins on top.

"What kind of car is that?" One of Joey's pals sniggered.

"Is that yours, Joey?" The boys all laughed.

"Go on, honey." I pushed Joey up to the front.

Red faced, Joey handed his car to the judge, and the judge placed it at the top of the ramp along with the others. He looked at the penguins and winked at Joey.

THE PAYOFF

"Let's wind them up for good luck." He wound up one of the penguins. Even though it was glued in place, the little penguin still wobbled back and forth, as if it were treading water.

The judge laughed, and wound up the rest of them, placing the little car on the starting line just as the race began. Down the ramp flew the little iceberg, its penguins prancing. People pointed and laughed.

"Go, penguins, go!" they shouted. "Go, penguins, go!"

To everyone's enormous surprise—especially Joey's—the little car placed third. Joey got a medal, and I got a big hug.

THE WAY THROUGH

"I can't believe it, Mom!"

I laughed. "Neither can I!"

But the best was yet to come. After all the races were over, the overall prizes were handed out. Grand Prize went to the sleekest, shiniest bullet car there, built by a Boy Scout whose father just happened to be a master carpenter. *Yeah, right*, I thought.

"Next up, the prize for the Most Original derby car," the Boy Scout leader announced. "Now which car do you think that will be?"

"Penguins! Penguins! Penguins!" the crowd roared.

"That's right! The prize for Most Original Car goes to Joey and his Penguins, from Troop 32!"

Joey beamed. The Boy Scout leader handed him his little silver cup and asked, "How in the world did you come up with this, Joey?"

Joey looked at me and smiled. "Me and my mom did it. Together."

"That's great! With an imagination like that, you'll go far, Joey! Congratulations!"

THE TRUE TEST

On the ride home, Joey and I stopped for ice cream. Over hot fudge sundaes, we relived every glorious moment of the Pinewood Derby.

"This is the best night ever, Mom!" said Joey, his face streaked with chocolate.

"I'm just glad it worked out," I told Joey.

Joey looked down at his ice cream. "You know, Mom, the car I made with Dad never won anything."

"I see," said I, praying for the good grace not to gloat.

"But our iceberg car totally rocked!"

I laughed. "Come on, time to go."

Back home, Joey washed his face, brushed his teeth, and put on his pajamas. He placed his prize-winning race car on the bookcase above his bed: a place of honor for the little iceberg car, blessed by the grace of God.

"Time for prayers," I told him.

"Okay," Joey said and scampered into bed. "God bless my Pinewood Derby car and Mom and Grandma and Grandpa and Mrs. Harper my teacher and Charlie my best friend and, uh, amen."

"And your dad," I said gently.

"And Dad."

"Amen."

RETURN TO THE NEW NORMAL

Joey looked at me. "I can't wait to tell him all about it, Mom. Nathan and Tyler, too."

"I see," I said, and kissed my son good night.

USING THE HERO'S JOURNEY IN YOUR OWN WORK

The hero's journey approach to the three-act structure is fun to work with. It's classic storytelling that outlines the hero's transformation—or dramatic arc—in the same way that humans have been telling these stories for millennia. Outline your hero's transformation according to the hero's journey and your story will resonate with readers, just as the myths of old do.

To identify the steps of your hero's journey, ask yourself the following questions, stage by stage.

ACT ONE (BEGINNING)

THE STATUS QUO: What constitutes your hero's ordinary world? All work and no play? Single and looking for love in all the wrong places? Stuck in the suburbs dreaming of Paris?

THE CATALYST: What happens to wake up your character? Does he get fired? Flunk an exam? Find out his wife is having an affair? Get kidnapped? Get dumped? Murder his boss? Meet a cute girl? Get a new job offer out of town?

DENIAL: Does your hero act on this catalyst right away? Or balk? What excuses does she come up with to ignore what's happening? Why does she fail to act?

ENCOUNTER WITH THE GURU: Who's your hero's mentor, advisor, or confidante? His mother? His boss? Sibling? BFF? Pastor? Priest? Rabbi? How does this person guide your hero?

ACCEPTANCE AND ACTION: What happens to change your hero's mind? Why does she accept what's happening and decide to act now? What does she do? Where does she go? What new world must she enter?

ACT TWO (MIDDLE)

TRIALS AND TRIBULATIONS, FRIENDS AND FOES: Who does your hero meet on his journey, in this new world? Who are his friends? His foes? How do they help—or hinder him? What new skills must he master? What lessons must he learn? What obstacles must he overcome?

THE EDGE OF THE ABYSS: What's the big challenge that faces your hero now? How will she prepare for it—mentally, physically, and spiritually? What are her plans?

THE PLUNGE: What plunge does your hero take? Does he risk declaring his love? Storming the castle? Righting a wrong? What fears must he overcome? How does he confront death—literally or metaphorically?

THE PAYOFF: How is your hero's brave plunge rewarded? Booty? Buried treasure? Fame? Fortune? Sex? Love? Commitment? What's your hero's Holy Grail?

ACT THREE (END)

THE WAY THROUGH: Who's chasing your hero now? Are your hero's enemies or demons hot on her heels? How will your hero prepare for the next test, the biggest one of all?

THE TRUE TEST: What is the test that will prove once and for all that your hero has truly learned his lesson? How will your hero pass this test? Why will he pass?

RETURN TO THE NEW NORMAL: What is the symbol of your hero's victory? A diamond ring? A crown? A Swiss bank account? Now that your hero is home safe and sound, her transformation complete, how will she celebrate that transformation? A wedding? A reunion? A graduation? An island in the Caribbean? Keys to the city? A grateful nation?

You can use the answers to these questions to help you think through the stages of your own hero's transformation and step them out in your own three-act structure. It's important to note that these steps do not necessarily have to appear in this exact order, nor do they all have to appear in your story. For example, in some stories the Encounter with the Guru comes earlier in the narrative, or not at all. The hero's journey is meant to be used as a guide, not a straightjacket.

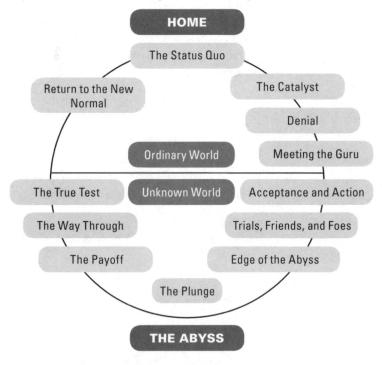

HOW MANY SCENES MAKE A NOVEL?

Okay, we've broken the three-act structure down into big scenes, plot points, and the hero's journey. We've seen how structure can play out in short stories and fairy tales as well as novels and memoirs and films. We've even examined samples of story questions and structure as revealed in the excerpt from *Fixing Freddie* and the story "God Bless Dad … Again."

But plotting a single scene or short story is one thing; plotting a long-form story is another. It is certainly true that the longer the work, the more challenging it is to build a solid structure. But there are guidelines you can follow when plotting a three-act structure for novels, memoirs, and films.

Most long-form stories have between fifty to one hundred scenes, depending on length. For your first draft, you should aim for at least sixty scenes.

- **ACT ONE**: fifteen scenes
- **ACT TWO**: thirty scenes
- **ACT THREE**: fifteen scenes

The following chart is a graphic representation of the three-act structure, broken down by scenes and plot points.

THREE-ACT STRUCTURE: Sixty Scenes

Act One: The Beginning | Act Two: The Middle | Act Three: The End

FUN WITH INDEX CARDS, PART I

At this point you have everything you need to build your sixty-scene three-act structure. You've identified your plot and subplots, your theme and variations on theme. You know your protagonist and your antagonist, as well as your secondary characters. You know what your big scenes and plot points are, and you may have identified the steps of your hero's journey as well. You can now brainstorm scenes for your story.

I like to do this with sixty blank index cards. I write down my ideas for scenes on the cards—one card per scene. This way I can shuffle them around until I find the most dramatic order. You can also use a notebook, sticky notes, or a software program. But whatever your approach, don't stop brainstorming until you have sixty ideas for scenes. Here are some instructions to help get you started.

1. Grab a stack of at least sixty blank index cards. If you already have a first draft completed, go through your manuscript and write down the scenes on the index cards. If you don't, brainstorm ideas for scenes and write each down on a separate card.

2. When you have written on fifty to sixty cards, stop and arrange them into three piles: Act One (Beginning), Act Two (Middle), and Act Three (End). Start with your big scenes, then fill in with the scenes between the big scenes.

3. If you get stuck, remember that every genre has its obligatory scenes: scenes that you'll most likely need to write, given the conventions of the genre and readers' expectations. For example, if you're writing a romance, you'll likely need to write these requisite scenes: meet-cute, first kiss, first fight, breakup, reconciliation, wedding, and so on. If you're writing a mystery, you might need: Murder 1, discovery of Body 1, introduction of sleuth, first clue, Murder 2, discovery of Body 2, sleuth interviews suspects, sleuth confronts murderer, and so on.

   Every genre has its obligatory scenes—and beginning with those can fuel your plotting imagination. How will you incorporate these obligatory scenes in your story? What will you do to make yours unique, since the reader has by definition seen these scenes before? Or will you play against these scenes, turn the table on the genre, and make your own conventions?

THE BEGINNING OF THE END

In this chapter, we've studied the three-act structure and its big scenes and plot points, and you've made a preliminary effort to plan out your story scene by scene. You have the sixty scenes you need to build your plot—or at least a fair number of them. With these scenes in hand, you can refine this first outline of your plot, weaving in your themes, building suspense, and deepening the emotional impact of your story.

In the next chapter, we'll see how everything we've explored in this book so far—plot and subplot, theme and variation of theme, character, story questions, big scenes and plot points, the three-act structure, and the hero's journey—comes together in one masterwork: *The Maltese Falcon* by Dashiell Hammett.

> "A story should have a beginning, a middle, and an end, but not necessarily in that order."
>
> —Jean-Luc Godard

CHAPTER SIX

CASE STUDY:
The Maltese Falcon

> "The Maltese Falcon *broke the barrier of the genre: it was, and is, a work of art.*"
>
> —Ross Macdonald

Case studies are one of the best ways to look at the complexities of plot and theme, because they allow you to see every piece of one puzzle, as opposed to many pieces of different puzzles. And what is plot if not a puzzle? No matter what your genre, you are building a story out of pieces of plot, scenes that illuminate your themes, characters, and worldview.

While these pieces need not fit together so perfectly in some genres, in others a good and even surprising fit is essential. Crime fiction is one of the most demanding genres in this regard. When it comes to plot, readers of this genre are as spoiled as they are sophisticated. They've cut their teeth on the stories of such masterful plotters as Agatha Christie, Sir Arthur Conan Doyle, Ngaio Marsh, Raymond Chandler, and John Le Carré, among others. Not to mention Edgar Allan Poe, the father of the detective story and the inspiration for the most prestigious award in crime writing, the Mystery Writers of America's Edgar Award.

That's why we'll be looking at Dashiell Hammett's *The Maltese Falcon* as our case study. This timeless story is generally acknowledged as the best detective novel of all time. And for good reason, given its intricacies of plot, theme, and character.

In examining *The Maltese Falcon*, we'll be taking a scene-by-scene look at one of the most cleverly plotted stories of all time. By analyzing this classic in terms of its theme, variations on theme, plot, and subplot, you'll learn to construct—and deconstruct—your own stories, as well as the bestsellers in your genre. And, perhaps most important, you'll have fun doing it.

> *"The Maltese Falcon is not only probably the best detective story we have ever read, it is an exceedingly well-written novel."*
> —The (London) Times Literary Supplement

If you don't know this story yet, I encourage you to pick up a copy; I promise you one of the best reads you've experienced in a long time. (Vintage publishes a very nice edition.) You can also watch the 1941 movie based on the book; it's a very faithful adaptation on most counts. Directed by John Huston, *The Maltese Falcon* made a leading man of Humphrey Bogart, who had previously been typecast as a thug or villain. It's an interesting exercise to compare the novel to the noir film—and a most enjoyable one at that. But nothing compares to reading the novel itself.

You don't need to read the book or see the movie to understand and appreciate all we'll discuss in this chapter. But if you do, you'll be glad you did (and you won't care about the spoilers you'll also find in this chapter). No story will teach you more about plot, dialogue, character, theme, and economy—all elements even more critical in today's market than they were when the story appeared in a five-part serialization in the September 1929 to January 1930 issues of the pulp magazine *Black Mask*. (The book came out in 1930.) That's why the novel still engages readers today; its plot is as compelling as any modern story, and its themes are as relevant now as they were nearly a century ago.

WRITER AT PLAY

Host a Dashiell Hammett night with your book club or writers group. Read *The Maltese Falcon* and discuss its plot, subplots, theme, and variations on theme. Talk about the characters and why this book is regarded as a classic. As an alternative, host a movie night and watch the 1941 film version with Humphrey Bogart and Mary Astor.

WHAT'S IT ALL ABOUT, SAM SPADE?

Let's start by taking a look at what *The Maltese Falcon* is about. In terms of broad strokes, *The Maltese Falcon* follows its genre.

1. Someone gets murdered.
2. The detective hero investigates the murder.
3. The murderer is brought to justice.

But Hammett tweaks these basic plot elements in a manner all his own. Sam Spade, the detective hero, is not simply a puzzle solver like Sherlock Holmes or Hercule Poirot. Spade is an existential hero who lives by his own code: the first of an archetype that has come to be known as the hard-boiled detective.

The "someone" who gets murdered is his own partner, Miles Archer— and that hits Spade very close to home. He feels he must act. And this holds true even when his investigation reveals that the murderer may be the woman he loves.

This code of honor speaks to the big themes of the story: love and loyalty, truth and betrayal.

By definition, detective stories concern a search for the truth: Whodunnit? And in this way, *The Maltese Falcon* is a typical detective story. But it's also about the truth that Sam Spade lives by and the loyalty he feels to his partner, dead or alive. In short, the story is about Spade's search for the truth about who killed his partner, and his dogged pursuit leads to a terrible choice—love or loyalty.

But there's more to this story, as we can tell by the title itself: *The Maltese Falcon*. This priceless treasure is what all of the story's antagonists are chasing after—and that pursuit is driven by greed. Greed is often the motive for murder in mysteries, but whether you are writing a mystery or a romance or a science fiction epic, you should look to the motivation of your villain(s) for additional themes that may mirror or challenge your hero's themes.

If we were to identify proverbs, quotes, and sayings that embody the themes of *The Maltese Falcon*, these might be among them.

- "Fool me once, shame on you. Fool me twice, shame on me."
- "Truth will out."
- "A half-truth is a whole lie."
- "Buy the truth, and sell it not."
- "Everybody lies."
- "A leopard never changes its spots."
- "People always revert to type."

- "To thine own self be true."
- "You are what you do."
- "A good name is better than riches."
- "All that glitters is not gold."
- "Money isn't everything."
- "Money is the root of all evil."
- "Crime doesn't pay."
- "You can't buy loyalty."
- "Birds of a feather flock together."

But Hammett also provides us with his own set of proverbs for *The Maltese Falcon,* proverbs that reflect his hero's solitary code of ethics.

- "When your partner is killed, you're supposed to do something about it."
- "Never ask a dog to catch a rabbit and let it go."
- "When someone in your detective agency gets killed, it's bad business to let the killer get away with it."

The best storytellers make the old adages their own—and Hammett is one of the best.

> *"I've been as bad an influence on American literature as anyone I can think of."*
>
> —Dashiell Hammett

THE USP OF *THE MALTESE FALCON*

The Maltese Falcon was a huge commercial success, first for *Black Mask,* the pulp magazine that published the book in serialization, and then for book publisher Alfred A. Knopf. The first film version, starring Ricardo Cortez as Spade, garnered good reviews and box office receipts. The 1941 film with Humphrey Bogart was a blockbuster for Warner Brothers, Edward G. Robinson played Spade on the radio, *The Adventures of Sam Spade* ran on television from 1946 to 1951, and the quintessential hard-boiled private eye character has been spoofed in countless parodies of the genre—from 1975's *The Black Bird* starring George Segal to Neil Simon's popular 1976 comedy, *Murder by Death*, starring Peter Falk.

And today *The Maltese Falcon* continues to win new readers, generation after generation.

What's the secret to this success? Sure, it's well written and entertaining, but the reason it remains one of the most popular private eye novels of all time lies in its unique selling proposition (USP): Sam Spade.

In Sam Spade, Hammett created a new kind of hero, an iconic archetype: the existential gumshoe who's influenced every hard-boiled detective since—from Raymond Chandler's Philip Marlowe in *The Big Sleep* to Nic Pizzolatto's nihilistic police detective Rustin Cohle in HBO's *True Detective*.

Create a new kind of hero—one who transcends your genre—and you have yourself one heck of a USP. Talk about the same but different: *The Maltese Falcon* is just like every other best-selling crime novel of its day, but different in its one-of-a-kind hard-boiled hero.

It is worth noting that, unlike his other crime-writing peers, Hammett himself had been an operative for the Pinkerton National Detective Agency—and that informed his creation of Sam Spade.

> "Spade has no original. He is a dream man in the sense that he is what most of the private detectives I worked with would like to have been and in their cockier moments thought they approached. For your private detective does not—or did not ten years ago when he was my colleague—want to be an erudite solver of riddles in the Sherlock Holmes manner; he wants to be a hard and shifty fellow, able to take care of himself in any situation, able to get the best of anybody he comes in contact with, whether criminal, innocent bystander or client."
>
> —Dashiell Hammett

THE FIRST LINE AND THE LAST LINE

In a significant way, Sam Spade is an all-American hero. His work ethic is singularly American, as is his belief that letting Archer's killer get away with murder would be "bad for business." Spade is all about his work—and this theme runs through the book from beginning to end. When we first meet Spade, he's at work. And when we see him at the end of the novel, he's at work.

Similarly the first line of the novel speaks to Spade's character.

> Samuel Spade's jaw was long and bony, his chin a jutting *V* under the more flexible *V* of his mouth.

We see in this Dickensian characterization a stubborn man with a strong jaw. We know from the first line that he won't easily sacrifice his principles. We just don't know what those principles are yet—or how they will be tested over the course of the story.

In the last line of *The Maltese Falcon*, Spade is back at his desk, and he says:

> "Well, send her in."

And life goes on for Sam Spade.

"X MEETS Y" AND "THE ONLY TROUBLE IS . . ."

Describing *The Maltese Falcon* in these high-concept Hollywood terms is an interesting exercise. You can think of this classic as an *X meets Y* equation: "Hemingway meets Carroll John Daly" or "Hercule Poirot meets the Pinkerton National Detective Agency."

If you prefer *The only trouble is ...*, you can think of *The Maltese Falcon* as: "A private detective takes on a new case. The only trouble is, his partner is murdered that same night." Or: "A private detective falls in love with his new client. The only trouble is, she's trouble."

These devices only hint at theme, so let's devise a theme statement for *The Maltese Falcon* that can incorporate Spade's unique code of ethics.

> Private detectives Sam Spade and Miles Archer take on a new case for a gorgeous client **[plot]**. When Archer is murdered **[plot]**, Spade vows to catch his partner's killer **[theme]**—and is pulled into a dangerous hunt for a priceless artifact known as the Maltese Falcon **[plot]**. Caught up in a web of greed, betrayal, and murder **[plot and theme]**, Spade's dogged search for the truth leads to a terrible choice—love or loyalty **[plot and theme]**.

This statement speaks to theme, but it can't account for all the themes and variations on theme that Hammett has woven into the novel. Bubble charts for the themes of truth and loyalty and love and greed will allow us to dig deeper.

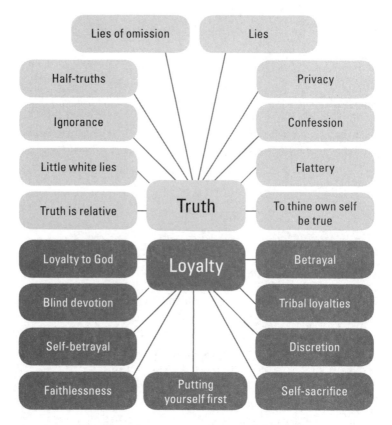

The Maltese Falcon is as rich in plot and subplots as it is in theme and variations on theme. Let's examine their interrelationships, as we did with *Pride and Prejudice* in chapter two.

LOVE: Love is a theme woven throughout this detective novel. Iva Archer loves her husband's partner, Sam Spade, and in her love for him she shows up at inopportune times to badger Spade. Spade loves Brigid O'Shaughnessy, and Brigid loves him, too—and it is this love that gives the novel its bittersweet ending. Thursby loves Brigid—and in the end he dies for it. Gutman loves Wilbur "like a son," and perhaps more accurately as a lover, but turns on him in a minute.

HATE: Wilmer Cook hates Spade, because Spade humiliates him by seeing through his amateurish effort to tail him, taking his guns away, serving him up as the fall guy, and knocking him out cold, among

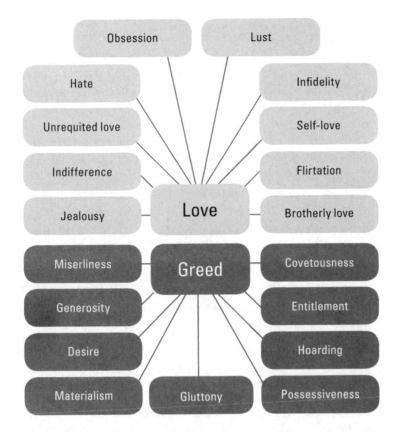

other things. Gutman, Cairo, and Wilmer love and hate each other, the implication being that they are a sexual threesome. Iva hates Brigid, Effie hates Iva, and Spade didn't think much of his partner, Miles Archer.

INFIDELITY AND FAITHLESSNESS: Spade is having an affair with his partner's wife, Iva. His partner, Miles Archer, would have slept with Brigid if she hadn't killed him first. Faithlessness is the name of the game among the crew chasing the Maltese Falcon; they're all scheming behind each other's backs and shifting alliances throughout the course of the story.

UNREQUITED LOVE: Iva loves Spade, but he doesn't love her. Thursby loves Brigid, but she doesn't love him—and she uses his love for her as bait, from the time they leave Hong Kong until he dies.

LUST: This novel is full of lust, fulfilled and unfulfilled—and who's sleeping with whom influences the plot. Spade lusts after Iva and has an affair with her. Spade lusts after Brigid and sleeps with her. Brigid offers herself to Spade, and the implication is that she does that whenever she wants something from a man, be it Thursby or Spade. Effie appears to lust after Spade, but she also admires Brigid, an admiration which some read as sexual interest. At the time when the novel was written, homosexuality was rarely written about overtly—but the implication is that Cairo is gay and Gutman is bisexual (readers are given hints that he's bedded his daughter, Rhea, as well as Wilmer and Cairo). Spade calls Wilmer a "gunsel," a slang term for homosexual. Gutman says he loves Wilmer "like a son," which many read as "lover." But Wilmer also shows an interest in Rhea Gutman. Whether or not Rhea really is Gutman's daughter is again a matter of interpretation. But regardless of how you read these relationships, it's obvious when Spade finds Rhea drugged in the hotel room, her torso punctured with pinpricks, that something is going on.

JEALOUSY: Iva gets jealous when she sees Spade with Brigid and sends the police to his apartment. Spade's secretary is jealous of Iva's relationship with Spade.

FLIRTATION: Brigid flirts with everyone—but her flirtation with Spade is ultimately her downfall. Iva's flirtation with Spade is a full-fledged affair. Spade flirts with Brigid, Iva, and even Effie.

INDIFFERENCE: Spade is detached; not much touches him. He's indifferent to Archer's feelings, so much so that he sleeps with his wife. He's indifferent to Iva's love for him. Even his feelings for Brigid are not strong enough to penetrate the detachment with which he solves the case and brings her to justice.

GREED: The Maltese Falcon is a priceless treasure that brings out the greed in virtually everyone who knows anything about it—and most of them are willing to kill for it. Even Spade doesn't seem immune—and yet in the end he hands over the $1,000 to the police along with Brigid.

COVETOUSNESS: Spade covets his partner's wife. Iva covets Spade. Wilmer, Cairo, Gutman, and Brigid all covet the Maltese Falcon.

GLUTTONY: Gutman is referred to as the "fat man" throughout the story—and great detail is given to the physical description of his girth.

DESIRE: Desire drives nearly everyone in this story—the desire for sex, love, and the Maltese Falcon.

OBSESSION: Gutman is obsessed with the bird and has been chasing it for seventeen years—and he's not the only one running all around the world after the treasure. Spade is obsessed with bringing his partner's killer to justice, no matter who it is.

TRUTH: Every detective story is a search for the truth—and this one is no exception. Spade needs to find out the truth about his partner's death, no matter what the cost. That's quite a challenge, as discovering the truth means seeing through the lies—and nearly everyone lies in this story.

LIES, HALF-TRUTHS, AND LIES OF OMISSION: Brigid lies about who she is and what she wants when she first comes to Spade's office. She lies to Archer, luring him to his death. She lies to Spade about her part in Archer's death, one among many lies she tells. Spade lies to the cops when they ask him about Brigid, and he lies to Brigid when he searches her apartment. Gutman, Cairo, and Wilber lie to each other and to Spade. Even the Maltese Falcon is, in the end, a lie.

CONFESSION: The cops and the district attorney press Spade to confess to the crime(s); Spade presses Brigid to tell him the truth over and over again throughout the story.

BETRAYAL: Spade betrays his partner, Miles Archer, by sleeping with his wife. He betrays Iva by sleeping with Brigid. Iva betrays Spade by telling the police Spade may have killed her husband so Spade could marry her. Gutman betrays Wilmer, and Wilmer kills him for it.

PRIVACY AND DISCRETION: Spade's interaction with the cops and the DA centers around the themes of discretion and privacy. Spade defends his clients' privacy when the police question him about the case, citing his discretion as his right as a private detective. Yet he sends Iva to talk to attorney Sid Wise and then pressures Sid to reveal what she told the lawyer in confidence.

LOYALTY AND TRIBAL LOYALTIES: The theme of loyalty is central to this story. Effie is loyal to Spade. Spade is disloyal to Archer as a man, when he sleeps with his wife, but Spade is loyal to Archer as his partner when he tracks down his killer. The cops stick together, as do the mobsters—and characters betray those kinds of tribal loyalties at their peril. Most important, Spade's code of ethics is a form of tribal loyalty; someone has killed his partner, and he has to do something about it.

DEVOTION: Thursby is devoted to Brigid—and that blind devotion costs him his life. Wilmer is devoted to Gutman, until Gutman sets him up as the fall guy. Effie is devoted to Spade, even when he sleeps with Iva and turns in Brigid. Sid and Spade are devoted to one another, out of a mutual respect for their commitment to work. Effie's mother is devoted to Effie, and Spade honors that. Spade is devoted to his work, which is another reason he feels he has to bring Archer's killer to justice.

SELF-LOVE: Spade may love Brigid, but he loves himself more. He knows that he couldn't live with himself if he let his partner's killer go free—and he tells her as much.

TO THINE OWN SELF BE TRUE: Ultimately this is the philosophy that drives Spade. He lives by a code of his own making, unmoved by conventional morality and behavior. At the end of the novel, he enumerates all the reasons he has to turn Brigid in—and why not doing so would be betraying himself.

> "To swipe the immortal lines uttered by Sam Spade in The Maltese Falcon, a great mystery should take 'the lid off life and let [you] look at the works.'"
>
> —Dashiell Hammett

THE MALTESE FALCON THEMES CHART

As you can see, in his unsentimental way Hammett is as clever a weaver of plot, subplots, theme, and variations on theme as Jane Austen is. Similarly he threads his various subplots—Spade and Iva; Spade and Brigid; Archer and Brigid; Thursby and Brigid; Gutman, Cairo, and Wilmer; Spade and Sid; Spade and Effie; Spade, the cops, and the DA—so they relate to one another as well as to the main plot and themes. Let's take a look at how the main plot and main subplots, themes, and variations on themes might appear on *The Maltese Falcon* Themes Chart.

THE MALTESE FALCON THEMES CHART

Variations on Theme
Flirtation, Infidelity, Betrayal, Jealousy, Covetousness, Lust, Unrequited Love, Indifference

Variations on Theme
Love, Lust, Lies, Betrayal, Flirtation, Self-love, Confession, To Thine Own Self Be True

Subplot D
Sam and Iva

Subplot A
Sam and Brigid

Main Themes:
Truth and Loyalty

Main Plot:
Sam solves his partner's murder and brings the killer to justice

Subplot C
Sam and the Law
(Cops, the DA, Sid)

Subplot B
The Hunt for the Maltese Falcon
(Brigid, Thursby, Wilmer, Gutman, Captain Jacobi, Cairo, Kemidov)

Variations on Theme
Privacy, Discretion, Tribal Loyalties, Half-Truths, Lies of Omission, Hate

Variations on Theme
Greed, Obsession, Lies, Betrayal, Devotion, Desire, Covetousness, Gluttony

SAM SPADE: A WALKING CONTRADICTION

Just like Hamlet and other great characters of literature, Sam Spade is a walking contradiction.

Romantic	Pragmatic
Idealistic	Cynical
Tender	Tough
Cowardly	Brave
Philosophical	Passionate
Loyal	Disloyal

Detached	Committed
Liar	Truth seeker
Hates women	Loves women
Loner	Lover
Disciplined	Messy
Observant	Proactive
Brainy	Brawny

Just as we saw in Hamlet's character, Spade's contradictory traits compete for dominance within him. And just like with Hamlet, Spade's contradictory impulses propel the plot.

- He's a romantic who lives by his own code of honor; he's a pragmatist who does what he needs to do to get the job done.
- He's idealistic about his calling as a detective; he's cynical about the world in which he practices that calling.
- He can be tender, as when he tries to save the drugged girl in Gutman's hotel suite; he'd as soon hit you as look at you if he feels you deserve it.
- He can be a coward, as he is when he avoids Iva rather than deal with her, pawning her off on Effie; he's brave in the face of getting beat up, drugged, etc.
- He's philosophical about human nature; he's passionate about work and women.
- He's committed to finding his partner's killer in the name of loyalty; he sleeps with his partner's wife.
- He's detached, distancing himself from everyone around him; he's committed to his work and bringing his partner's killer to justice.
- He's not above obscuring the truth, telling half-truths, and lies of omission, as well as outright lies, when dealing with everyone from cops to criminals; he will stop at nothing to discover the truth about Archer's murder.
- He loves women, all kinds of women, from Effie to Brigid; he often treats them roughly and badly—not to mention as sexual objects.
- He's a loner whose relationships consist mostly of colleagues, enemies, frenemies, and hookups; he falls in love with Brigid O'Shaughnessy.

- He intellectualizes everything; he reacts emotionally and aggressively.
- He cares for Brigid; he breaks her heart and turns her in.
- He's disciplined about his work; he's messy in his relationships.
- He's strong and proactive; he's observant and world-weary.
- He's smart as a whip; he's as apt to punch you out as outsmart you.

BRIGID O'SHAUGHNESSY: A WALKING CONTRADICTION

As in most crime fiction, the antagonist in *The Maltese Falcon* is the murderer. But when Dashiell Hammett introduced the enigmatic and beautiful schemer Brigid O'Shaughnessy, he created the iconic femme fatale of noir fiction—the bad girl with the gorgeous gams who leads the hero into big trouble. Just like our hero—and her mark—Sam Spade, she's a walking contradiction.

Tentative	Bold
Soft	Hard
Well-dressed	Stripped naked
Innocent	Guilty
Honest	Liar
Good	Evil
Hot	Cold
Pretty on the outside	Ugly on the inside
Naïve	Manipulative
Romantic	Ruthless
Loves men	Uses men
Tender	Tough
Loyal	Disloyal
Lover	Sees sex as a weapon

Brigid O'Shaughnessy is as complex a character as our hero—and thus she's a worthy adversary. Just as her contradictory traits compete for dominance within her own character, these pairs of opposites face off with those contradictory traits of Sam Spade and provoke much of the conflict between them.

- When she first appears in Spade's office as Miss Wonderly, she's described as tentative and shy and soft-spoken; as Brigid

O'Shaughnessy she boldly offers to give up her body to him in exchange for the priceless bird.

- She's all soft and feminine in that "school girl manner" Spade teases her about; she kills Archer in cold blood without hesitation.
- She wears very smart and sensuous clothes—from silk crepe dresses to satin gowns—which are described at great length, and which suit her respective aliases; she strips herself naked in the bathroom to prove to Spade that she has not stolen the $1,000 bill.
- As Miss Wonderly, she's all sweetness and innocence; as Brigid O'Shaughnessy she tells Spade flat out that "I'm not innocent."
- She makes several flirtatious statements to Spade that sound like a line but turn out to be completely true in a different context, including the aforementioned "I'm not innocent," as well as "I haven't lived a good life;" she tells lie after lie after lie, starting with her name—first she's Miss Wonderly, then she's Miss Leblanc, then she's Brigid O'Shaughnessy.
- At first she comes across as the good sister trying to find her errant sibling; later we find out that she is nobody's good anything.
- She's a very sexy, hot lady, who has most men eating out of her hand—even Spade is not immune to her smoldering sexuality; we see later that she can turn her charm on—and off—even as she shoots you at point-blank range.
- She's a beautiful woman; as the proverb goes, "beauty is only skin deep"—and below that lovely skin is a dark soul.
- She's naive enough to believe that she can charm Spade into letting her get away with murder; she manipulates Thursby and Archer and does her best to manipulate Spade as well.
- She's a romantic when it comes to Spade, and we (nearly) believe that she loves him, at least as much as she is capable of loving anyone; she's absolutely ruthless in her pursuit of the Maltese Falcon.
- She loves men, at least physically, over and over again; she uses men—Thursby, Archer, even Spade—to get what she wants.
- She's very tender with Spade, a tenderness that may or may not be real; she's tough enough to survive among the likes of Thursby, Gutman, Cairo, and Wilber, and give them a run for their money.

- She professes loyalty to Spade, and certainly she is loyal to her own aims; in the end, she betrays everyone, except Spade—and he knows he can never trust her not to betray him in the future.
- She's good enough in bed to seduce man after man; she uses her sexual wiles as a weapon to induce men to do her bidding.

Of course, Brigid is just one of many antagonists in *The Maltese Falcon*. Spade is challenged by the criminals chasing the bird, by the cops and the DA, and even by his mistress and his secretary. All provide great fodder for the main plot and subplots as well as the theme and variations on theme. Let's take a look at the bubble chart below outlining the characters in Spade's world.

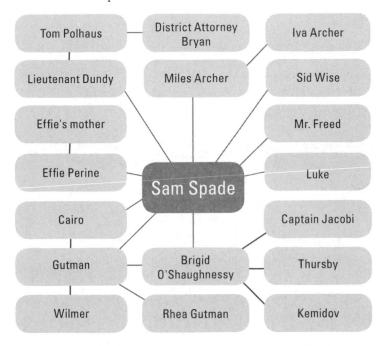

THE BIG SCENE BREAKDOWN

Now that we've taken a good look at *The Maltese Falcon's* theme and main plot, subplots, and variations on theme, as well as the protagonist, antagonist, and secondary characters, let's break down the story into its big scenes.

ACT ONE
- **INCITING INCIDENT**: Archer is murdered (Murder 1), as is Thursby (Murder 2).
- **PLOT POINT 1**: Cairo offers Spade $5,000 to find the Maltese Falcon.

ACT TWO
- **MIDPOINT**: Gutman drugs Spade. Spade wakes up and goes back to the office.
- **PLOT POINT 2**: Enter the man with the Maltese Falcon (Murder 3).

ACT THREE
- **CLIMAX**: Spade turns in Brigid.
- **DENOUEMENT**: Spade is back at the office with Effie and Iva.

As you can see, the plot points in *The Maltese Falcon* align with those of many crime novels, from introducing the crimes to solving the crimes and bringing the criminals to justice.

THE MALTESE FALCON: THE ULTIMATE MACGUFFIN

A *MacGuffin* is a term popularized by film director Alfred Hitchcock to describe any object, goal, event, or character in a story that drives the plot, motivating the characters to get it, control it, conceal it, or crush it. Examples include:

- Bilbo's ring (*The Lord of the Rings* by J.R.R. Tolkien)
- Helen of Troy, "the face that launched a thousand ships" (*The Iliad* by Homer)
- France (*Henry V* by Shakespeare)

And, of course, the Maltese Falcon in *The Maltese Falcon*.

The debate over the true definition of a MacGuffin seems ongoing and never-ending, but here are a couple of broad guidelines to follow when you're dreaming up your own holy grail: (1) Make it something—or someone—hard to get, and (2) make it something—or someone—well suited to your genre.

THE MALTESE FALCON STATUE: THE ULTIMATE MACGUFFIN

In *The Maltese Falcon*, the bird turns out to be a lead fake. But Hammett allegedly based his Maltese Falcon on the real artifact known as the Kniphausen Hawk. The bejeweled statuette is a ceremonial pouring vessel that dates from 1697. Originally created for George William von Kniphausen, Count of the Holy Roman Empire, the priceless vessel is now the prized property of the Duke and Duchess of Devonshire.

Ironically the props of the Maltese Falcon created for 1941 film starring Humphrey Bogart are now ranked among the most significant movie props of all time, along with Dorothy's ruby slippers and Marilyn Monroe's subway dress—and as such are now also worth a fortune. There are two such Maltese Falcon props, one of which sold for $398,500 to a private collector back in 1994. The other sold for a remarkable $4,085,000 at auction in 2013.

A MACGUFFIN BY ANY OTHER NAME

Alfred Hitchcock credits screenwriter Angus McPhail as the man who coined the term *MacGuffin*, based on an old schoolboy joke that went like this.

> A man is riding on a train when a second gentleman gets on and sits down across from him. The first man notices the second is holding an oddly shaped package.
>
> "What is that?" the first man asks.
>
> "A MacGuffin, a tool used to hunt lions in the Scottish highlands."
>
> "But there are no lions in the Scottish highlands," says the first man.
>
> "Well then," says the other, "that's no MacGuffin."

> *"I'm one of the few—if there are any more—people moderately literate who take the detective story seriously. I don't mean that I necessarily take my own or anybody else's seriously—but the detective story as a form. Someday somebody's going to make 'literature' of it ... and I'm selfish enough to have my hopes."*
>
> —Dashiell Hammett

A DETECTIVE BY ANY OTHER NAME

Dashiell Hammett had a bit of fun naming the characters in *The Maltese Falcon*. This Dickensian device is one you might want to try in your novel—with subtlety, of course. Here are some of the best names in the novel, ones that relate directly to its themes and variations on theme.

- **SAM SPADE:** The dogged detective who keeps digging until he finds his partner's murderer.
- **GUTMAN:** The corpulent villain whose greed for the Maltese Falcon knows no bounds. He is also known as "the fat man."
- **SID WISE:** The astute attorney who calls Spade on his shenanigans, serving as a sort of moral compass for our hero.
- **MISS WONDERLY/MISS LEBLANC/MISS O'SHAUGHNESSY:** The slippery beauty goes from "wonderful" to "pure white" (or a "blank") to "a person of uncertain origin." And of course Brigid is the name of the classic Celtic Triple Goddess, made up of three sisters—Brigit the Poetess, Brigit the Smith, and Brigit the Healer.
- **LIEUTENANT DUNDY:** The dunderheaded cop who's always in Spade's face.

SAM SPADE AND THE HERO'S JOURNEY

As we've seen, Sam Spade is an iconic hero who's served as the inspiration for countless private detective protagonists. So it might prove very useful to deconstruct *The Maltese Falcon* in terms of the hero's journey—and examine how Spade fits the hero model.

ACT ONE

THE STATUS QUO: Private detective Sam Spade meets with a new client, the beautiful Miss Wonderly (later known as Brigid O'Shaughnessy), in his office.

THE CATALYST: Spade's partner, Miles Archer, is found murdered. Not long afterward, the man Archer was tailing, Floyd Thursby, is also murdered.

DENIAL: The cops think Spade killed Archer and/or Thursby. Brigid asks Spade to protect her.

ENCOUNTER WITH THE GURU: Spade visits his attorney Sid Wise. (Note the lawyer's last name.)

ACCEPTANCE AND ACTION: Cairo offers Spade $5,000 to find the Maltese Falcon.

ACT TWO

TRIALS AND TRIBULATIONS, FRIENDS AND FOES: Spade begins his investigation.

THE EDGE OF THE ABYSS: Spade runs into trouble with the cops, the DA, and Cairo, Gutman, and Wilmer. He sleeps with Brigid.

THE PLUNGE: Wilmer confronts Spade, guns loaded. Spade takes away the guns, and they go see Gutman. Gutman tells Spade the story of the Maltese Falcon—then drugs him. As Spade goes down, Wilmer kicks him in the head.

THE PAYOFF: Captain Jacobi shows up with the bird.

ACT THREE

THE WAY THROUGH: Spade hides the bird and puts his plan in place.

THE TRUE TEST: The showdown in the apartment with Gutman. The bird turns out to be a fake. Cairo and Gutman take off for Constantinople and Wilmer slips out. Spade calls the police on them. He confronts Brigid about Archer's murder and turns her in.

RETURN TO THE NEW NORMAL: Sam Spade is back in his office. Only his name appears on the door now. He's survived the loss of his partner—and the loss of his love.

> "Sam Spade is the friend we need in trying times. He is our taunting big brother, our brutal father, the schoolyard bully who has seen the error of his ways and now defends us. He is the man we want in our corner because he will stop at nothing to save us, or, if need be, avenge us. It is Spade's humanity that we feel, and which Hammett so brilliantly illuminates, and it is that humanity to which we respond."
>
> —Robert Crais

THE MALTESE FALCON, SCENE BY SCENE

The Maltese Falcon is a great story to study at the scene level because it breaks down into about sixty scenes—just like the sixty scenes we talked about in chapter five.

As a refresher, most long-form stories have between fifty to one hundred scenes, depending on length. For your first draft, you should aim for at least sixty scenes.

- **ACT ONE**: fifteen scenes
- **ACT TWO**: thirty scenes
- **ACT THREE**: fifteen scenes

As you look at the following scene-by-scene breakdown of *The Maltese Falcon*, remember that, just as every step in the hero's journey may not appear in every story or in precisely the same order, the number of scenes per act can vary as well. The fifteen-thirty-fifteen formula is an approximation, as we'll see in the deconstruction of Dashiell Hammett's classic.

THE MALTESE FALCON: A SCENE-BY-SCENE BREAKDOWN

ACT ONE

1. Miss Wonderly comes to Sam Spade and Miles Archer's office in San Francisco to hire them to find her baby sister, who's run

away from New York with a man named Floyd Thursby. Archer will tail Thursby when he meets Miss Wonderly at the St. Mark that evening.

2. A phone call in the middle of the night alerts Spade to a death, and he calls a cab.

INCITING INCIDENT

3. Spade goes to the crime scene, where Detective Tom Polhaus and his fellow cops are investigating the murder of Spade's partner, Archer, who's been found shot through the heart with a Webley-Fosbery automatic revolver.

4. Spade calls his secretary, Effie, and asks her to tell Archer's wife about her husband's murder.

5. Spade goes home and has a drink. Tom Polhaus and Lieutenant Dundy drop by to interrogate Spade about Thursby, who was shot four times in the back after Spade left the scene of the Archer murder.

6. The next morning Archer's widow, Iva, is waiting for Spade at his office. Iva kisses him. He sends her home.

7. Effie tells Spade that Iva had just gotten home when she arrived to tell her about Archer the night before.

8. Spade goes to the St. Mark, but Miss Wonderly has checked out.

9. Back at the office Effie tells Spade that Miss Wonderly left word that he should meet her at the Coronet, where she's staying under the name Miss Leblanc.

10. Spade goes to see Miss Wonderly/Miss Leblanc, who tells him her real name is Brigid O'Shaughnessy. She says she met Thursby in Hong Kong and is scared now that he's dead. She asks him to protect her from the police.

11. Spade goes to visit attorney Sid Wise.

ACT TWO

PLOT POINT ONE

12. Joel Cairo offers Spade $5,000 to find the priceless Maltese Falcon. After Effie leaves, Cairo pulls a gun on Spade. Spade knocks him out. When he comes to, Spade agrees to take the

job and gives Cairo his gun back. Cairo turns it on Spade, so he can search Spade's office.

13. Wilmer tails Spade when he goes to find Cairo at the theater. Cairo claims he doesn't know him.

14. Spade loses the tail and goes home, where he finds his apartment has been searched.

15. Spade tells Brigid about Cairo's bid for the bird, and she offers up her body to him.

16. Spade and Brigid go to his apartment. Iva is waiting outside for him—and Spade tells her to go home. Spade tells Brigid the Flitcraft story. Cairo shows up, and he and Brigid fight. Spade intervenes.

17. The cops show up at Spade's door. Cairo calls for help, and the cops go in. Cairo and Brigid tell tales, and Spade says it's all a joke. Cairo and the cops leave. Brigid kisses Spade.

18. The next morning Spade takes Brigid's key while she's asleep and goes to search her place.

19. Spade goes back to his apartment, makes Brigid breakfast, and then escorts her home.

20. Spade goes to the Belvedere to see Cairo, where he runs into Wilmer, whom he believes works for Gutman. Spade gives Wilmer a message for Gutman and gets the hotel detective to throw him out.

21. Cairo comes back to the hotel and tells Spade that the cops grilled him all night about the murders.

22. Spade asks Effie to put Brigid up at her place. They leave the office in separate cabs.

23. Iva shows up at the office, tells Spade that she lied to the police and Archer's brother, Phil, about Spade and his possible involvement in Archer's murder. He sends her to Sid Wise.

24. Spade visits Gutman, who refuses to tell him what's up with the bird. Spade throws his drink against the wall, threatens Gutman and Wilmer, and tells Gutman he has until 5:30 P.M. to wise up.

25. Spade goes to see Sid Wise about Iva.

26. Effie tells Spade that Brigid never made it to her house.

27. Spade finds the cab driver, who says he dropped Brigid off at the Ferry Building.
28. Spade searches Brigid's apartment again.
29. An armed Wilmer comes to Spade's office to bring him to Gutman. Spade tricks him and takes away his pistols.
30. Gutman tells Spade the story of the Maltese Falcon—and drugs Spade's drink. Spade passes out.

MIDPOINT

31. Spade arrives at the office with a head injury. Effie has been waiting for him. She agrees to ask her professor cousin about the Maltese Falcon.
32. Spade goes home and cleans up. He goes to the Coronet, but Brigid is not there. He goes to the Belvedere, but Gutman is not there.
33. Spade has breakfast with the hotel detective.
34. The hotel detective and Spade search Cairo's room, where Spade finds a news clipping from the *Call* about a ship.
35. Spade finds the previous day's *Call*. He checks the shipping news and then makes five phone calls.
36. Effie tells Spade her cousin confirmed the Maltese Falcon's existence, and that there's a ship called the *La Paloma* on fire down at the pier.
37. Spade has lunch with Polhaus, who tells him about Thursby's ties to the mob.
38. Spade goes to see the DA, who tries to threaten him into talking.
39. Spade calls Gutman's hotel and Cairo's hotel, but neither is in.
40. Spade takes on a new case for a theater owner.
41. Effie guilts Spade into going to the boat to find Brigid.
42. Spade returns to the office, where Effie tells him the hotel detective has called to say Cairo is back.
43. Spade goes to the hotel, but he's too late. Cairo is gone.
44. The hotel detective and Spade search the trunk Cairo left behind, but it's empty.
45. Spade returns to the office and tells Effie that by the time he got to the boat, Brigid was long gone.

ACT THREE

PLOT POINT TWO

46. A big bleeding man barges into the office carrying a package—and falls down.
47. Spade tells Effie to lock the door and then searches the man, who's dead. He opens the package—it's the bird. The phone rings, and Effie picks it up. It's Brigid, and she says she's in danger. Spade leaves with the package, telling Effie to call the cops.
48. Spade takes a cab to the terminal, where he checks the bird at the parcel room there, and then puts the claim check in a stamped envelope and drops it in a mailbox.
49. Spade finds a drugged girl in Gutman's suite. He revives her, and she tells him that she's Gutman's daughter, Rhea. She sends him to Burlingame to save Brigid.
50. Spade calls the ER and tells them about the drugged girl.
51. Spade calls for a car and driver to meet him at John's, where he has dinner.
52. The driver parks not far from the house in Burlingame, and Spade tells him to keep the car running.
53. The house appears vacant. Spade has the landlord down the street let him in the house. It's empty.
54. Spade goes to the Alexandria. The hotel desk clerk tells him there was no drugged girl in Gutman's room.
55. Spade calls Effie. He goes to her house and she tells him that the cops grilled her about the dead captain but that they didn't know anything about the bird—and she didn't tell them anything.

CLIMAX

56. Spade goes back to his apartment, where Brigid is waiting outside for him. They go into the apartment, and Cairo, Gutman, and the tail, Wilmer, are all there, guns loaded.
57. Spade tells them they need a fall guy; they agree on Wilmer. Gutman gives Spade $10,000 in an envelope. Someone steals a grand when Spade's not looking. Spade takes Brigid into the bathroom, where she strips to prove she doesn't have it. Spade forces Gutman to give him the $1,000. They stay up all night

waiting for the bird. In the morning Effie brings the Maltese Falcon. Gutman takes a knife and scrapes the enamel off the bird—revealing lead. Cairo, Brigid, and Gutman all start yelling; they decide the Russian has tricked them, and Cairo and Gutman head for Constantinople to get it. Wilmer slips out. Gutman pulls a pistol on Spade and demands the money back; Spade gives it all back except for $1,000.

58. Cairo and Gutman leave.

59. Spade calls the cops, tells them Wilmer killed Thursby and Jacobi, and that Cairo and Gutman were in on it. He confronts Brigid, who admits she killed Archer. The cops show up, and he turns her in.

DENOUEMENT

60. The next morning Spade goes to his office. Iva shows up, and Effie sends her in to see him.

CALLING OUT SCENES BY NAME

One of the interesting devices Dashiell Hammett uses is chapter names. He breaks the story into twenty chapters—and each has a name.

1. Spade & Archer
2. Death in the Fog
3. Three Women
4. The Black Bird
5. The Levantine
6. The Undersized Shadow
7. G in the Air
8. Horse Feathers
9. Brigid
10. The Belvedere Divan
11. The Fat Man
12. Merry-Go-Round
13. The Emperor's Gift
14. La Paloma

Chapter names add a fun and thematic element to the story. You might consider applying this technique to your story as well, especially if they are related to your USP.

WRAPPING IT ALL UP

One of the most intriguing aspects of *The Maltese Falcon* is the story that Sam Spade tells Brigid O'Shaughnessy in chapter seven while they are waiting for Cairo to arrive at Spade's place. It's a story that embodies the themes of the book that we've discussed: privacy, discretion, faithlessness, tribal loyalties, to thine own self be true, people don't change, reverting to type, once a liar, always a liar, a world with or without rules, etc. Known as the Flitcraft story, the tale is one of the many elements that set *The Maltese Falcon* apart and contribute to the transcending of its genre. Hammett is a minimalist, as befits his genre, but in writing the Flitcraft story he gives his work a nuanced and layering effect that is at the same time completely accessible. And he does it through theme. You can do the same thing, no matter what your genre.

Let's finish up this case study by reviewing the Flitcraft story.

THE FLITCRAFT STORY

A man named Flitcraft had left his real estate office, in Tacoma, to go to luncheon one day and had never returned. He did not keep an engagement to play golf after four that afternoon, even though he had taken the initiative in making the engagement less than half an hour before he went out to luncheon **[impulsivity]**. His wife and children never saw him again **[disloyalty, betrayal, abandonment]**. His wife and he were supposed to be on the best of terms **[love, fickleness, loyalty]**. He had two children, boys, one five and the other three **[paternal love, tribal loyalties]**. He owned his house in a Tacoma suburb, a new Packard, and the rest of the appurtenances of successful American living **[reliability, security, conventionality, conformity]**.

Flitcraft had inherited seventy thousand dollars from his father, and with his success in real estate, was worth something in the neighborhood of two hundred thousand dollars at the time he vanished **[wealth, security, success]**. His affairs were in order, though there were enough loose ends to indicate that he had not been setting them in order preparatory to vanishing **[reliability]**. A deal that would have brought him an attractive profit, for instance, was to have been concluded the day after the one on which he disappeared **[impulsivity, abandonment]**. There was nothing to suggest that he had more than fifty or sixty dollars in his immediate possession at the time of his going **[thrift]**. His habits for months past could be accounted for too thoroughly to justify any suspicion of secret vices, or even of another woman in his life, though either was barely possible **[loyalty, conventionality, conformity]**.

"He went like that," Spade said, "like a fist when you open your hand."

When he had reached this point in his story the telephone-bell rang.

"Hello," Spade said into the instrument. "Mr. Cairo? ... This is Spade. Can you come up to my place—Post Street—now? Yes, I think it is." He looked at the girl, pursed his lips, and then said rapidly: "Miss O'Shaughnessy is here and wants to see you."

Bridget O'Shaughnessy frowned and stirred in her chair, but did not say anything.

Spade put the telephone down and told her: "He'll be up in a few minutes. Well, that was in 1922. In 1927 I was with one of the big detective agencies in Seattle. Mrs. Flitcraft came in and told us somebody had seen a man in Spokane who looked a lot like her husband **[duplicity, abandonment, betrayal, people don't**

change]. I went over there. It was Flitcraft, all right. He had been living in Spokane for a couple of years as Charles—that was his first name—Pierce **[privacy; discretion; faithlessness; once a liar, always a liar; lies of omission; self-love; putting yourself first]**. He had an automobile-business that was netting him twenty or twenty-five thousand a year, a wife, a baby son, owned his home in a Spokane suburb, and usually got away to play golf after four in the afternoon during the season **[people don't change, reverting to type, tribal loyalties, living a lie]**."

Spade had not been told very definitely what to do when he found Flitcraft. They talked in Spade's room at the Davenport. Flitcraft had no feeling of guilt **[infidelity, betrayal, faithlessness, lack of remorse, indifference, entitlement, self-love, putting yourself first]**. He had left his first family well provided for, and what he had done seemed to him perfectly reasonable. The only thing that bothered him was a doubt that he could make that reasonableness clear to Spade. He had never told anybody his story before, and thus had not had to attempt to make its reasonableness explicit **[confession, rationalization, morality]**. He tried now.

"I got it all right," Spade told Bridget O'Shaughnessy, "but Mrs. Flitcraft never did. She thought it was silly. Maybe it was. Anyway, it came out all right. She didn't want any scandal, and, after the trick he played on her—the way she looked at it—she didn't want him **[faithlessness, infidelity, betrayal, deception, abandonment, moving on]**. So they were divorced on the quiet and everything was swell all around.

"Here's what happened to him. Going to lunch he passed an office-building that was being put up—just the skeleton. A beam or something fell eight or ten stories down and smacked the sidewalk alongside him **[death, fate, world without rules]**. It brushed pretty close to him, but didn't touch him, though a piece of the sidewalk chipped off and flew up and hit his cheek. It only took a piece of skin off, but he still had the scar when I saw him **[fear, trauma, damage]**. He rubbed it with his finger—well, affectionately—when he told me about it. He was scared stiff of course, he said, but he was more shocked and really frightened **[fear, shock]**. He felt like somebody had taken a lid off life and let him look at the works **[fate, world without rules, the meaning of life—or lack thereof]**."

Flitcraft had been a good citizen and a good husband and father, not by any outer compulsion, but simply because he was a man who is most comfortable in step with his surroundings **[conventionality, security, complacency]**. He had been raised that way **[family, tradition, tribal loyalties]**. The people he knew were like that. The life he knew was a clean orderly sane responsible affair **[order, conventionality, conformity]**. Now a falling beam had shown him that life is fundamentally none of these things **[chaos, existentialism, nihilism, fate]**. He, the good citizen-husband-father, could be wiped out between office and restaurant by the accident of a falling beam. He knew then that men died at haphazard like that, and lived only while blind chance spared them **[luck, fate, skepticism, anarchism]**.

It was not, primarily, the injustice of it that disturbed him: he accepted that after the first shock. What disturbed him was the discovery that in sensibly ordering his affairs he had got out of step, and not into step, with life **[conformity, truth seeking, reality, entitlement]**. He said he knew before he had gone twenty feet from the falling beam that he would never know peace again until he had adjusted himself to this new glimpse of life **[chaos, anxiety, entitlement, self-love, putting yourself first, adaptability]**. By the time he had eaten his luncheon he had found his means of adjustment. Life could be ended for him at random by a falling beam: he would change his life at random by simply going away **[change, adaptability, faithlessness, self-love, putting yourself first]**. He loved his family, he said, as much as he supposed was usual, but he knew he was leaving them adequately provided for, and his love for them was not the sort that would make absence painful **[love, marriage, family, loyalty, devotion, indifference, betrayal, entitlement, self-love, putting yourself first]**.

"He went to Seattle that afternoon," Spade said, "and from there by boat to San Francisco **[escape, truth-seeking, to thine own self be true]**. For a couple of years he wandered around and then drifted back to the Northwest, and settled in Spokane and got married **[love, marriage, conventionality]**. His second wife didn't look like the first, but they were more alike than they were different **[people don't change, reverting to type]**. You know, the kind of women that play fair games of golf and bridge and like new salad-recipes **[conformity, conventionality, domesticity]**. He wasn't sorry for what he had done **[confession, guiltlessness, entitlement, adaptability, remorse]**. It seemed reasonable enough to him. I don't think he even knew that he had settled back naturally into the same groove he had jumped out of in Tacoma **[people don't change, reverting to type, conformity, conventionality]**. But that's the part of it I always liked. He adjusted himself to beams falling, and then no more of them fell, and he adjusted himself to them not falling **[entitlement, adaptability, people don't change, reverting to type, self-love, putting yourself first]**."

THE CASE STUDY AS PREPARATION

In this chapter, we've taken an exhaustive look at the structure and thematic elements of *The Maltese Falcon*. We've seen how cleverly Hammett wove his plot, subplots, themes, and variations on theme throughout his story, as well as how tightly he structured it—scene by scene. It's a masterful tapestry—and one that serves as an excellent model for you to refer to as you create a scene-by-scene breakdown of your own story.

"When you write, you want fame, fortune and personal satisfaction. You want to write what you want to write and feel it's good, and you want this to go on for hundreds of years. You're not likely ever to get all these things, and you're not likely to give up writing and commit suicide if you don't, but that is—and should be—your goal. Anything else is kind of piddling."
—Dashiell Hammett

CHAPTER SEVEN
PLUS AND MINUS SCENES

"Real suspense comes with moral dilemma and the courage to make and act upon choices. False suspense comes from the accidental and meaningless occurrence of one damned thing after another."

—John Gardner

Now that we've seen how all the pieces of a plot can come together seamlessly in a storyline, as they do in *The Maltese Falcon*, it's time to take another look at the scene-by-scene breakdown you've developed for your own story. We'll explore how you can make that breakdown better in every way and scrutinize the emotional landscape of your story as it unfolds.

In the most compelling plots, each scene is charged—with emotion, action, and theme—creating an emotional landscape that drives the story. This takes the reader along for an exciting ride. Whether you end up with a roller coaster ride or a boring detour to nowhere depends on how you orchestrate your scenes. We'll look at the ups and downs you can plug in to your structure—and how you can charge them to best effect. You will also master the art of electrifying your scenes with plus and minus charges and ordering them to best advantage. In chapter four we talked about the big and little story questions that drive the action in a storyline's scenes. You can think of plus and minus scenes as positive and negative answers to those story questions.

I'll also share some invaluable tricks to help you make each scene as powerful as possible within the context of the storyline: identifying the POV character's objective in each scene, heightening the emotional impact, and milking the action.

The first step is to examine the "pluses" and "minuses" you can use to charge your scenes through emotion, action, theme, and more.

DESIGNATING SCENES AS "PLUSES" OR "MINUSES"

There are a number of ways in which a given scene can be classified as positive or negative—that is, marked with a plus or a minus sign. Let's go through them one by one.

EMOTION

Every scene must be charged with emotion. Whether this is positive or negative emotion depends on how your POV character feels by the end of the scene.

First, determine the POV character for the scene. If you're writing your story from a single point of view—either in first or third person—then you already know who your point of view character will be. If you are writing your story in multiple points of view, then you'll need to decide whose POV will be the best for this particular scene. You'll need to make this decision for every scene, and it's a critical one. The answer often lies in finding the character who is most affected by what happens in that scene—the character who has the most at stake. Making that decision is half the battle.

Once you know which POV character stands to gain or lose the most in a given scene, it's easy enough to figure out if that character is losing or gaining something—physically, emotionally, spiritually—by the end of the scene. You might find that in some scenes, the POV character will gain one thing only to lose another (thus giving both "plus" and "minus" charges to the scene).

Let's return to the scenes we talked about in chapter four, only this time, we'll consider these scenes from the context of emotion.

ROMEO AND JULIET BY WILLIAM SHAKESPEARE
SCENE: The balcony scene

QUOTE: "O Romeo, Romeo, wherefore art thou Romeo?"

POV: Dramatic (third-person objective)

This is a love scene in which both parties, Romeo and Juliet, express their love for one another for the first time. It's a plus for Romeo and a plus for Juliet.

EMOTIONAL CHARGE: Positive +

THE PRINCE OF TIDES BY PAT CONROY

SCENE: The dinner scene

QUOTE: "Now this is food, Lila. Simple food, but good."

POV: Tom (first person)

This is a suspenseful scene in which Tom's mother serves her belligerent husband doctored-up dog food, while her kids watch in disbelief—and fear. It's terrifying and hilarious at the same time—and in the end, she pulls it off, much to the giddy relief of the children. It's a win for the kids and their mother.

EMOTIONAL CHARGE: Positive +

PRIDE AND PREJUDICE BY JANE AUSTEN

SCENE: The scene at the ball

QUOTE: "She is tolerable; but not handsome enough to tempt me…"

POV: Elizabeth Bennet (third person)

In this scene, Elizabeth Bennet overhears Mr. Darcy insulting her behind her back. She laughs it off with her friends, but she is offended nonetheless.

EMOTIONAL CHARGE: Negative –

THE WORLD ACCORDING TO GARP BY JOHN IRVING

SCENE: The scene at the hospital

QUOTE: She felt more receptive than prepared soil—the nourished earth—and she had felt Garp shoot up inside her as generously as a hose in summer (as if he could water a lawn).

POV: Jenny Fields (third person)

In this scene, Jenny Fields, Garp's mother, conceives her son in a most ingenious way, through both resourcefulness and ruthlessness. She's a woman who desperately wants a baby, and in this scene she successfully impregnates herself—with a little help from a dying man. It's as funny and poignant and heartbreaking as it is exhilarating—for Jenny and the reader.

EMOTIONAL CHARGE: Positive +

THE HUNGER GAMES BY SUZANNE COLLINS

SCENE: The scene at the lottery

QUOTE: "I volunteer as tribute!"

POV: Katniss Everdeen (first person)

This is a critical set-up scene in which Katniss Everdeen insists on taking her little sister, Prim's, place when her name is called in the lottery. This action is fraught with emotion. Katniss and the reader are relieved that Prim will not have to participate in the Hunger Games, but now Katniss must risk her own life in the Hunger Games instead.

EMOTIONAL CHARGE: Positive + and Negative –

GAME OF THRONES BY GEORGE R.R. MARTIN

SCENE: The funeral scene

QUOTE: "I am Daenerys Stormborn, daughter of dragons, bride of dragons, mother of dragons, don't you see?"

POV: Dany (third person)

In a climactic scene, Dany walks into her dead husband's funeral pyre and emerges the queen of the dragons. From certain death to resurrection and royalty—that's a pretty positive outcome.

EMOTIONAL CHARGE: Positive +

THE GIRL WITH THE DRAGON TATTOO BY STIEG LARSSON

SCENE: The scene with the tattoo

QUOTE: "I am a sadistic pig, a pervert, and a rapist."

POV: Lisbeth (third person)

In this scene, Lisbeth Salander turns the table on her abuser and brands him with a warning to his unsuspecting victims. It's revenge served cold—and hot—and allows Lisbeth to mete out justice to the man who abused her.

EMOTIONAL CHARGE: Positive +

POINT OF VIEW IN *THE MALTESE FALCON*

If you've read *The Maltese Falcon*, you may have noticed that Dashiell Hammett chose to write his masterwork in third-person objective point of view. This is the camera's point of view, following Spade throughout the story. Spade is in every scene; we only see what Spade sees, but we do not get inside his head.

Sustaining third-person objective POV throughout an entire novel is very tough, and few writers attempt it. Hammett employs it to good effect here; its detached quality contributes to the story's existentialist themes. Fair warning: Don't try this at home.

WRITER AT PLAY

Just for fun—and profit—go through the scene-by-scene breakdown of *The Maltese Falcon* in chapter six. Mark each one negative or positive, depending on how the scene affects our hero, Sam Spade.

"I love writing. I love the swirl and swing of words as they tangle with human emotions."

—James A. Michener

READING FOR WRITERS

If you're having trouble filling out your storyline, there are a couple of reference books that may prove useful to you. Here are a few invaluable volumes that may help take the guesswork out of your plotting efforts.

- *Plot Outlines of 101 Best Novels*. My copy of this classic was published by Everyday Handbooks, Harper & Row in 1962. It's out of print now, but there are used copies available online.
- *The Thirty-Six Dramatic Situations* by Georges Polti. This is another classic—and the good news is that it's still in print.
- *The Uses of Enchantment: The Meaning and Importance of Fairy Tales* by Bruno Bettelheim. Whether you want to rewrite a fairy tale or just enjoy a deeper understanding of your favorite tales, this is a must-have for your bookshelf.

THEME

Scenes can also be positively or negatively charged through theme as well, and some themes can elicit both "plus" and "minus" reactions from the reader. Other themes will have an obviously positive or negative charge and can be used accordingly for specific scenes that need one or the other.

ROMEO AND JULIET

THEME: true love

POSITIVE SCENE: In the balcony scene from *Romeo and Juliet*, the theme of true love is reinforced as the lovers devote themselves to each other.

NEGATIVE SCENE: The lovers ultimately die for true love. Juliet takes a potion that makes her appear to be dead as part of a plot to marry Romeo. In a series of miscommunications and misunderstandings, Romeo believes Juliet is actually dead and poisons himself in her tomb. Juliet, upon waking, discovers her dead lover's body and commits suicide.

THE PRINCE OF TIDES

THEMES: love, loyalty, dysfunctional families, changing male and female roles

POSITIVE SCENE: The clever and beautiful wife outwits her boorish husband, much to the amusement of their terrified children.

NEGATIVE SCENE: When the clever and beautiful wife turns off the television so that her boorish husband can sing "Happy Birthday" to his twins on their tenth birthday—and he slams her head into the television set. The children come to her defense, and he goes after them.

PRIDE AND PREJUDICE

THEME: obstacles to love

POSITIVE SCENE: Elizabeth and Mr. Darcy declare their love to one another, acknowledging that they have overcome the obstacles to love—namely pride and prejudice—and can now enjoy a future together.

NEGATIVE SCENE: When Mr. Darcy alienates Elizabeth Bennet, the course of true love is not running smoothly.

THE WORLD ACCORDING TO GARP

THEMES: love, death, sex, and feminism

POSITIVE SCENE: Jenny Fields conceives her beloved son—by taking advantage of a dying man.

NEGATIVE SCENE: Her beloved son dies too young, assassinated by a member of a radical feminist extremist group.

THE HUNGER GAMES
THEMES: power, loyalty, love, independence
POSITIVE AND NEGATIVE SCENE: The novel's themes are reflected in the scene in which Katniss volunteers as tribute. The government enforces the lottery and puts on the Hunger Games (negative); Katniss demonstrates loyalty and love for her sister and an independent streak when she volunteers for the Games (positive); Katniss must now face almost certain death by participating in the Games (negative).

A GAME OF THRONES
THEMES: power, violence, the endless cycle of life and death
POSITIVE SCENE: In the last scene of the book, Dany overcomes death on her husband's funeral pyre by sacrificing and resurrecting herself, and helping birth the dragons. In doing so, she secures her position as queen. It's a dramatic—and thematic—end to the first book in the best-selling series.
NEGATIVE SCENE: When Dany tries to save her husband from death with the maegi's black magic, she loses her child and is forced to put her half-dead husband out of his misery herself.

THE GIRL WITH THE DRAGON TATTOO
THEMES: violence (particularly against women), corruption
NEGATIVE SCENE: Lisbeth's abuser is her state-appointed guardian, charged with protecting her—and yet he rapes her.
POSITIVE SCENE: Lisbeth turns the tables on him—and strikes a blow against corruption and violence against women.

GOAL
In each scene, the POV character should have a goal: take that hill, talk to that girl, test that limit. If by the end of the scene the POV character achieves her goal—or comes closer to achieving it—the scene has a positive outcome. A plus sign. If she fails to achieve that goal—or is further than ever from achieving it—the scene has a negative outcome. A minus sign.

In the balcony scene in *Romeo and Juliet*, it's Romeo's goal to observe Juliet—and he gets that and more. When Tom's mom serves up the dog food for dinner in *The Prince of Tides*, her goal is to prove to her children that her husband is no more discerning than a dog when it comes to the finer things in life—which she does, thanks to a few culinary tricks. In *Pride and Prejudice*, every single girl is at the ball in search of a suitable husband—and Mr. Darcy is one of the most eligible men there. His dismissal of Elizabeth's charms is a blow to her own prospects.

In *The World According to Garp*, when Jenny Fields decides that she wants a baby without the bother of a relationship, she sets out to get pregnant with a minimum of emotional and physical connection—and she does. At the lottery in *The Hunger Games*, Katniss's goal is to not get selected—but when Prim's name is called, Katniss's goal shifts to saving her little sister from certain death, thereby risking her own. When her husband dies, Dany's goal is to take his place as leader of his *khalasar*, and to birth the dragons. She achieves both in the cleansing fires of the pyre. When Lisbeth tattoos her assailant in *The Girl with the Dragon Tattoo*, her goal is to mark him as the beast he is and get revenge. She succeeds.

ACTION

As we've seen, a scene is by definition a "continuous action"—and that action can be viewed as positive or negative, depending on the POV character's perspective. Romeo and Juliet profess their love for one another—a positive action for both, at least at this point in the story. But it's an action that ultimately has tragic consequences for them and their families. Tom's mother wins the battle in the dinner scene in *The Prince of Tides*, but it's one victory in a long, bitter marital war in which the children are the casualties. For Elizabeth Bennet and Mr. Darcy, the incident at the ball marks the first of many conflicts and misunderstandings the couple must forgive, forget, and figure out before they can live happily ever after.

In *The World According to Garp*, Jenny Fields's action is as morally ambiguous as it is inventive, but in so doing she conceives the hero of the story, whose life is as unconventional as his conception. Katniss's impulsive act at the lottery saves her sister and sets the stage for our heroine's fight to the death at the Hunger Games. In *A Game of Thrones*, when her husband dies, Dany enters the fire as a girl-widow and emerges as the queen of the dragons. It's an action that seems suicidal to all who watch, but she's confident in her ability to pull it off—and she does.

WRITER AT WORK

Watch your favorite movie in the same genre as your story. As you view the film, mark each scene in terms of pluses and minuses. Ask yourself these questions: What is the POV character's emotion in this scene? What is the theme? Goal? Action? What happens? Achieve or fail? Plus or minus? Positive aspect of theme or negative aspect of theme? Plus or minus? When the movie is over, notice the pattern of pluses and minuses throughout the structure of the film. Consider how this pattern might compare to the pattern of pluses and minuses in your own story. **NOTE:** This is a good exercise to do with your writers group.

> "I have these huge black foam boards on the wall, and tacked to them, I have these white punch cards with my story ideas, scenes, and notes."
>
> —Robert Crais

> "The weird thing is that working within an established story was actually kind of liberating. You know the beginning and middle and end, more or less, so there's less pressure to figure all that out."
>
> —Dave Eggers

"BORROWING" INSPIRATION

If you're having trouble coming up with a plot, you can always do what Shakespeare did: "borrow" one from a colleague. Shakespeare "borrowed" (some say "stole") most of his ideas for his plays from the work of his contemporaries. Thanks to copyright law, you can't steal the plots of your contemporaries—or any copyrighted work— and you shouldn't. That said, works in the public domain are fair game. So you can rewrite Jane Austen's *Emma* and call it *Clueless*, as screenwriter Amy Heckerling did. You can imagine a modern retelling of *Wuthering Heights*, as Alice Hoffman did in *Heaven on Earth*. Or restage Shakespeare's *Romeo and Juliet* as a musical, as Leonard Bernstein did in *West Side Story*. Or build an entire film studio on remakes of works in the public domain, as Disney has done with dozens of films over the years—from *Snow White* to *John Carter*.

If it worked for Walt Disney and William Shakespeare, it may work for you.

> *"He took all his plots from old novels and threw their stories into a dramatic shape, at as little expense of thought as you or I could turn his plays back again into prose tales."*
>
> —Lord Byron on Shakespeare

FUN WITH INDEX CARDS, PART II

Remember: To keep your reader engaged throughout the course of your story, you need to mix up the pluses and minuses of your plot.

To do this, examine your plot scene by scene. Take out those sixty (or more) index cards on which you wrote the brief summaries of the scenes that make up your novel. It's time to consider each scene in terms of its charge.

The scene is a positive/plus scene if:

- Your protagonist gets what he wants.
- Your protagonist feels better than when the scene began.
- Your protagonist takes positive action.
- The action in the scene represents a positive aspect of the theme.
- The plot has moved forward in a positive way for the hero.

If the scene is positive, then mark that card with a plus sign.

If the reverse is true—your protagonist doesn't get what he wants, he feels worse than when the scene began, the action represents a negative aspect of theme, or the plot has taken a bad turn, mark the card with a minus sign.

Review all of your scene cards this way and mark them accordingly: plus or minus. Now organize your cards according to act: Act One, Act Two, and Act Three. Once you have arranged your index cards by act, order them within that act. Try to alternate plus and minus scenes if and when you can. *Note:* This is a pacing trick that works. More on this in chapter ten.

Once you've determined a strong order for your scenes, transcribe the scenes in the Theme-Based Plot Structure worksheet that follows. After you've filled this out, you'll be able to see your entire plot scene by scene within the same document. Ask yourself: What works? What doesn't work? Could you shuffle any scenes for better dramatic effect?

WRITER AT PLAY

Choose two of Shakespeare's plays, one tragedy and one comedy. Read them for plus and minus scenes, and observe how the pattern of pluses and minuses differs according to the ending. Does the play with the happy ending contain more plus scenes? Does the play with the tragic ending contain more minus scenes? How do these respective patterns compare to your comedy—or tragedy?

"[Comedies], in the ancient world, were regarded as of a higher rank than tragedy, of a deeper truth, of a more difficult realization, of a sounder structure, and of a revelation more complete. The happy ending of the fairy tale, the myth, and the divine comedy of the soul is to be read, not as a contradiction, but as a transcendence of the universal tragedy of man. ... Tragedy is the shattering of the forms and of our attachments to the forms; comedy, the wild and careless, inexhaustible joy of life invincible."

—Joseph Campbell

ACT ONE	
Main Plot	
+	
-	
+	
-	
+	
-	
+	
-	
Subplot A	
+	
-	
Subplot B	
+	
-	
Subplot C	
+	
-	

PLOT POINT 1

ACT TWO, PART ONE	
Main Plot	
+	
-	
+	
-	
+	
-	

+	
-	
Subplot A	
+	
-	
Subplot B	
+	
-	
Subplot C	
+	
-	
MIDPOINT	
ACT TWO, PART TWO	
Main Plot	
+	
-	
+	
-	
+	
-	
+	
-	
Subplot A	
+	
-	
Subplot B	
+	
-	

Subplot C	
+	
-	

PLOT POINT 2

ACT THREE

Main Plot	
+	
-	
+	
-	
+	
-	
+	
-	
Subplot A	
+	
-	
Subplot B	
+	
-	
Subplot C	
+	
-	

CLIMAX

DENOUEMENT

To access a printable version of this worksheet, visit www.writers digest.com/plot-perfect-worksheets.

Now that you've taken a stab at organizing your scenes into three acts and ordering your plus and minus scenes to best dramatic effect, you may find yourself staring at holes in your plot or worrying that you have yet to structure your story in the most compelling manner. In the next chapter, we'll examine your story structure act by act and explore ways to ensure that the beginning, middle, and end of your story engages readers—and keeps them up all night reading every word through the last page.

> *"I start with the history, and I ask myself, 'What are the great turning points? What are the big dramatic scenes that are essential to telling the story?'"*
>
> —Ken Follett

CHAPTER EIGHT

ACT-BY-ACT
Tips and Tricks

> *"I start at the beginning, go on to the end, then stop."*
> —Anthony Burgess

There's an old adage in publishing: *The first page sells the book, the last page sells the next book.* And all those pages in between provide the reading experience that earns you an audience.

Each of the three acts—beginning, middle, and end—comes with its own challenges, obstacles, and pitfalls.

Typically there are three main problems that plague the manuscripts I've reviewed in more than twenty years as an agent, acquisitions editor, and writing teacher. (They've also plagued my own manuscripts, in my role as a writer.) There's one for each act.

- The beginning is bloated and boring.
- The middle sags.
- The end is rushed.

When I work with writers to prepare their stories for the submission process, these are the big structural issues that most need to address. There are others as well, and in this chapter we'll examine the tips and tricks that can help each act stand on its own and function within the plot as a whole. With your scene lists in hand, you'll apply what you've learned about plus and minus scenes, subplots and secondary characters, and theme and variations on theme to make sure that all three acts work in concert to create the most dramatic plotline possible. You'll also learn how to make each part of your story seduce your readers, over and over again—scene by scene, page by page, and line by line.

We'll start where the reader starts: at the beginning.

STARTING AT THE BEGINNING

> "In literature and in life we ultimately pursue, not conclusions,
> but beginnings."
>
> —Sam Tanenhaus

The next time you're in a bookstore, watch the way people browse for books. (And, yes, please do frequent brick-and-mortar bookstores as well as online booksellers.) Study after study shows that people look at the cover first—and if they like what they see, they will turn the book over and read the back-cover copy (and the flaps as well, if it's a hardcover). If they still like what they see, they will open the book to the first page and begin to read. If they like what they read in those first lines, they will buy the book. If what they read doesn't grab them, they will put the book down and pick up another. This buying decision process takes no more than a minute on average.

That's why the beginning is so important. If you don't write a compelling opening, readers—be they agents, editors, critics, or consumers—will never make it past the first page.

This is more important now than ever before. In today's fast-paced cacophony of media, you need to grab your reader's attention within 140 characters. When an agent or editor reads your work, you have between 140 characters and 250 words—if you're lucky—to grab their attention. That's a single line, paragraph, page, *scene*.

THE NUMBERS GAME

Everyone always complains—with some justification—that agents and editors take forever to respond to queries and submissions. That said, don't underestimate the sheer volume of the stories being pitched to agents and editors at any given moment.

As an acquisitions editor, I received several hundred e-mails a day. In my first two weeks as an agent, I received more than one thousand queries. And they just keep coming ...

All agents and editors are similarly swamped—that's why your material must be good enough to stand out. The good news is that the good material *does* stand out.

The beginning is the first part of your story that agents, editors, and readers see. And if it doesn't work, you've lost your chance with that agent, editor, or reader—maybe forever. So it needs to be better than good.

THE TOP TEN REASONS WE STOP READING

At our agency, we ask that queries include a synopsis and the first ten pages. I typically skip synopses and go right to the first ten pages, because:

1. Even great writers sometimes can't write compelling synopses, and I don't want to miss any great writers.
2. It's the writing that counts. The first ten pages show me if the writer has mastered the craft and *if the writer has a story to tell.*

So I've read a lot of first ten pages. Or, rather, I've *started* reading a lot of first ten pages.

Nine times out of ten I don't make it through.

> *"The best time to plan a book is while you're doing the dishes."*
> — Agatha Christie

It's easy for agents, editors, and readers to say no to your story. *No* to signing another writer whose work will need polishing, preparing, and pitching (thinks the agent). *No* to accepting another project that will need pitching to pub board, shepherding through editing and production, promoting to the salespeople, booksellers, and beyond (thinks the editor). *No* to shelling out another twenty-five bucks on a book when the rent is due (thinks the reader).

So don't give us any reason at all to stop reading, to say no to your story. Here are some of the most significant reasons we'll stop reading.

1. **NOTHING HAPPENS**. You're using the beginning as a "warm up," writing to tell yourself what you need to know to write your story. But odds are your reader doesn't need to know any

of it. You need to start in media res—that is, in the midst of something happening. Something needs to happen on page 1. Something compelling.

2. **WE'VE SEEN IT BEFORE.** If your opening scene is one we've seen a million times before—your heroine going for a run, your hero waking up in bed, your antagonist on a plane—then you need to either start with something more compelling or find a way to make the scene *different* and therefore more compelling. The former is by far the safer bet.

3. **IT DOESN'T HAVE A STRONG VOICE.** Most readers are a sucker for voice—and will follow it anywhere.

4. **WE'RE BORED.** Maybe there's something happening, but it's not significant enough to maintain our interest. Make sure that your opening action is worthy of the first pages.

5. **WE'RE NOT CONNECTING WITH ANY OF THE CHARACTERS.** We want to see your hero in action. We want to fall in love with your hero and go where he goes, do what he does, learn what he learns. If we can't do this from the beginning, we'll stop reading.

6. **WE CAN'T TELL WHAT KIND OF STORY WE'RE READING.** It's imperative that you make it clear what kind of story you are telling. Mystery fans want to know they're reading a mystery right away. Ditto for readers of every genre. You can make this clear in a number of ways. For example, if you're writing a mystery, beginning with a murder is always a good way to go. If you can't drop a body on the first page, then at least establish a sense of foreboding so that we know a murder will happen soon.

7. **WE DON'T CARE WHAT HAPPENS NEXT.** Remember your story questions—and scatter them through your scenes.

8. **THE PLOT IS UNBELIEVABLE OR FULL OF CLICHÉS.** Again, this is where "the same, but different" comes into play. You have to transcend the conventions of your genre—not simply regurgitate them.

9. **THE DIALOGUE DOESN'T SOUND LIKE "REAL PEOPLE."** Bad dialogue leaves the reader laughing—even when it's not funny.

10. **THERE ARE TYPOS, SPELLING, AND GRAMMATICAL ERRORS.** Enough said (at least until chapter fifteen).

THE TOP TEN REASONS WE KEEP READING

Just as there are reasons we'll stop reading, there are reasons we'll keep reading. When you're working on your beginning, keep these in mind.

1. **SOMETHING HAPPENS**. Make sure something compelling happens—and you can ensure it does by incorporating story questions, the inciting incident, the catalyst, plot point 1, etc.
2. **THE STORY IS TOLD IN A STRONG VOICE**. Think Holden Caulfield in *The Catcher in the Rye*, Bridget Jones in *Bridget Jones's Diary*, Charlie in *The Perks of Being a Wallflower*.
3. **THE LEVEL OF CRAFT IS HIGH**. Knowing how to tell a story is as important as the story itself.
4. **THE CHARACTERS MAKE ME FEEL SOMETHING**. Reed Farrel Coleman, three-time Shamus award winner and two-time Edgar-nominated author of the Moe Prager mysteries, says he always aims to evoke a feeling of poignancy in his opening pages. What feeling does your opening evoke? What happens to create that feeling?
5. **THE WRITER HAS GAINED OUR CONFIDENCE**. This you do by writing with authority and confidence. The stronger the action, the easier it is to write with authority and confidence.
6. **WE WANT TO KNOW WHAT HAPPENS NEXT**. Story questions are the secret here; plant them early and keep them coming.
7. **THERE'S SOMETHING UNIQUE ABOUT THE STORY/STORYTELLER**. This speaks to your USP, which should be on display in your opening pages, as well as through the remainder of the book.
8. **IT'S CLEAR WHAT KIND OF STORY IS BEING TOLD**. Readers want to know that they're reading the kind of story they like.

Plot Perfect

If you've written a romance, then the beginning must read like a romance—otherwise you'll confuse your readers. A confused reader is a lost reader.

9. **THERE'S A MARKET FOR THIS KIND OF STORY.** This is a consideration for agents and editors more than readers. Having a strong USP is critical in this regard.

10. **THE PROSE IS CLEAN, CLEAR, AND CONCISE.** The cleaner, clearer, and more concise your prose, the more direct your communication with your readers. And the more professional you appear to people in publishing.

"The thing should have plot and character, beginning, middle, and end. Arouse pity and then have a catharsis. Those were the best principles I was ever taught."

—Anne Rice

WHAT *NOT* TO DO IN THE BEGINNING

Elmore Leonard, the prolific "Dickens of Detroit," produced some of the most compelling popular fiction ever written—forty-five novels and nearly as many Western and crime short stories, including "Road Dogs," "Up in Honey's Room," "The Hot Kid," "Mr. Paradise," and "Tishomingo Blues." Many of his books have been made into movies, including *Get Shorty, Out of Sight, Rum Punch* (which became Quentin Tarantino's *Jackie Brown),* and *Touch* (my personal favorite of his novels). He was known for his cinematic storytelling and wicked-good dialogue, and for leaving out "the part readers tend to skip." He lived by a number of writing rules, two of which are particularly relevant to our discussion of what *not* to do in the beginning.

Elmore Leonard's Rule 1: Never Open a Book with Weather.

No reader wants to wade through a meteorological report to get to the heft of your story. Not to mention that we've seen this "the sun shone down on Main Street" opening way too many times. So, generally speaking, it's a bad idea to start with the weather.

That said, if you must start with the weather, then the weather needs to work for you and your story.

Make the weather:

- **BAD. VERY BAD.** Thunder, lighting, downpours, hail storms, dense fog, hurricanes, tornadoes, typhoons, monsoons, flash floods, high winds, heat waves, droughts, dust storms, wildfires, nor'easters, blizzards, thunder snow, avalanches, mudslides, sinkholes, tsunamis, volcanic eruptions, earthquakes—any sort of severe weather or natural disaster will do.

- **PROPEL YOUR PLOT.** The worse the weather, the more the plot possibilities. Bad weather is the inciting incident for many a swell story: the cyclone that carries Dorothy away from Kansas in L. Frank Baum's *The Wonderful Wizard of Oz*, the storm at sea that blows the ship off course in Johann David Wyss's *The Swiss Family Robinson*, the drought that sends the Joad family on the road west to California in John Steinbeck's *The Grapes of Wrath*.

- **AFFECT YOUR HERO—IN A BAD WAY.** You can open with bad weather if that bad weather is bad news for your hero. That cyclone lands Dorothy smack on the Wicked Witch of the East—and sets up her showdown with the Wicked Witch of the West. The storm at sea forces the family to live on an island as castaways far from civilization in *The Swiss Family Robinson*. And the drought that turns Oklahoma in the Dust Bowl is to blame for the Joads's tragic trek to California.

- **SET THE TONE.** And no, we don't mean, "It was a dark and stormy night." You can see the risk that you take when you start with the weather. It's a cliché waiting to happen. But if you do it skillfully, you can use weather to set the tone. Think of the storm conjured up by Prospero in *The Tempest* by Shakespeare, setting the mood for all the magic to come.

- **SPEAK TO THEME**. Weather can speak to theme, as well as to tone. Think of Rick Moody's acerbic classic *The Ice Storm*, in which the calm and cool façade of wealthy Connecticut suburbia in 1973 obscures the perfect storm of sex, drugs, and suicide raging behind closed doors. Weather can also be a part of an image system (or symbology) that you weave throughout your story, as Alice Hoffman does so seamlessly and beautifully in *The Ice Queen*.

RULES ARE MADE TO BE BROKEN, PART I

Leave it to Elmore Leonard to break his own rules—and do so it beautifully. Check out the opening of one of his most popular novels, *Get Shorty*.

> When Chili first came to Miami Beach twelve years ago, they were having one of their off-and-on again cold winters: thirty-four degrees the day he met Tommy Carlo for lunch at Vesuvio's on South Collins and had his leather jacket ripped off. One his wife had given him for Christmas a year ago, before they moved down here.

In this opening, Elmore Leonard gives us the weather—and so much more. We get a sense of Chili, the cool character who may have come south to Miami but still hangs out with gangsters at Italian restaurants and bemoans the loss of his leather jacket. We get the feeling that we're in for a good ride with Chili—and we are.

WRITER AT PLAY

Watch a movie in which weather plays a significant role. Pay attention to the way the direction, cinematography, art direction, acting, and set design reinforce the tone and theme suggested by the meteorological phenomena. Here are some you might enjoy.

- *Body Heat*, directed by Lawrence Kasdan (a remake of *Double Indemnity*, based on the James M. Cain novel of the same name)

- *Insomnia,* directed by Christopher Nolan
- *Delores Claiborne,* directed by Taylor Hackford (based on the novel by Stephen King)
- *Smilla's Sense of Snow,* directed by Bille August (based on the novel by Danish author Peter Hoeg)
- *Les Diaboliques,* directed by Henri-Georges Clouzot (based on the novel *Celle qui n'était plus,* also known as *She Who Was No More* by Pierre Boileau and Thomas Narcejac)

> *"People have forgotten how to tell a story. Stories don't have a middle or an end anymore. They usually have a beginning that never stops beginning."*
>
> —Steven Spielberg

Let's take a look at another one of Elmore Leonard's rules, one that you break at your peril.

Elmore Leonard's Rule 2: Avoid Prologues.

I know, I know, you read novels with prologues all the time. Some of your favorite books have prologues. And you'd be happy to list them all for me.

Whatever. First, let me reveal a dirty little secret about prologues and introductions: Most readers skip them. Why? Because they know prologues are often just self-indulgent notes from the author—and they're usually right. (Editors let authors get away with using prologues because they know readers will skip them anyway.) In the case of prologues, readers usually skip them because they know that the real story doesn't start until chapter one—*after* the prologue. (Never underestimate your readers. They're as smart as you are, if not smarter.)

That said, you can begin your story with a prologue if you feel you must. But if you want readers to actually read it, you will need to use a little subterfuge. As soon as the readers see the word *prologue,* they yawn. Or worse, they run. So whatever you do, don't call it a prologue. Try one of these options instead.

- Swap out the word *prologue* for a time or place reference.
  - *Berlin, 1939*

- *Five Years Earlier*
- *3012 CE*
- Use a device that can reveal time, place, and any information you need to communicate. Such devices can include:
  - news clippings
  - diary entries
  - trial transcripts
- Apply a different format to set it apart. You can use italics, breaks, and other graphic means of telling the reader that this part of the story is special. *Note:* If you use italics, keep it short. Reading italics is hard on the eyes, and many readers may opt out without even knowing why.

RULES ARE MADE TO BE BROKEN, PART II

Again, Elmore Leonard breaks his own rules, but he does it with style—and with one of the devices we've been talking about. This is the opening to Leonard's novel *The Hunted*.

This is the news story that appeared the next day, in the Sunday edition of the *Detroit Free Press*, page one:

Four Tourists Die
In Israeli Hotel Fire

TEL AVIV, March 20 (AP)—A predawn fire gutted an eight-story resort hotel Saturday, killing four tourists and injuring 46 others, including guests who leaped from upper-story windows to escape the flames. No Americans were killed, but two were reported injured, including an Ohio woman who jumped from the fourth-floor window.

By using the device of a news clipping, Leonard sets the stage for his story, reveals the information the reader needs, and avoids the dreaded word *prologue*.

Now let's explore some other risky ways to start your story. You should avoid these clichéd and boring methods if at all possible.

Don't Start with a Dream

So many stories start with dreams that pulling it off in an original way is darn near impossible. I personally feel so strongly about this that even were you able to come up with a means of making your dream opener work, I wouldn't read far enough to know it's working. As soon as I realize you're starting with a dream, I stop—and you've lost me. I know from the many "critique the first page" events I've participated in with agents, editors, and other publishing professionals that I am not alone in this. So the safest advice I can give you is this: Just don't do it. After all, do you really want readers to meet your hero while he's flat on his back, asleep? Who wants a hero like that? Better for readers to meet your protagonist while she's awake, alive, and active!

That said, here are two examples of stories in which opening with a dream works.

> Last night I dreamt I went to Manderley again.
> —*Rebecca*, Daphne du Maurier

This is a classic opener—and trying this yourself would only call attention to your lack of originality.

> He has forgotten something, he knows that for sure when he wakes up. Something he dreamt during the night. Something he ought to remember.
> —*Faceless Killers*, Henning Mankell

Mankell, Swedish creator of the popular Kurt Wallander mysteries, opens with a dream that's not really a dream. It sets the mood and hints at a darkness that came in the night. This is atmospheric writing at its best—and it's one of the reasons Mankell is an internationally known best-selling author.

If you can finesse your dream opener as smoothly as Mankell, go ahead and give it a try.

Don't Start with a Character Alone

Another red flag is starting with a character alone. Too often a character alone is a character alone, thinking. Again, this is not a proactive way to begin, nor is it a compelling way to introduce your protagonist.

If you begin with a character alone, that character better be doing something pretty fascinating, like:

- robbing a bank
- starting a fire
- spying on a lover
- finding a corpse
- planting a bomb
- quitting a job
- uncovering a secret
- leaving a spouse

You get the idea.

HOW MANY CHARACTERS MAKE A SCENE?

Once you've completed your scene-by-scene outline, you need to go through and think about how many characters are in each scene. Too many writers create too many scenes with only one or two characters. That's understandable; logistically, it's easier to juggle one or two characters at a time, but ultimately it makes for a boring read. Be sure that you have a good mix in terms of number of characters in your scenes.

- Rarely leave your characters alone, unless they are doing something really interesting.
- Be sure to have lots of two-, three-, four-, and more character scenes as well.
- Remember that many of a story's biggest scenes require a large cast: battles, parties, weddings, funerals, graduations, etc.

Don't Start with a Phone Call

This is another opener that we've seen a million times before. It's also another one of my pet peeves, because often it's just a matter of lazy writing. Surely you can come up with a more gripping opening for your story.

Let's face it: The phone call in the middle of the night is a cliché. As are texts, tweets, e-mails, and instant messages, voice mails, and

Skype calls. If you must begin with any of these, find a way to make it different. Go ahead; surprise me—and your reader!

A GREAT FIRST LINE

Earlier we discussed the importance of first lines in regard to theme. But there's another reason to start with a great first line: Not only can it set the stage for a great opening for your story, but it can also set the stage for the actual writing of a great opening for your story. A great first line will help you start on the right track—and set the right trajectory for your plot.

Let's take a look at some first lines that do just that.

> It was one hell of a night to throw away a baby.
> —*In the Bleak Midwinter* by Julia Spencer-Fleming

This novel went on to win virtually every award in its genre—because the rest of the story lives up to that intense and intriguing first line.

> It is a truth universally acknowledged, that a single man in possession of a good fortune, must be in want of a wife.
> —*Pride and Prejudice* by Jane Austen

This thematic first line stands the test of time; even after two hundred years, its wit, truth, and foreshadowing delight readers.

> January 23, 2004
> Abby Reynolds braked her truck on the icy highway, startled by what she imagined she saw at the side of the road.
> —*The Virgin of Small Plains* by Nancy Pickard

This is bad weather at its best, setting the perfect mood for the intriguing mystery that won the Agatha and Macavity awards as well as Edgar and Anthony nominations.

> Lolita, light of my life, fire of my loins.
> —*Lolita* by Vladimir Nabokov

What an unforgettable opening to a disturbing story that prepares us for the obsession to come. Not to mention that Lolita's character is so well drawn that the word itself became synonymous with a certain kind of child temptress.

I drove out to Glendale to put the new truck drivers on a brewery company bond, and then I remembered this renewal over in Hollywoodland. I decided to run over there. That was how I came to this House of Death, that you've been reading about in the papers.

—*Double Indemnity* by James M. Cain

James M. Cain gives us, in so few words, a slightly dodgy hero, a slightly seedy setting, and a major promise of scary things to come.

I was sitting in a taxi, wondering if I had overdressed for the evening, when I looked out the window and saw Mom rooting through a Dumpster.

—*The Glass Castle* by Jeannette Walls

This startling opening of Walls's best-selling memoir prepares us for the fact that when it comes to this dysfunctional family, nothing is at it seems.

The missing girl—there had been unceasing news reports, always flashing to that achingly ordinary school portrait of the vanished teen, you know the one with the rainbow-swirl background, the girl's too straight, her smile too self-conscious, then a quick cut to the worried parents on the front lawn microphones surrounding them, Mom silently tearful, Dad reading a statement with quivering lip—that girl, that *missing* girl, had just walked past Edna Skylar.

—*Promise Me* by Harlan Coben

I defy anyone not to keep reading after this classic Coben opening. He takes the situation we've all seen before—a missing girl—and manages to engage *and* surprise us.

You would think it would be impossible to find anything new in the world, creatures no man has ever seen before, one-of-a-kind oddities in which nature has taken a backseat to the coursing pulse of the fantastical and the marvelous. I can tell you with certainty that such things exist, for beneath the water there are beasts as huge as elephants with hundreds of legs, and in the skies, rocks thrown alit from the heavens burn through the bright air and fall to earth.

—*The Museum of Extraordinary Things* by Alice Hoffman

Alice Hoffman's opening is rich in theme, atmosphere, and fairy tale anomalies. It's a seduction that will pull the reader right into what John Gardner called "the fictive dream."

> The office of the university president looked like the front parlor of a successful Victorian whorehouse. It was paneled in big squares of dark walnut, with ornately figured maroon drapes at the windows. There was maroon carpeting and the furniture was black leather with brass studs. The office was much nicer than the classrooms; maybe I should have worn a tie.
> —*The Godwulf Manuscript* by Robert B. Parker

The voice of Robert B. Parker's sardonic hero opens the first of the wildly successful Spenser novels. Parker's Zen-like prose is clean, clear, and precise, and readers fall in love with Spenser immediately

> If you really want to hear about it, the first thing you'll probably want to know is where I was born, and what my lousy childhood was like, and how my parents were occupied and all before they had me, and all that David Copperfield kind of crap, but I don't feel like going into it, if you want to know the truth.
> —*The Catcher in the Rye* by J.D. Salinger

Meet Holden Caulfield, the teenage protagonist of *The Catcher in the Rye*—the character who comes to symbolize adolescent angst and rebellion for generations of young people.

WRITER AT WORK

If you're having trouble with your beginning, pull ten of your favorite novels in your genre (published in this century) off your bookshelf and read the opening pages. See how these writers pull it off—and extrapolate.

YOUR ACT ONE CHECKLIST

We've spent a lot of time on beginnings in this chapter. That's because if your beginning doesn't grab your reader, the rest doesn't really matter. Here's a checklist you can use to make sure that your beginning works.

- What actually happens?
- Why will the reader care about or relate to the characters?
- How do you want the reader to feel? What have you done to evoke that feeling?
- Have you used all the elements of fiction at your disposal—setting, plot, character, theme, and so on?
- Have you chosen the right POV and voice?
- Is your inciting incident strong enough? The catalyst? Plot Point 1?
- Does the dialogue ring true?
- Are the story questions strong enough to keep the reader turning pages?
- Is it clear what kind of story you're telling?
- What makes this beginning different from others of its ilk?
- Is it well written and well edited?

TACKLING THE MIDDLE

> "A novel with a bad middle is a bad book. A bad ending is something I've just gotten in the habit of forgiving."
>
> —Lev Grossman

> "[Writing a novel] is like driving a car at night. You never see further than your headlights, but you can make the whole trip that way."
>
> —E.L. Doctorow

In literature, as in life, our middles can give us trouble. They're not as sleek or as strong or as sexy as they should be. They're a little flabby and frowsy and unformed. While we may know our beginning and our ending, we're often a little unsure of our middle. We don't see Act Two as clearly as we see Act One and Act Three. Just like the hero in the hero's journey, we must face the trials and tribulations of the second act.

But that's not necessarily a bad thing; there's no reason to panic. You have strategies, tricks, and tips you can use to help you navigate that grand desert you must cross to get to the other side of Act Two.

But first, let's examine the most common faults, failings, and flaws that plague many middles. Fair warning: It's a short list of foibles.

THE TOP THREE REASONS ACT TWO DOESN'T WORK

1. Not enough happens.
2. Not enough happens.
3. Not enough happens.

Fortunately all the work you've done on your main plot and subplots, theme and variations on theme is now about to pay off big-time; for it's the subplot that will save your middle every time. And the more subplots you have, the more story threads you have to weave through Act Two. If you find yourself with a weak middle, then beef up the subplots you've already planned and add more as needed. You can have a half dozen subplots or more, depending on the kind of story you're writing. A good general rule: Aim for at least two to four subplots as you plan your story.

SECOND ACTS: A TIME FOR LOVE, LEARNING, MACGUFFINS, MAYHEM, AND MURDER

As we have noted, keeping the plot moving in the second act is often a matter of beefing up or adding subplots, creating scene sequences, and using devices. There are certain kinds of subplots, scene sequences, and devices that are particularly good for strengthening second acts. Let's take a look at each in turn.

The Love Subplot

In many genres, one of the significant subplots of the story revolves around a love interest. In a mystery, for example, the protagonist's love life is often a strong secondary thread that runs through the story, providing a respite from the more serious and violent main plot. Think of the film *Witness,* the 1985 American thriller directed by Peter Weir and written by William Kelley, Pamela Wallace, and Earl W. Wallace. The film's second act is illuminated by the moving love story between Philadelphia police detective John Book (played by Harrison Ford) and the young Amish widow, Rachel Lapp (played by Kelly McGillis). Their relationship carries the second act—and ultimately elevates a run-of-the-mill crime story into an Oscar-nominated classic whose original screenplay earned the Writers Guild of America Award for Best

Original Screenplay and the Mystery Writers of America's 1986 Edgar Award for Best Motion Picture Screenplay.

Other mysteries with a romantic subplot that add freshness and fuel to the story include Julia Spencer-Fleming's Clare Fergusson/Russ Van Alstyne mysteries, Hank Phillippi Ryan's Jane Ryland series, and Robert B. Parker's Jesse Stone series.

If you're writing a love story, you may think this strategy doesn't apply to you. But in love stories, it's often the secondary love story, involving secondary characters, that serves as the big subplot in Act Two. Consider the romantic subplot in *Pride and Prejudice* involving Elizabeth Bennet's friend Charlotte and Mr. Collins, or all of the romantic subplots involving her sisters.

In *When Harry Met Sally*, the romantic subplot between Sally's best friend, Marie, and Harry's best friend, Jess, mirrors Harry and Sally's relationship, and their wedding provides the setting for a big confrontation between our hero and heroine.

Another subplot strategy for love stories is to build out the subplots involving your lovers' previous relationships. Again, you only have to look to Jane Austen to see how invaluable these subplots can be. In *Sense and Sensibility*, Marianne Dashwood's main romance with Colonel Brandon is thwarted by her dalliance with Willoughby, just as her sister Elinor Dashwood's relationship with Edward is nearly undone by his secret engagement to Lucy.

No matter what kind of story you are writing, you may love what a romantic subplot can do for your second act. How can you build the love story in your novel? Which secondary characters can you enlist to mirror the principal characters? How can you use these subplots to enliven the middle of your story?

The Learning Scene Sequence

In many stories, the protagonists must acquire certain knowledge or master certain skills and prove they've done so successfully before they can face the climactic challenge that awaits them in Act Three. (In movies, this is often a montage.) Such preparation and testing can drive much of the action in Act Two. This can take many forms.

- Luke Skywalker learns to fence with the lightsaber in *Star Wars*.
- Elizabeth Gilbert learns to meditate and forgive herself in India in *Eat Pray Love*.
- Rocky gets into shape—physically, mentally, and spiritually—for the big fight in *Rocky*.
- Ren teaches Willard to dance in *Footloose*.
- The girls go through Carrie's closet in *Sex in the City*.
- Mia Thermopolis goes from Greenwich Village awkward teen to princess in *The Princess Diaries*.

Ask yourself what your protagonist must learn—and how that learning will be tested in your story. Brainstorm ways to dramatize the mastery of skills and the acquiring of knowledge, as well as the testing of those skills and knowledge.

> *"When I'm deciding to read a book, I never open to the first chapter, because that's been revised and worked over eighty-eight times. I'll just turn to the middle of the book, to the middle of a chapter, and just read a random page, and I'll know right away whether this is the real deal or not."*
>
> —Carl Hiaasen

The MacGuffin Device

We've already seen the significant role that MacGuffins can play in a plot in our analysis of *The Maltese Falcon*. MacGuffins can also help you get through Act Two. In *The Wizard of Oz*, the film could conceivably be over once Dorothy arrives at the Emerald City. But the Wizard tells her he won't help her get back home to Kansas until she brings him the broomstick of the Wicked Witch of the West. That broomstick is the MacGuffin that drives the rest of the story. (*Note:* In L. Frank Baum's original *The Wonderful Wizard of Oz*, the Wizard says they must kill the witch, not fetch the broomstick.)

In crime fiction, MacGuffins are often treasures, secrets, malevolence—something worth killing for. In science fiction and fantasy, MacGuffins can be weapons, mystical artifacts, technologies—something worth dying for. In romance, MacGuffins run the gamut from objects, like the emerald in the film *Romancing the Stone*, to emotions, like Emma's persistent desire to play the matchmaker in Jane Austen's *Emma*.

Does your story have a MacGuffin? Are you using it to best effect? If you don't yet have a MacGuffin, consider how you might weave one into your plot. How could that MacGuffin help you make your Act Two more exciting and compelling?

The Mayhem and Murder Subplots

"When in doubt, have a man come through the door with a gun in his hand."

—Raymond Chandler

Sometimes the best approach to Act Two is to throw caution to the wind and go for broke. Do something unexpected. Shake things up. Bring in a man with a gun or an ex-wife with a grievance or a sibling with a persecution complex. Put someone in jail or on trial or on a boat to China. Think sex and violence, weddings and funerals, bombs and bombshells.

If you're writing a mystery, another body ups the ante for detective and villain alike. If you're writing a romance, an old flame turns up the heat on our happy couple. If you're writing a domestic drama, a holiday gathering can set the stage for a family meltdown.

Make a list of the things you could do in Act Two to throw your protagonist off balance in every aspect of her life, physically, emotionally, and spiritually. The harder you are on her, the better your story will be. Remember: What doesn't kill your hero makes your story stronger.

> *"Plot is tremendously important to me: I can't stand books where nothing happens, and I can't imagine ever writing a novel without at least one murder."*
>
> —Ned Beauman

ACT TWO CHECKLIST

The middle is where a lot of writers get stuck, stories slow down, and readers bail. We've discussed many ways in which you can ensure your middle propels the plot and engages readers in the process. Here's a list of questions to ask yourself to make sure your Act Two fires on all cylinders.

- What actually happens?
- Have you beefed up your existing subplots? Have you added more?
- Have you considered a strong love subplot?
- What does your protagonist have to learn to proceed successfully? How will you dramatize that preparation and testing?
- Do you have a MacGuffin you could insert into Act Two?
- What about sex and violence? Is it time for an untimely death or a hot night between the sheets?
- Who could show up uninvited in Act Two to give your heroine more grief?
- Is there a big event—battle, wedding, funeral—you can use to drive your plot through the middle?
- What surprising turn of events can you plot for Act Two?
- Which of your characters has a secret that could be revealed in Act Two?
- Have you used all the elements of fiction at your disposal: setting, plot, character, theme, and so on?

- Are the story questions strong enough to keep the reader turning pages?
- Is it well written and well edited?

CROSSING THE FINISH LINE TO THE END

For a writer, there's nothing more exciting or exhilarating than that glorious race to the finish line. After tens of thousands of words, the end is in sight, and like a horse galloping home to the food and shelter of the barn, you just can't wait to get there. Your fingers fly across the keys and the pages pile up and you start planning the many ways in which you will reward yourself when you finish the story that has held you captive all this time.

Which is why so many third acts seem rushed and raw and relatively unsatisfying. Remember that old publishing adage we discussed at the beginning of this chapter: *The first page sells the book; the last page sells the next book.* Now it's time to make sure your ending is as good as your beginning.

If the ending doesn't rock, the rest doesn't matter. I know, I know, I said that about the beginning, too, but it's just as true for your ending. From the point of view of agents, editors, and readers, the only thing worse than taking the time to sit down and read a book with a terrible opening is taking even more time to sit down and read a book all the way to its terrible ending. This is when people throw books across the room in disgust—or in the case of unpublished manuscripts housed in Word docs, hit the delete key in disgust.

On the other hand, there's nothing more gratifying to agents, editors, and readers alike than forsaking all other forms of entertainment and investing several hours in a good story only to be rewarded by a finale that satisfies, surprises, and even haunts them. Remember the first time you read the ending of F. Scott Fitzgerald's *The Great Gatsby*? Or Alice Walker's *The Color Purple*? Or John Irving's *The World According to Garp*?

We all have our favorite stories, and those stories have great endings or they wouldn't be our favorites. There are the endings that delight us (*Emma* by Jane Austen), the endings that disturb us (*My Sis-*

ter's Keeper by Jodi Picoult), and the endings that haunt us (*Never Let Me Go* by Kazuo Ishiguro).

You, too, can make sure that *your* ending delights, disturbs, or haunts your readers. There are certain mistakes you can avoid making, as well as certain techniques and tricks you can use to craft an Act Three that moves readers and sends them to the bookstore for your next work.

As an agent, I hear editors' feedback on what they believe is working and not working in writers' stories. As an editor and teacher, I help writers make the most of the final pages of their manuscripts. And as a writer, I try to craft effective endings to my own stories. The following techniques, tips, and tricks are those I've culled from all this expertise and experience from editors, agents, teachers, writers, and readers.

> *"I want an ending that's satisfying. I'm more of a classical writer than a modernist one in that I want the ending to be coherent and feel like an ending. I don't like when it just seems to putter out. I mean, life is chaotic enough."*
>
> —Jeffrey Eugenides

PLAY BY THE RULES

Rule 1: Don't Rush It

When I wrote my first (practice) novel many years ago, I was lucky enough to be able to give the first draft to *New York Times* best-selling author Pamela Jekel. She read my manuscript and gave me some of the best advice I've ever received as a writer. She pointed out that I had failed to dramatize the biggest moments in my story, and those moments I had tried to dramatize were woefully inadequate. She warned me that I might be avoiding the writing of the big scenes because I was anxious about writing them. She also told me to "milk the drama" in my scenes, and that most of my scenes should be at least *twice as long.*

In short: I was rushing it. I was a reporter, taught to write lean—and to leave myself out of my writing. But both that leanness and that distance were working against me as a novelist. I had to train myself to slow down, take my time, and milk the drama.

The same issues plague other writers, too—and they may be plaguing you as well. Even if you do fully dramatize your scenes in Act One and Act Two, as you approach the finish line you may quicken your pace—and give short shrift to the drama in Act Three.

DOUBLE YOUR DRAMA

Select one of your big scenes from Act Three. How long is it? Challenge yourself to make it twice as long. (Hint: You do this by making sure that you have fully dramatized it.) See what that looks like. Is it better? Worse? Bring your "before" and "after" versions to your writers group, and see what they say.

Rule 2: The Protagonist Drives the Action

Another common failing that editors especially are quick to point out is the ending where the hero does not drive the action. This may seem obvious, but you'd be surprised how often it is not the case.

- The sleuth does not figure out who the murderer is. Someone else does, or the murderer confesses before the sleuth can figure it out.
- The woman in jeopardy *is* in jeopardy but is rescued rather than saving herself. Even if she has help, your heroine needs to do the lion's share of the work involved in saving herself.
- The hero is absent at the climax of the story. This should never, ever happen. Even Dustin Hoffman shows up at the wedding in *The Graduate.*
- A deus ex machina saves the day. *Deus ex machina* is Latin for "god in the machine," and is used to describe a character or thing that enters the story in a godlike fashion and solves a previously unsolvable problem. Think of the British naval officer finding Ralph on the beach at the end of William Golding's *Lord of the Flies.*

Act Three is the time when your hero gets all the good action, lines, and—more often than not—the love interest. If you were casting the film version of the story, this part is the reason the famous movie star agrees to sign on to the project. It's chock-full of swell acting opportunity and emoting as the story comes to its dramatic conclusion and the hero learns his lessons and becomes the man he was destined to become, thereby embodying the themes of the work. Examples include Katniss Everdeen in *The Hunger Games*, Elizabeth Bennet in *Pride and Prejudice*, and Michael Corleone in Mario Puzo's *The Godfather*.

Act Three is where that starring role lands the actor an Oscar. Think of Jack Nicholson as the misanthropic Melvin Udall in *As Good as It Gets*, as he struggles to become "a better man," a man worthy of the lovely Carol Connelly, played by Helen Hunt. Or Natalie Portman as the ambitious ballerina Nina Sayers in *Black Swan*, who drives her body, mind, and spirit to the limit to be the most perfect Swan Queen ever.

Make sure that your protagonist gets the opportunity to win the Oscar for appearing in your story. Or, if you prefer sports analogies to film, give your protagonist the plays worthy of the Most Valued Player award in your plot.

> "Discovering the 'impossible' ending to a new book makes me sick with joy and relief."
>
> —Chuck Palahniuk

Rule 3: Make Sure Your Antagonist Gets His or Her Due

In your zeal to describe the triumph (or failure) of your protagonist, you may have neglected to give your antagonist his due. The most satisfying endings are those where both the antagonist and the protagonist have their spot in the sun. In *The Silence of the Lambs*, Clarice Starling rescues Catherine, her abductor Buffalo Bill is killed, and Hannibal Lecter escapes to kill—and eat—again.

Rule 4: Tie up Your Loose Ends

The good news is that all of your subplots carried you through Act Two in style. The bad news is that now you have to tie up all the loose ends from all of those subplots. In your rush to the finish line, you may very well have dropped some threads of your story.

Loose ends drive agents, editors, and readers crazy. Publishers have rejected many a well-told story because of the questions left unanswered in said stories. Go through and tie up those loose ends—or risk losing your readers and being labeled a careless writer.

> *"It is the loose ends with which men hang themselves."*
> —Zelda Fitzgerald

Rule 5: Add a Twist If You Can

There's nothing like a good twist to ensure a memorable Act Three. Pulling off a good twist—one that readers don't see coming—isn't easy. But if you can do it, do it.

The best way to pull off a good twist is to remember that there are two stories: the one you are telling your readers, and the one you are *not* telling your readers. In a murder mystery, for example, there's the story the reader sees about the solving of the crime. But you as the writer already know the story of the crime—that's the story you're *not* telling your readers. You can use this knowledge to mislead readers, distracting them so that they don't see the twist coming and yet planting enough clues along the way that the ending doesn't seem to come out of nowhere. This is a subtle trickery, because the best twist endings are as inevitable as they are surprising.

In some genres, such as crime fiction and science fiction, a good twist can make the difference between getting published and not getting published. That said, a good twist will improve your story no matter the genre. Think of "The Gift of the Magi," the moving love story written by O. Henry, who made his reputation as a writer based on his ingenious plot twists. Other stories known for their surprising endings include:

- *The Murder of Roger Ackroyd* by Agatha Christie
- *Fight Club* by Chuck Palahniuk
- *Ender's Game* by Orson Scott Card
- *A Dream of Wessex* by Christopher Priest
- *Life of Pi* by Yann Martel
- *Gone Girl* by Gillian Flynn
- *The Time Traveler's Wife* by Audrey Niffenegger

Rule 6: Don't Cut Off Your Ending

When you are writing a series, it's tempting to simply cut off the story in Book One and plan to pick up where you left off in Book Two. This is a cheat that will not win you any praise from agents, editors, or readers. Each book in a series needs to stand alone, and this is especially true for Book One—because if Book One doesn't work, there won't be a Book Two.

Think of the original *Star Wars* (now known as *Star Wars Episode IV: A New Hope*). It ends with the ceremony in which Luke Skywalker and his pals are honored for destroying the Death Star, a scene that brings the story to a satisfying conclusion. We know, of course, that although this battle is won, the war will rage on (when *The Empire Strikes Back*). But George Lucas does not cheat us out of this successful resolution, and we're able to revel in the happy ending. (Of course, he does cut off *The Empire Strikes Back* rather abruptly, but by then the movies were so successful and the anticipation for the third film to follow so great, nobody cared. We should all be so lucky.)

Having sold several multiple book deals in which the writer had to address this issue before I could shop the book, I can assure you that if you are writing a series, you'll want to make sure each book in the series stands alone, on its own, and gives the reader a full and satisfying reading experience. In fact, most series deals are negotiated based on a completed Book One and, at minimum, outlines of the remaining books in the series. These outlines typically indicate both the overall dramatic arc of the whole series as well as the individual plots for each book in the series.

> "I better make the plot good. I wanted to make it grip people on the first page and have a big turning point in the middle, as there is, and construct the whole thing like a roller coaster ride."
>
> —Mark Haddon

Rule 7: Leave Us with a Great Last Line

As we discussed in chapter eight, readers will carry a great last line with them long after they finish your story. The perfect last line is like a sweet snippet of melody or a captivating lyric from a popular song, one that slips into your consciousness at the oddest moments and won't leave.

Most important, this last line is your final opportunity to drive home the theme of your story. We've talked about some great last lines, and you've taken a stab at writing yours earlier in this book, in chapter one.

But let's take a look at some more classic last lines, the ones that stay with you.

> But, in spite of these deficiencies, the wishes, the hopes, the confidence, the predictions of the small band of true friends who witnessed the ceremony, were fully answered in the perfect happiness of the union.
>
> —*Emma* by Jane Austen

I ran with the wind blowing in my face, and a smile as wide as the valley of Panjsher on my lips. I ran.

—*The Kite Runner* by Khaled Hosseini

It is not often that someone comes along who is a true friend and a good writer. Charlotte was both.

—*Charlotte's Web* by E.B. White

The creatures outside looked from pig to man, and from man to pig, and from pig to man again; but already it was impossible to say which was which.

—*Animal Farm* by George Orwell

But the effect of her being on those around her was incalculably diffusive: for the growing good of the world is partly dependent on unhistoric acts; and that things are not so ill with you and me as they might have been is half owing to the number who lived faithfully a hidden life, and rest in unvisited tombs.

—*Middlemarch* by George Eliot

My husband remained there some time after me to settle our affairs, and at first I had intended to go back to him, but at his desire I altered that resolution, and he is come over to England also, where we resolve to spend the remainder of our years in sincere penitence for the wicked lives we have lived.

—*Moll Flanders* by Daniel Defoe

After a while I went out and left the hospital and walked back to the hotel in the rain.

—*A Farewell to Arms* by Ernest Hemingway

When the long winter nights come on and the wolves follow their meat into the lower valleys, he may be seen running at the head of the pack through the pale moonlight or glimmering borealis, leaping gigantic above his fellows, his great throat a-bellow as he sings a song of the younger world, which is the song of the pack.

—*The Call of the Wild* by Jack London

But wherever they go, and whatever happens to them on the way, in that enchanted place on the top of the Forest, a little boy and his Bear will always be playing.

—*The House at Pooh Corner* by A.A. Milne

For it is the dawn that has come, as it has come for a thousand centuries, never failing. But when that dawn will come, of our emancipation, from the fear of bondage and bondage of fear, why, that is a secret.

—*Cry, the Beloved Country* by Alan Paton

And it may be that love sometimes occurs without pain or misery.

—*The Shipping News* by Annie Proulx

"My test of a good novel is dreading to begin the last chapter."
—Thomas Helm

WRITER AT WORK

What was the last book that haunted you, that you hoped would never end? Ask yourself what you loved about that reading experience and what made that story so satisfying. Write those thoughts down.

Now, take that book and reread the last three chapters. Analyze how these chapters contribute to that remarkable reading experience, paying particular attention to:

- the action
- the events
- the last chapter
- the last page
- the last line

Write down why you think these elements work so well. Consider how you can use the techniques the author of the book uses to make the ending of your story as fulfilling to your readers.

YOUR ACT THREE CHECKLIST

The end is where you prove to your reader that your story means something. It's where your plot and theme, subplots and variations on theme all come together in a climactic clamor of conflict and meaning. But Act Three is where a lot of writers hold back and pull their literary punches, and in so doing they miss the opportunity to make the lasting impression that the best endings leave on readers.

We've discussed many ways in which you can ensure that your ending rocks your story and brings it home. Here's a list of questions to consider when creating the best possible ending for your story.

- What actually happens?
- Is the action big enough?
- Do you rush it? Act Three should take up about one-fourth of your story. (Act One: one-quarter at fifteen scenes; Act Two: two-quarters at thirty scenes; Act Three: one-quarter at fifteen scenes)
- Do you give your protagonist an ending worthy of an Oscar-winning performance?
- Does your villain get what's coming to him?
- Have you forgotten your subplots? Have you tied up all of your loose ends?
- Have you pulled out all the stops for your ending?
- Have you worked in a good twist that will surprise your readers?
- Have you crafted a great last line that speaks to theme?
- Have you made sure that your hero plays the biggest role in Act Three, driving the plot to its fireworks ending?
- How does your hero pass his final test? What lessons has he learned? How do those relate to your theme?
- What's the worst that could happen to your heroine? Do you make it happen? How do you get her out of it?
- Have you dramatized the big moments in Act Three?
- Are the story questions strong enough to keep the reader turning the pages? Do you answer the big story question of the book?
- Is your story the first in a series? Does it stand alone? Did you gracefully plant the setup for the next story in the series in the end of the first story?
- Is Act Three well written and well edited?

BEGINNING, MIDDLE, END ... AGAIN

We've taken a hard look at each act of your story, and we've analyzed what's working and what's not working in each section. You've gone through your scene-by-scene breakdown and made sure that the storyline holds together and that your main plot and main theme, subplots, and variations on theme all work together to create a cohesive whole. In the next chapter, we'll focus on the elements of fiction—tools that will help tackle the actual writing of each scene as you bring your structure to life on the page. If you already have a first draft, you can use these tools to polish your work and fix the issues that often keep manuscripts from finding a home with a publisher.

Either way, you'll be putting it all together in Part Three.

> "You know you've read a good book when you turn the last page and feel a little as if you have lost a friend."
>
> —Paul Sweeney

PART III

PUTTING IT ALL TOGETHER

"To produce a mighty book, you must choose a mighty theme. No great and enduring volume can ever be written on the flea, though many there be that have tried it."

—Herman Melville

IDENTIFY THE CENTRAL THEME THAT DRIVES YOUR PLOT
HEROES, VILLAINS, AND SUPPORTING CHARACTERS
PLOT VS. ORGANIZING PRINCIPLE
VARIATIONS
TWISTS AND TURNS
FIND YOUR USP
LAYERS
CATALYST
THE TAPESTRY OF STORY
WEAVE PLOT AND SUBPLOT
BUILD STRONG ARCS FOR YOUR MAIN CHARACTERS
PACING
ACTION IS CHARACTER
PLUS AND MINUS SCENES

THE TAPESTRY OF STORY

"Storytelling is ultimately a creative act of pattern recognition. Through characters, plot, and setting, a writer creates places where previously invisible truths become visible. Or the storyteller posits a series of dots that the reader can connect."

—Douglas Coupland

Creating a great plot is like weaving a tapestry, in which all the threads—voice, action, point of view, tone, style, setting, conflict, dialogue, and more—must be woven together in a seamless pattern to create the whole. Working in concert, these elements of fiction can help you move the story forward, establish genre, highlight voice, describe setting, reveal character, set the tone, and, most important, speak to theme.

This careful weaving begins and ends with theme. In this chapter, we'll explore how you can use theme to create a story tapestry that not only holds together, but that moves readers on many levels. Let's examine each thread in that tapestry, one by one.

THE VOICE OF THEME

If you are a writer with a strong and unique voice, it can set your book apart—and make readers fall in love with you. Remember the first time you read *The Catcher in the Rye* by J.D. Salinger? Odds are you fell in love with Salinger's voice right away. (Or maybe you didn't. Certainly I didn't. When I read it the first time as a teenager, I thought *The Catcher in the Rye* was lame. But when I read it again twenty years later, after raising two boys, I thought it was brilliant. It was as if Salinger were breaking open the inside of the male adolescent brain for all the world to see, helping confused mothers like me get a clue.)

Which just goes to prove my point.

When a writer is telling a story to best effect, his voice rings with his themes—and his themes echo throughout his voice. Consider Salinger, whose themes of adolescence, honesty, authenticity, and the pretense and hypocrisy of adult life are all bound up in his one-of-a-kind voice, whether he's writing about Holden Caulfield or Franny and Zooey.

THE VOICES IN YOUR HEAD

If you are confused about the difference between your writer's voice and the various voices of your POV characters, you are not alone. This can be a bewildering distinction for many writers.

Think of it this way: Your voice is your voice no matter which character's POV you're writing. Take John Irving, whose unique voice reflects his comic approach to the tragedy that is life. His colorful characters range from the saintly Jenny Fields of *The World According to Garp* to the vile Mr. Rose of *The Cider House Rules*. But his voice remains his own, from character to character and story to story.

The same is true of Charles Dickens and Jane Austen and countless other authors.

Think of your favorite writers and the constancy of their voices over the course of their careers in storytelling.

WRITER AT PLAY

Choose a story from the following list. All are by storytellers whose voices are redolent with theme. It can be one you've already read and loved or one that you haven't read. Either way, read it; while you do, consider the ways in which voice and theme mirror each other.

- *Gone Girl* by Gillian Flynn
- *Bridget Jones's Diary* by Helen Fielding
- *The All-Girl Filling Station's Last Reunion* by Fannie Flagg
- *Me Talk Pretty One Day* by David Sedaris
- *Durable Goods* by Elizabeth Berg
- *The Book Thief* by Markus Zusak

- *Bird by Bird* by Anne Lamott
- *Interview with the Vampire* by Anne Rice
- *Practical Magic* by Alice Hoffman
- *Catch-22* by Joseph Heller
- *Slaughterhouse-Five* by Kurt Vonnegut
- Any work by Shakespeare

How does your voice reflect your theme? And how do you know if it does or not? As an agent, I often meet talented writers who have yet to sell their stories because they have yet to find their voice. Or they are fighting the truth about their own voice. Finding your voice is like finding the right partner. Sometimes you like someone, but you know it's just not going to work out—because the right person feels like *home,* and for whatever reason, this person does not feel like home.

Finding your voice is finding your home. Your true north. I have a client who's published a lot of nonfiction, wonderful how-to books about the secrets of living an authentic life. And yet, her novels never rang true. A seasoned traveler, she set her stories in the cultural milieus of her favorite foreign places, locales she knew well but could not call home, even when she wanted to. These novels were technically proficient, but the voice was not her own. She was trying on the voices of other cultures, other customs, other writers. And as her voice was not her own, neither were her themes. She continued to publish the successful nonfiction that reflected her values and traditions, and to write novels that didn't quite work. Meanwhile she bought a little farm and started writing a blog about life on the land. I—and thousands of readers—loved her blog and told her so. As her agent, I told her this was where her juice was— she'd found her fictive voice. (Of course, she'd never lost it; she used it when writing her nonfiction. But her love of "the other" blinded her to it in her own storytelling.) I encouraged her to write a novel set on the farm and tell it in her authentic (blogger's) voice. Which she did— and was promptly rewarded with a three-book deal! All because she found her voice. The lesson is this: Figure out who you are and what you care about, and you'll achieve that happy marriage of voice and theme. These other writers have done the same.

- Philip Roth
- Janet Evanovich
- Mark Twain
- Woody Allen
- Dorothy Parker
- Maya Angelou
- Ray Bradbury
- Elizabeth Berg
- And many more!

THEMATIC TONE

"I particularly admire Mark Twain and Jerome K. Jerome, who wrote in a certain tone of voice which was humane and understanding of humanity, but always ready to annotate its little foibles. I think I'd lay my cards down on that and say that it's that that I'm trying to do."

—Terry Pratchett

Tone speaks to the emotion, atmosphere, and mood of your story. This is why the right tone is critical to communicating the themes of your story. Think of Stephen King, whose clever use of tone tells readers right away that they are in for a scary ride. His themes are about what scares us—and his tone tells us we're about to be scared.

Or think of P.G. Wodehouse, whose lighthearted and funny tone has been compared to that of a musical comedy—without the music. (Which is not surprising, given that he was also a popular playwright and lyricist who wrote fifteen plays and more than 250 songs for some thirty musical comedies.) Or Anne Rice, whose darkly sensual tone sets the stage for her darkly sensual vampire novels, which are all about love, sex, and death, not to mention immortality, existentialism, and what it means to be human.

Other writers with pitch-perfect tones include:

- Voltaire
- Jonathan Swift
- David Sedaris

- Edgar Allan Poe
- William Faulkner
- Anais Nin
- Emily Brontë
- Henry James
- Shirley Jackson
- Edith Wharton
- John Steinbeck

What is the tone of your novel—and how does it reflect the themes of your story? How do you achieve that tone? Say you're writing a police procedural. Your tone could be spare and bleak, like that of Henning Mankell's Wallander novels, whose pessimistic themes revolve around the xenophobia and dark underbelly of Swedish "über-civilized" society. Or maybe you're writing a gothic romance and you are aiming for a tone that's, well, gothic—just as in *The House at Riverton* by Kate Morton. Or your story may be a coming-of-age novel whose confessional, vulnerable tone reflects the anxiety and insecurity of adolescence and the pain of growing up, as in Stephen Chbosky's *The Perks of Being a Wallflower*.

Study the tone in stories by authors in your genre and deconstruct how the tone relates to the theme. Think about how you can achieve the same effects.

THE DIFFERENCE BETWEEN VOICE AND TONE

Tone is not the same thing as voice, even though they are very closely related and very often confused. It's the difference between you as a personality and the particular mood you're in. You are always you (voice), even when you're happy, sad, angry, and so on (tone).

"I never plot out my novels in terms of the tone of the book. Hopefully, once a story is begun it reveals itself."

—Alice Hoffman

THEME AS STYLE

Style is not the same thing as tone. As we've seen, tone reflects the atmosphere, mood, and emotion of the writing. Style deals more with the way in which you put words together, structure your sentences, and use punctuation. It's the words you choose—and why you choose them. The right style can reinforce your theme, just as wearing the right clothes on the outside can reflect who you really are on the inside.

Certain writers are known for their style, and often that style is so unique that it's gone on to influence generation after generation of writers since. James Joyce and Cormac McCarthy are particularly notable in terms of their style.

James Joyce was the literary genius who played with language with the uninhibited passion of a child playing with his toys and pioneered the so-called stream of consciousness style of writing fiction. This no-holds-barred ebullience reflects his themes, which include the stages of a man's life, the search for identity, the nature of faith, and "love's bitter mystery." Check out *Ulysses* and *Finnegan's Wake*, if you haven't already. *Note:* Don't try to understand it, at least not the first time you read it. Just let his extraordinary language wash over you—and *feel* it.

Cormac McCarthy, the acclaimed author of such classics as *No Country for Old Men*, *The Road*, and the Border trilogy, has credited James Joyce as the main influence on his work (with nods to William Faulkner and MacKinlay Kantor as well). The Pulitzer Prize winner, known for his bleak, poetic style, favors declarative sentences that can run on and on and on, without benefit of punctuation—just as Joyce's do. In fact, McCarthy writes by his own set of punctuation rules: no quotation marks, no semicolons, and only the rare colon. McCarthy's style reflects his dark and nihilistic themes of death, violence, and the struggle between good and evil.

> *"I believe in periods, in capitals, in the occasional comma, and that's it."*
>
> —Cormac McCarthy

Joyce and McCarthy are very different writers, even though they share some stylistic techniques. Ultimately their styles are as different as their themes. They both write superb prose, but while Joyce's lovely language paints life as a beautiful, melancholy mess that is ultimately worth living, McCarthy's lovely language paints life as a nihilistic exercise in violence and death.

We all can't be James Joyce or Cormac McCarthy—and we shouldn't want to be. There are plenty of great writers known for their style in every genre.

- Annie Proulx
- Ernest Hemingway
- Virginia Woolf
- Pat Conroy
- Kurt Vonnegut
- Alice Hoffman

Study the style of your favorite writers in your genre. Note how the elements of their styles—specificity, imagery, rhythm, word choice, sentence structure, and so on—relate to their themes. Then read a page of your own work, and see how it compares. Are you making the most of these elements of style?

> *"Style means the right word. The rest matters little."*
>
> —Jules Renard

READING FOR WRITERS

Here is some of the best advice on style and writing, from writers who know what they are talking about.

- *The Elements of Style* by William Strunk Jr., E.B. White, and Roger Angell
- "How to Write with Style" by Kurt Vonnegut
- *Three Uses of the Knife: On the Nature and Purpose of Drama* by David Mamet
- *Ernest Hemingway on Writing* edited by Larry W. Phillips
- *How to Write a Sentence* by Stanley Fish
- *How to Write* by Gertrude Stein
- *On Writing* and *One Writer's Beginnings* by Eudora Welty

SETTING: THE BIG PICTURE

"Rule one: Write about settings you're familiar with."

—Jeffery Deaver

The best settings are so critical to the theme and action of the story that, when well chosen and fully realized, they become characters as well—characters without whom the story could not be told. Choosing an intriguing setting gives you an opportunity to take readers to a place they've never been before or don't know much about. Such settings engage readers, as these writers proved in their popular stories.

- *THE HUNT FOR RED OCTOBER.* Tom Clancy's exciting techno-thriller introduces a fascinating setting most of us probably don't know much about: a nuclear submarine. Talk about all amped up and nowhere to go—now that makes for an exciting ride!
- *THE BONFIRE OF THE VANITIES.* Tom Wolfe reveals the greed, racism, and self-indulgence that rules the upper classes in the 1980s in New York City—the city that never sleeps.
- *MYSTIC RIVER.* Dennis Lehane knows Boston, and his psychological thriller explores the themes of love, faith, family, and tribal loyalties in a town all too familiar with the negative and positive aspects of them all.
- *THE WONDERFUL WIZARD OF OZ.* It's all about setting for L. Frank Baum's heroine Dorothy, who must make her way out of the magical and menacing Land of Oz and find her way home.
- *NINETEEN EIGHTY-FOUR.* George Orwell gives us a frightening and yet wildly prophetic vision of the future—a dystopian setting where Big Brother is always watching and privacy is a thing of the past—that science fiction writers everywhere have been trying to outdo ever since.
- *READING LOLITA IN TEHRAN.* Azar Nafisi's memoir shows us another side of life in the Islamic Republic of Iran—the female side—and speaks to themes of literature, personal freedom, feminism, and the power of art.
- *A PASSAGE TO INDIA.* E.M. Forster's spellbinding story about an English girl whose journey to India in the early twentieth

century challenges everything she knows about India, her own country, and herself. It's a novel that explores the mystical as well as the social and political aspects of a multifaceted country and its colonial rulers.

- *PEYTON PLACE.* Grace Metalious's classic soap opera set the bar for every other story written about a picture-perfect small town with terrible secrets to tell.
- *ONE FLEW OVER THE CUCKOO'S NEST.* Ken Kesey set his heartbreaking story about the institutionalized degradation that robs patients of their individuality, freedom, and humanity in an Oregon mental hospital.
- *THE NO. 1 LADIES' DETECTIVE AGENCY.* Alexander McCall Smith's strong and incorruptible Precious Ramotswe investigates cases with intelligence, integrity, and industry in Botswana, a place few of us knew anything about before this bestselling series was released.
- *DELORES CLAIBORNE.* There's a reason Stephen King sets many of his stories in his native Maine, a place where the summers are brief and the winters are long and sunlight is in short supply. Here he explores the darker side of human nature and the lengths to which mothers will go to protect their children in a thriller set in a small town in Maine during a solar eclipse.
- *THE PILLARS OF THE EARTH.* Ken Follett's mammoth historical bestseller about the building of a gothic cathedral in twelfth-century Kingsbridge, England, during the Anarchy explores the themes of love, faith, ambition, power, and revenge.

When you choose a setting for your novel, make it somewhere special. Someplace you know well or can get to know well enough to show us a side we don't know. Think of the many faces of Los Angeles as revealed by her writers: the dark underbelly of her sunny streets in James Ellroy's *L.A. Confidential*, the grim reality of daily life in South Central in Walter Mosley's *Walkin' the Dog*, or the search for good food and good enlightenment in affluent Los Feliz in central L.A. in Michelle Huneven's *Jamesland*.

Show us a face of your setting that we have not seen before. And make sure that it's closely related to your theme, so much so that it can become a character in your story.

> *"As a writer, I'm driven by settings. Others are driven by characters or predicaments, but with me, settings come first."*
> —Jim Lynch

SETTING: SCENE BY SCENE

Just as you should choose your overarching setting in a place we haven't seen before (or find a way to make a known place different, if we have seen it before), you should also set *each scene* somewhere we haven't seen before. Watch out for settings such as these, which we have seen too many times before.

- houses
- apartments
- offices
- restaurants
- cars
- airports
- schools
- malls
- places of worship

If you must set a scene in a familiar place, find a way to make it different. And make that difference relate to theme.

> *"For my first three books the setting (or place if you will) has always been a given—N.J. and the Dominican Republic and some N.Y.C.— so from one perspective you could say that the place in my work always comes first."*
> —Junot Díaz

THE ULTIMATE SETTING: WORLD BUILDING

The right setting can make all the difference in more ways than one. In science fiction and fantasy, choosing a setting often means creating a whole new world in another time, galaxy, or dimension. This world building is only as effective as the themes that inform it.

The king of world building is undoubtedly J.R.R. Tolkien, who created Middle-earth in *The Lord of the Rings* in painstaking detail, setting the standard for generations of SF/fantasy writers to come. This elaborate crafting incorporates such themes as mythology, religion, and history, as well as the nature of good and evil, friendship, loyalty, war, death, and immortality.

If Tolkien is the king of world building, then J.K. Rowling must be the queen. In her Harry Potter series, she introduces the world of Muggles, Wizards, and Hogwarts School of Witchcraft and Wizardry. With every succeeding book in the series, she builds upon the foundation of her world, adding new creatures, rules, mythologies, histories, and more. As her world—and the characters in it—mature with each book, so do the themes that inform that setting.

If your setting requires world building, think about how the various aspects of that world can speak to your themes and variations on theme.

> *"It's place that interests me, and the social and economic situation in a place—how people live, how they make their living, the culture—but the story comes from place."*
>
> —Annie Proulx

HUMOR AND THEME

> *"Writers must describe the terrible. And one way to describe the terrible is to write comically, of course."*
>
> —John Irving

Whether you're writing a comedy or a tragedy, a lighthearted love story or a dark noir thriller, a coming-of-age novel or a memoir, you can use humor to help drive home your themes and variations on theme.

Some plots are inherently funny or ironic, and for such stories the related themes are obvious.

- A nineteenth-century American travels back in time to sixth-century England (*A Connecticut Yankee in King Arthur's Court* by Mark Twain)

- A fast-talking lawyer must tell nothing but the truth for twenty-four hours (*Liar Liar* by Paul Guay and Stephen Mazur)
- An unfashionable young woman becomes the personal assistant to the demanding editor of a high-fashion magazine (*The Devil Wears Prada* by Lauren Weisberger)
- A street-smart Detroit cop comes to Beverly Hills to investigate a murder (*Beverly Hills Cop* by Daniel Petrie Jr.)
- A struggling writer trying to make it in New York City signs on as a Christmas elf at Macy's department store (*Holidays on Ice* by David Sedaris)
- A deadline-driven FedEx manager is stranded on an island with nothing but time to kill (*Cast Away* by William Broyles Jr.)

Some stories may not have an inherently comic premise, but they are written by authors with a fine sense of irony, which can be just as laugh-out-loud funny. Think of anything by Jane Austen, Anne Tyler, or Beverly Cleary.

Even if you are writing a story with serious themes, adding humor can help shine a mirror of truth on the terrible absurdities of life. Think of anything by John Irving, Christopher Moore, or Kurt Vonnegut.

When you're writing your story, ask yourself if you can use humor in one or more of the following classic ways.

1. Funny premise (*Big* by Gary Ross and Anne Spielberg)
2. Wise-cracking best friend (Ron Weasley in J.K. Rowling's Harry Potter series)
3. Mistaken identity (Shakespeare's *A Midsummer Night's Dream*)
4. Misunderstanding (*Persuasion* by Jane Austen)
5. Comedy = Tragedy + Time (*Heartburn* by Nora Ephron, or anything by Woody Allen)

When it comes to engaging the reader, a little humor can be your best friend. So go ahead, make 'em laugh.

"A man's got to take a lot of punishment to write a really funny book."

—Ernest Hemingway

THEMATIC POINT OF VIEW

Choosing the right point of view can reinforce your themes. What's more, often it's the POV that makes a story "the same, but different"—and a bestseller. Let's look at the thematic implications of these stories' POVs.

- **THE LOVELY BONES.** What sets Alice Sebold's *The Lovely Bones* apart from the usual murder story is its point of view. It's told from the POV of the young victim herself, which really brings home the themes of the novel: loss, memory, guilt, and responsibility.

- **THE ART OF RACING IN THE RAIN.** This classic novel by Garth Stein is so much more than just another dog story. I admit that I put off reading this novel for a long time because I couldn't bear to read a book told from a dying dog's POV, but it's one of the reasons it's among my favorite stories now. And ultimately the dog tells us what it means to be human.

- **MR. BRIDGE AND MRS. BRIDGE.** The his-and-her POVs of these companion volumes by Evan S. Connell are both the conceit and the genius of these completely different renditions of the same marriage. The dual POVs remind us, as the author intended, that there are three sides to every marriage: his, hers, and the truth.

- **GONE GIRL.** Gillian Flynn crafted her break-out bestseller about a marriage gone very, very wrong by telling it from alternating his-and-her POVs, and in so doing presents us with the dark side of his, hers, and the truth.

- **ROOM.** Telling this story of a woman and child held prisoner in a small shed from the point of view of the child gives Emma Donoghue's story about love, loss of innocence, and the "cruel truth of the world" a poignancy readers will not soon forget.

- **WICKED.** In retelling *The Wonderful Wizard of Oz* from the Wicked Witch of the West's POV, Gregory Maguire challenges readers to consider the true nature of beauty, good versus evil, and reality itself—and creates a new subgenre in the process.

> *"You could tell* The Handmaid's Tale *from a male point of view. People have mistakenly felt that the women are oppressed, but power tends to organize itself in a pyramid. I could pick a male narrator from somewhere in that pyramid. It would be interesting."*
>
> —Margaret Atwood

You may choose to tell your story from a unique POV, as with *The Lovely Bones* or *The Art of Racing in the Rain*. Or you may decide that telling your story from multiple POVs would work better and allow you to use the multiple-POV device to personify or mirror your main theme and variations on theme. As is true of many SF/fantasy stories, George R.R. Martin does this most effectively in *A Game of Thrones*. Love stories often alternate between his-and-her POVS. And in crime fiction, stories often go back and forth between the villain's, victim's, and hero's POVS.

CHARACTER AS THEME

In chapter three, we talked about how your hero, villain, and secondary characters can reflect various aspects of your themes. As you write your story, use those characters to bring your themes to life.

> *"You need characters who want things. They want love, they want recognition, they want happiness."*
>
> —Candace Bushnell

Do it right and you can create an original and appealing character that readers love and want to read about again and again. That's when you succeed in creating a series character, like these favorites.

- Stieg Larsson's *The Girl with the Dragon Tattoo*
- Ian Fleming's James Bond series
- Arthur Conan Doyle's Sherlock Holmes series
- Lee Child's Jack Reacher series
- Janet Evanovich's Stephanie Plum series

Series characters like these represent important themes like courage, resourcefulness, wit, and intelligence—all qualities that we hope to discover in ourselves.

YOUR THEMES IN ACTION

"Never confuse movement with action."

—Ernest Hemingway

If you can write stellar action scenes, you can sell your work. Readers love a character who *does* something; proactive heroes dominate the bestseller list and high-concept films based on those bestsellers. That's because when you think high concept, you think action—and with good reason. Here's a list of some of the most successful action stories.

- The Jason Bourne novels by Robert Ludlum
- "The Minority Report" by Philip K. Dick
- The Jack Ryan novels by Tom Clancy
- The Hunger Games trilogy by Suzanne Collins
- *The Princess Bride* by William Goldman
- *The Godfather* by Mario Puzo
- The Jack Reacher novels by Lee Child

These stories give us action heroes we can't help but love and *keep them moving*. It's something to remember as you weave your story tapestry together, no matter what your genre.

WHAT'S HIGH CONCEPT?

"High concept" is a Hollywood term for a Big Idea—one that is easily communicated in just a few words.

- *Speed*: *Die Hard* on a bus.
- *Jaws*: Big shark terrorizes small town.
- *Titanic*: Star-crossed lovers meet on a sinking ship.
- *Elf*: An adopted "elf" leaves the North Pole for New York to find his birth father.
- *Schindler's List*: The true story of a playboy who saves 1,100 Jews by putting them to work in his factory in World War II.
- *The Hangover*: Three pals must find the groom they lost during a bachelor party in Las Vegas.
- *Snakes on a Plane*: Duh.

> *"I think all art comes out of conflict. When I write, I am always looking for the dramatic kernel of an event, the junctures of people's lives when they go in one direction, not another."*
> —Joyce Carol Oates

THE THEMATIC NATURE OF CONFLICT

You don't have to blow stuff up in your story; not everyone is writing an action-adventure tale. But you do have to milk the conflict. As we've seen, conflict is the engine of drama, and weaving conflict through your storyline helps you keep the reader's attention.

But conflict tied to theme is the best kind of conflict, the kind that really moves the reader. Picture these compelling conflicts.

- McMurphy defying Nurse Ratched in Ken Kesey's *One Flew Over the Cuckoo's Nest*
- Mr. Knightly scolding Emma for hurting poor Miss Bates's feelings in Jane Austen's *Emma*
- Dr. Berger pushing Conrad Jarrett to reveal the truth about the sailing accident in Judith Guest's *Ordinary People*
- Lt. Kaffee confronting Col. Jessup on the stand in Aaron Sorkin's *A Few Good Men*

> *"Now, what is it which makes a scene interesting? If you see a man coming through a doorway, it means nothing. If you see him coming through a window—that is at once interesting."*
> —Billy Wilder

THE TYPES OF CONFLICT

Conventional literary wisdom says there are four types of conflict: the first four I've included in the following list. But modern theorists have since added three types of conflict, which I've included as well. No matter how you classify the conflict, being aware of it can prove useful when you're plotting.

The most successful stories employ at least two kinds of conflict, one of them always being inner conflict (the conflict between your hero and himself). The remaining types of conflict qualify as external conflict (the conflict between your hero and something outside himself).

Let's take a look at these seven types of conflict.

1. **MAN VS. MAN.** This is your classic hero-against-villain scenario, as with Tom Sawyer and Injun Joe in Mark Twain's *The Adventures of Tom Sawyer* or the battling spouses in Gillian Flynn's *Gone Girl*. Family squabbles can be a major source of conflict—from the ugly stepsisters taunting Cinderella about her lowly status to the dueling divorcing couple fighting to the death in Warren Adler's *The War of the Roses* (the devastating novel on which the successful 1989 film was based).

2. **MAN VS. SOCIETY.** This is your hero fighting a (usually) tyrannical system, as in Ken Kesey's *One Flew over the Cuckoo's Nest* or Suzanne Collins's *The Hunger Games*.

3. **MAN VS. NATURE.** When your hero finds himself at odds with nature, whether it's Robert Redford as Our Man alone at sea in J.C. Chandor's *All Is Lost* or Ahab in pursuit of Moby-Dick in Herman Melville's *Moby-Dick*.

4. **MAN VS. SELF.** Otherwise known as inner conflict, man vs. self is the main conflict in such stories as Helen Fielding's *Bridget Jones's Diary*, where the biggest obstacle the heroine faces is her own neurotic self. But in many stories, the hero may prove his own worst enemy as a result of his inner conflict—just as Hamlet is in Shakespeare's *Hamlet*.

5. **MAN VS. FATE OR GOD.** In classic mythology, the hero is always at the mercy of the fates or the gods, just as Odysseus is in Homer's *The Odyssey*. But even in contemporary stories, fate can play a significant role in the hero's life, as it does in Vikas Swarup's novel *Q&A*, which became the Oscar-winning film *Slumdog Millionaire*.

6. **MAN VS. PARANORMAL.** This type of conflict has generated an entire genre encompassing every possible kind of paranormal phenomenon, from vampires and demons to ghosts and UFOs. The classic man vs. paranormal conflict is Van Helsing against Count Dracula in Bram Stoker's *Dracula*.

7. **MAN VS. TECHNOLOGY.** This "man against machine" genre is one that reflects the age in which we live—and features such

conflicts as Sarah Connor and Kyle Reese against the cyborg in James Cameron and Gale Ann Hurd's *The Terminator*, and Theodore and his operating system in Spike Jonze's *Her*.

Think about the kinds of conflicts, large and small, external and internal, in your story. Do they resonate with your theme and variations on theme? Weave them through your storyline.

> *"There's a lot of conflict and darkness inside everybody's family. We all pretend to outsiders that it's not so, but behind locked doors, there are usually high emotions running."*
>
> —Salman Rushdie

DIALOGUE: THEME SPEAKS

Writing great dialogue is critical to telling a good story. And if you do it well, you may be on your way to the bestseller list. (After all, Elmore Leonard made his career on his ability to write great dialogue.) Readers love dialogue both in the story and on the page. To sharpen your own back-and-forth between your characters, study these masters of dialogue.

- Elmore Leonard
- Judy Blume
- Raymond Chandler
- Aaron Sorkin
- Shakespeare
- David Mamet

MAKE DIALOGUE DO DOUBLE AND TRIPLE DUTY

Conventional wisdom has it that good dialogue does two things: (1) It reveals character, and (2) it moves the plot forward. But the best dialogue does triple duty by tying directly into theme.

Let's take a look at some of the most memorable lines of dialogue ever. Note how they relate to the theme of their story.

DOROTHY: "There's no place like home." (*The Wonderful Wizard of Oz* by L. Frank Baum)

ANDY DUFRESNE: "You know what the Mexicans say about the Pacific? They say it has no memory. And that's where I want to finish out my life, Red. In a warm place that has no memory." (*Rita Hayworth and Shawshank Redemption* by Stephen King)

LADY BRACKNELL: "To lose one parent, Mr. Worthing, may be regarded as a misfortune; to lose both looks like carelessness." (*The Importance of Being Earnest* by Oscar Wilde)

BLAKE: "Put. That coffee. Down. Coffee's for closers only." (*Glengarry Glen Ross* by David Mamet)

SHUG: "I think it pisses God off if you walk by the color purple in a field somewhere and don't notice it." (*The Color Purple* by Alice Walker)

VINCENT: "Wonderful things can happen when you plant seeds of distrust in a garden of assholes." (*Glitz* by Elmore Leonard)

SHYLOCK: "If you prick us do we not bleed? If you tickle us do we not laugh? If you poison us do we not die? And if you wrong us shall we not revenge?" (*The Merchant of Venice* by William Shakespeare)

JANE EYRE: "I am not an angel, and I will not be one till I die: I will be myself. Mr. Rochester, you must neither expect nor exact anything celestial of me—for you will not get it, any more than I shall get it of you: which I do not at all anticipate." (*Jane Eyre* by Charlotte Brontë)

Try weaving theme throughout your dialogue. Let your characters say flat-out what they believe about themselves, each other, and the situations in which they find themselves. Just be sure to be entertaining as opposed to preachy.

> "I'm very much aware in the writing of dialogue, or even in the narrative, too, of a rhythm. There has to be a rhythm with it. … Interviewers have said, you like jazz, don't you? Because we can hear it in your writing. And I thought that was a compliment."
>
> —Elmore Leonard

THE DIALOGUE IN *THE MALTESE FALCON*

Dashiell Hammett was as good at dialogue as he was at everything else. And his dialogue was as rich in theme as it was in humor and pathos. Here are just a few of the best lines from this wonderful novel.

SPADE: Everyone has something to conceal.

SPADE: I don't know anything about women.

LT. DUNDY: I don't know that I'd blame you a hell of a lot—but that wouldn't keep me from nailing you.

SPADE: We didn't exactly believe your story. … We believed your two hundred dollars.

BRIGID: I won't be innocent.

BRIGID: Can I buy you with my body?

SID WISE: Why don't you get an honest lawyer—one you can trust?

SPADE: My clients are entitled to a decent amount of secrecy.

SPADE: Well, there's our fall guy. **GUTMAN:** You can have him.

SPADE: I don't care who loves who I'm not going to play the sap for you.

SPADE: When a man's partner is killed he's supposed to do something about it.

The best take-away from Hammett's dialogue is this: Be bold. Let your characters speak the truth—even when they're lying.

> *"What comes easiest for me is dialogue. Sometimes when my characters are speaking to me, I have to slow them down so that I'm not simply taking dictation."*
> —Richard Russo

THE ART OF THE BIG SPEECH

Remember the Flitcraft story Sam Spade tells Brigid O'Shaughnessy in *The Maltese Falcon*? As we've seen, that story is in effect a monologue in which the themes of Hammett's classic are revealed. Most stories have a moment in which the protagonist reveals himself—as well as the themes of his story. Here are some great examples.

- Ronny Cammareri's speech on the nature of love in John Patrick Shanley's *Moonstruck*: "Loretta, I love you. Not like they told you love is, and I didn't know this either, but love don't make things nice, it ruins everything … ."
- M'Lynn's graveside meltdown as she buries her daughter Shelby in Robert Harling's *Steel Magnolias*: "I'm fine, I'm fine, I'm fine … ."
- The impassioned speech in the courtroom by Atticus Finch in Harper Lee's *To Kill a Mockingbird*: "… Now I am confident that you gentlemen will review, without passion, the evidence that you have heard, come to a decision and restore this man to his family. In the name of God, do your duty. In the name of God, believe Tom Robinson."
- Erica Barry confronting Harry on the street after he dumps her in Nancy Meyers's *Something's Gotta Give*: "I don't want my bearings. I've had my bearings my whole goddamn life … ."

Each of these big speeches drives home the themes of the piece and spotlights the transformation that the protagonist is experiencing: falling in love, grieving a terrible loss, fighting injustice, or surviving a breakup.

Consider giving your own protagonist a big speech worthy of the themes you explore in your story—and have him or her deliver it at a pivotal moment in your story for the most impact.

THE SOLILOQUY OF ALL SOLILOQUIES

Shakespeare is the king of the Big Speech—and this one from *Hamlet*, spoken by Hamlet, is the best.

> To be, or not to be—that is the question:
> Whether 'tis nobler in the mind to suffer
> The slings and arrows of outrageous fortune
> Or to take arms against a sea of troubles

And by opposing end them. To die, to sleep—
No more—and by a sleep to say we end
The heartache, and the thousand natural shocks
That flesh is heir to. 'Tis a consummation
Devoutly to be wished. To die, to sleep—
To sleep—perchance to dream: ay, there's the rub,
For in that sleep of death what dreams may come
When we have shuffled off this mortal coil,
Must give us pause. There's the respect
That makes calamity of so long life.
For who would bear the whips and scorns of time,
Th' oppressor's wrong, the proud man's contumely
The pangs of despised love, the law's delay,
The insolence of office, and the spurns
That patient merit of th' unworthy takes,
When he himself might his quietus make
With a bare bodkin? Who would fardels bear,
To grunt and sweat under a weary life,
But that the dread of something after death,
The undiscovered country, from whose bourn
No traveller returns, puzzles the will,
And makes us rather bear those ills we have
Than fly to others that we know not of?
Thus conscience does make cowards of us all,
And thus the native hue of resolution
Is sicklied o'er with the pale cast of thought,
And enterprise of great pitch and moment
With this regard their currents turn awry
And lose the name of action. — Soft you now,
The fair Ophelia! — Nymph, in thy orisons
Be all my sins remembered.

You can use dialogue to create a similar soliloquy for your own protagonist.

Attend a play or watch a film known for its dialogue, preferably in your own genre. Here are some recommendations.

- *Glengarry Glen Ross* by David Mamet
- *When Harry Met Sally* by Nora Ephron
- *Fargo* by the Coen Brothers
- *Annie Hall* by Woody Allen
- *Pulp Fiction* by Quentin Tarantino
- *The Princess Bride* by William Goldman
- *Moonstruck* by John Patrick Shanley
- *Jerry Maguire* by Cameron Crowe
- *Shakespeare in Love* by Tom Stoppard
- *Cat on a Hot Tin Roof* by Tennessee Williams
- *August: Osage County* by Tracy Letts
- *Angels in America* by Tony Kushner

As you watch, write down your favorite lines. How do they relate to the themes of the film? Is there a monologue for the protagonist? If so, how does it relate to theme? What have you learned that you can apply to your own dialogue?

"My characters have to talk, or they're out. They audition in early scenes. If they can't talk, they're given less to do, or thrown out."

—Elmore Leonard

BACKSTORY: A CAUTIONARY TALE

You'll notice that I didn't include backstory in this look at the elements of fiction. That's because it slows down the story—and you don't want to slow down your story. You need to lose as much of it as possible. Here are some tips for getting rid of your backstory.

1. Much of the backstory is information you needed to know to write the story—*not* information the reader needs to know to read it. Reevaluate all of your backstory in this light. Remember: What appears on the page is just the tip of the iceberg.
2. Many writers weigh down their beginnings with backstory. This is not a dramatic way to begin. Whatever backstory you *truly* need should be woven skillfully and sparsely into the action. Jump right into the action—and weave the backstory into it.
3. If getting rid of the backstory seems impossible without losing a vital part of the story's structure, then ask yourself if you have started your story at the right place. If you can't eliminate the backstory and proceed from there, then maybe you should consider dramatizing the backstory, starting the story there, and then working your way to the present. It all depends on how you can best structure your story.

Backstory is often the downfall of many a good plot, bogging it down until it sinks under its own weight. Before you sink your plot, figure out how much backstory is really necessary to include, and how to include it without slowing down the story.

WRITER AT PLAY

Watch your favorite movie in the same genre as your story. As you view the film, note the scenes you most enjoy, the ones that contribute to your liking this movie so much. When the movie is over, deconstruct the scenes in terms of action, dialogue, character, originality, setting, and emotional impact. **NOTE:** This is a good exercise to do with your writers' group.

WEAVING IT ALL TOGETHER

Now that we've explored all of the elements that make up dramatic storytelling, you can use them to weave a compelling tapestry of story. This weaving is critical to capturing and maintaining the reader's interest.

Failing to weave this tapestry is one of the most common mistakes writers make—and it's one of the most common reasons manuscripts are rejected. Do not write in chunks of elements. That is, don't just insert a chunk of text that's mostly all description, followed by a chunk that's all narrative, backstory, or world building, and then a chunk that's all dialogue or action.

For your story to succeed, each scene needs to be a balance of character, dialogue, action, narrative, inner monologue, and setting, with all the elements woven together seamlessly.

It's ultimately a question of balance, and it's one best demonstrated through example. Let's take a look at an early scene from *Fixing Freddie*. I've called out each of the elements in brackets, revealing the pattern of threads that makes up the story tapestry.

> The Puppy Palace sat just inside the city limits of Bowlington in a large old Victorian home. **[setting]** Clean and cheerful, it looked more like a well-run daycare center than the sordid puppy mill of my imagination. **[voice]**
>
> "We're here for a puppy," Mikey told the sweet-faced, white-haired dog breeder at the front desk. **[dialogue]**
>
> "Are you now," she said, her voice full of Irish smiles. "Well, you've come to the right place, young man." She pointed to the left. "Why don't you take a look at the wee ones, then?" **[action, dialogue]**
>
> Mikey bounded down the hall toward the irresistible call of joyful puppy noise. **[action]**
>
> "Thank you," I said to the puppy lady, and hurried after my son.
>
> I found him in a big, bright room that had once been a sunporch. Playpens full of adorable puppies lined the walls. Tiny and fluffy and yappy little pooches, too lovely for words—a

stylish cacophony of eight-week-old Yorkies and Shih Tzus and Lhasa apsos. **[setting, style]** Toy poodles and Chihuahuas and Pekingese. All of whom would fit perfectly into a Kate Spade bag, even once they were full-grown. *If Paris Hilton were running a kennel*, I thought, *this would be it*. **[tone, voice]**

Mikey ran from one puppy to another, excited and happy. "Look at this one, Mom! Look at this one!" **[action, dialogue]**

They were all beyond cute, but I knew that these pretty puffy balls of beribboned fur were far too feminine for my boy. Oh, at twelve he might fall head over heels in love with one; but by fourteen he'd die of testosterone-driven embarrassment before he'd be seen walking such a girly dog in public. He certainly wasn't going to carry it around in his purse. If we went home with one of these trendy creatures, the chi chi canine would end up being mine—not Mikey's. And I already had a perfectly good dog in Shakespeare. **[theme, conflict, tone, style, voice]**

"They are darling," I said, noncommittal. I moved from playpen to playpen, desperately seeking a manly little dog. One who wouldn't look so good in a pink puppy tutu. **[dialogue, action]**

It had been a long time since I'd actually *purchased* a dog. Our pets had always come from the pound, ours for only a small donation and the cost of spaying when required. **[backstory]** But these designer pups were purebred beauties—with price tags to match. The average price of a puppy here was $500; some brought as much as $1,000. I calculated the state of my meager savings, recently depleted by the extra closing costs on the house that had run me $4,000 I had not expected. I still needed a washer and a dryer, curtains and rods, a dishwasher . . . and all the other sundries you needed when you moved into a new home. Not to mention as a proud homeowner I'd just doubled my monthly expenses in mortgages, taxes, and property insurance. The raise that came with my new job helped, but for the first time in forever I'd actually need the child support that by law I should receive but in fact rarely did. I'd informed my ex that he needed to start paying support more regularly now, but that was no guarantee I'd actually get it, short of hiring a pricey attorney in California to make it happen. More money I didn't have. I shut my eyes, and wondered—not for the first time—how I could possibly pull off the perfect suburban family life as a single mom. **[backstory, tone, style, voice, conflict, theme]**

"Mom?" **[dialogue]**

I opened my eyes to find Mikey standing before me, holding a wriggling white powder puff with two dark eyes and a pink tongue that licked Mikey's cheek with vigor. **[action]**

"Isn't she cute?" **[dialogue]**

"Yes," I said slowly, looking out of the corner of my eye at the price tag on the Bichon Frise's pen. $1,000. There went my washer and dryer. I turned my attention back to my son. "She's adorable *now*. But she won't be a puppy forever. She'll grow up into one of those frilly lapdogs. Are you really going to want a *girly* dog to call your own when you're fourteen ... sixteen ... eighteen?" I held my breath. **[dialogue, conflict]**

Mikey thought about that, then handed me the puppy. **[action]** "You may be right, Mom. We'll just have to get a bigger dog. A guy's dog, like a black lab or a golden retriever." He looked around. "I don't see any of those here. This is a small dog place." **[dialogue, conflict]**

"Whoa, buddy." I set the little Bichon Frise carefully back down in her pen. "We already have a big dog. And a cat. And you and me in the world's smallest house." **[action, dialogue, conflict]**

"But, Mom ... ." **[dialogue, conflict]**

"We agreed that you'd get a small dog. There has to be something here." I pushed Mikey toward the back of the room. "Let's keep looking." **[action, dialogue, conflict]**

I spotted a pair of dachshunds. "Now those are cute. But not *too* cute." **[action, dialogue]**

"I don't want a *wiener* dog, Mom." **[dialogue, conflict]**

"Okay, okay." I laughed. "How about this little pug? Pugs are great dogs." **[dialogue, conflict]**

Mikey leaned toward me. "I think they're kind of ugly," he whispered, so as not to offend the jowly little puppy. **[dialogue, conflict]**

"I see." We were nearly to the end of the line of pens—and running out of options. If I didn't find the right pup fast right here at the Puppy Palace, I'd soon be tripping over some drooling, lumbering, 200-pound Saint Bernard in my postage-stamp living room. *Please God*, I thought. **[conflict, tone, style, voice]**

And then I spotted him. The answer to my puppy prayers. A sweet, silky-eared beagle baby, sleeping peacefully in the midst of all the yipping and yapping of his fussy little puppy peers. **[action]**

"Look," I said to Mikey, "it's Snoopy!" **[dialogue]**

"Shush, Mom, he's sleeping." Mikey leaned over the pen to get a closer look. At the sound of my son's gentle voice, the little beagle opened his big brown eyes and looked right into Mikey's heart. He was a goner. **[action, dialogue]**

"See? You woke him up." **[dialogue, conflict]**

"That's okay," I said, smiling at Mikey's newly paternal tone. "Why don't you introduce yourself?" **[dialogue]**

Mikey reached in and pulled the drowsy dog up into his arms. "He's so soft. Feel his ears, Mom." **[action, dialogue]**

I scratched the puppy's sleek, russet-colored ears. He *was* cute. And he seemed so mellow. Mellow was good. We needed a puppy who wouldn't annoy his elders, namely Shakespeare and Isis. The affable Shakespeare might overlook some youthful antics, but the exacting Isis undoubtedly would not. That wise feline did not suffer any fools—read dogs—gladly. A harebrained hound could find himself on the wrong side of the cat's claws in a flash. **[action, theme, style]**

"Why don't you take him to our playroom?" The white-haired puppy lady appeared as if on cue to seal the doggie deal. **[dialogue, action]**

Mikey grinned. "Cool." **[dialogue, action]**

"It's the door just past the last pen." **[dialogue, setting]**

I watched my son cradle the little dog in his arms like the big baby he was and carry him carefully into the playroom. **[action, theme]**

"He's larger than these other puppies," I said, considering the relative size of the little balls of fluff yapping around us. **[dialogue, conflict]**

"He's a bigger breed. And he's older." **[dialogue]**

"Older?" I raised an eyebrow. **[dialogue, conflict]**

"He's six months old. Most of these puppies are six to eight weeks old." **[dialogue]**

I frowned. "Does that mean there's something wrong with him?" Surreptitiously I checked out the price tag on his pen: $500. I was *not* spending five hundred bucks on a defective dog. **[dialogue, action, conflict, theme]**

"It means he's had all his shots and is housebroken." She smiled at me. **[dialogue, action]** "Housebroken," I repeated. *What a beautiful word.* **[dialogue, action]**

"Let's see how they're doing together, shall we?" She led me into the playroom, where Mikey was on his hands and knees, giggling as his new best friend licked his face all over. **[dialogue, action, theme]**

"Yuck," I said. "Doggie cooties." **[dialogue]**

"Oh, Mom." Mikey rolled his eyes. The dog kept on licking. **[dialogue, action]**

"I guess he likes you." **[dialogue]**

"Yeah." Mikey laughed. "I like him, too. He's the one, Mom." **[dialogue, action]**

"Are you sure? We don't know anything about beagles." **[dialogue, conflict]**

"We don't need to know anything. He's a good dog." **[dialogue, theme]**

"We could go home, research beagles online, and then come back ... ." My voice trailed off.

"Mom!" **[dialogue, conflict]**

"We send puppies back to the breeder if we haven't sold them by the time they're six months old," said the puppy lady. "He's due to go back Monday." **[dialogue, conflict]**

"We'll take him," Mikey told her. Then he fixed me with his sternest gaze. "We're taking him, Mom." **[action, dialogue, theme]**

"How much is he?" I asked her, knowing full well I was about to shell out my dishwasher money for this loveable lump of fur. **[dialogue, action, conflict]**

"Usually five hundred," she said, "but since it's his last weekend, he's actually on sale." **[dialogue, action]**

I loved a good sale. "So?" **[dialogue, action]**

"Fifty percent off." **[dialogue, action]**

Only $250. Such a deal. Visions of dishwashers danced in my head. "Sold!" **[dialogue, action]**

The puppy lady smiled. **[action]**

Mikey whooped. **[action, theme]**

The startled puppy yelped. **[action, theme]**

And so the howling began. **[action, conflict, theme, tone, style, voice]**

WRITE TO YOUR STRENGTHS

We've talked about the power of voice, character, action, dialogue, and other elements and how they all relate to and inform your story. Know your strengths in these areas, and play to them. If your voice is particularly strong, readers will tune in to it as long as it tells a story. If your character is worthy, they'll follow her through thick and thin and fall in love with her. If the action in your story is tight and compelling, they'll stay engaged to see what happens next. If your dialogue is rich and realistic, they'll stick around to hear the next conversation.

But there's a caveat. Playing to your strengths can help keep your readers reading, but be careful not to rely on your strengths to the detriment of other elements. For example, many writers with a strong voice fall victim to this mistake; it's too easy to tell readers what's happening rather than *showing* them.

No matter what your strengths, make sure you focus on writing fully imagined scenes that constitute a well-balanced tapestry made up of all the elements.

As we've seen in this chapter, the best-told stories are tapestries, made up of gracefully interwoven threads of voice, tone, style, dialogue, action, setting, and more. You've learned to weave your story elements together into a storyline that simmers *and* shimmers.

In the next chapter, we'll examine ways to amp up the page-turning quotient in your shimmering tapestry. You'll learn the tricks and techniques of pacing—that all-important aspect of plot that transforms your story into a true page-turner.

"Destiny itself is like a wonderful wide tapestry in which every thread is guided by an unspeakable tender hand, placed beside another thread and held and carried by a hundred others."

—Rainer Maria Rilke

CHAPTER TEN

PACING:
The Secret to Creating a Page-Turner

> "The definition of a page-turner really aught to be that this page
> is so good, you can't bear to leave it behind, but then the next
> page is there and it might be just as amazing as this one."
>
> —John Burnside

Writing a page-turner is a tricky business. We've talked about how
critical story questions are to capturing and sustaining the reader's
attention. In many manuscripts, the biggest problem is a lack of narrative thrust. One scene does not logically lead to another. The writer
has failed to connect them, and so the reader cannot connect to the
storyline. The trick here is to present story questions that push the
action forward. We need to know what our protagonist's motives are,
what she or he wants in every scene so that we care what happens next.
Otherwise it reads as random scenes strung together, rather than as a
compelling narrative.

But story questions aren't the only weapons in your writer's pacing
arsenal. In this chapter, we'll look at the pacing problems that plague
many manuscripts and how to fix them. We'll also explore the many
ways in which you can improve the pacing of your stories—from ticking clocks and transitions to reversals, language, and more.

If you're thinking that these tools don't apply to you and your genre,
think again. Sometimes even writers of upmarket fiction, or those with
a strong command of the elements of fiction, can write stories that

never really take hold of their readers. And creating literary tension is essential to good storytelling, no matter the genre.

> *"I don't know if it's good or bad, but when I first started writing I imitated the narrative thrust of a movie. And as I worked, I learned what you can do in fiction that you can't do in movies, and vice versa."*
>
> —Kevin Wilson

When the pacing is off, a number of factors can be at play.

- The story moves too slowly.
- Not enough happens soon enough.
- It's all talk and no action.
- The writer could have established what needs to be established in half the pages.
- Something more needs to happen in each scene.
- Backstory or info dumps are slowing down the narrative.
- The reader doesn't care what happens next.
- The POV character's motivations are unclear or not strong enough.
- There's not enough conflict.
- There's no sense of urgency.

If any of your scenes are sluggish, consider whether any of the afore-mentioned factors may be weighing down your story.

WRITER'S BOOKSHELF

Writers have been churning out page-turners since the dawn of literature. From the Bible to Dan Brown's latest, *Inferno*, here's a thumbnail time line of the books that have kept countless readers turning those pages long into the night, past and present.

- The Bible
- *The Odyssey* by Homer
- *The Divine Comedy* by Dante
- *Hamlet* by Shakespeare

- *Moll Flanders* by Daniel Defoe
- *Pride and Prejudice* by Jane Austen
- "The Tell-Tale Heart" by Edgar Allan Poe
- *Little Women* by Louisa May Alcott
- *The Adventures of Sherlock Holmes* by Arthur Conan Doyle
- *And Then There Were None* by Agatha Christie
- *The Maltese Falcon* by Dashiell Hammett
- *Double Indemnity* by James M. Cain
- *Fahrenheit 451* by Ray Bradbury
- *In Cold Blood* by Truman Capote
- *To Kill a Mockingbird* by Harper Lee
- *Portnoy's Complaint* by Philip Roth
- *Eye of the Needle* by Ken Follett
- *The Godfather* by Mario Puzo
- *The Firm* by John Grisham
- *Patriot Games* by Tom Clancy
- *The Shipping News* by Annie Proulx
- *The Hunger Games* by Suzanne Collins
- *Gone Girl* by Gillian Flynn
- *Inferno* by Dan Brown

Reread your favorites, and take note of the pacing as you go through the books. What tricks and tips can you borrow from these classics?

TEN TOOLS FOR PACING

Once you've addressed the issues that may have been slowing down your story, you can concentrate on picking up the pace. There are a number of tools and techniques you can use to accomplish this. Let's take a look at each in turn.

1. CHOOSE YOUR POV WISELY

Point of view can be an effective means of building suspense, a critical aspect of pacing. There are two main ways to use POV to keep the readers turning pages.

- **UNIQUE POV.** As we've seen, a unique point of view offers readers a window into a world they may not have otherwise seen. In *The Lovely Bones,* the POV allows readers to experience a different perspective, that of the dead victim. They read on just to see what the dead heroine says next. In *The Art of Racing in the Rain*, readers see their own world—the world of humans—from the point of view of a nonhuman of great humanity, Enzo the dog. Here, too, Enzo's perspective on the human condition is compelling, and we love seeing our world through canine eyes.

- **MULTIPLE POVS.** Using multiple points of view has long been a technique used to build suspense and quicken the pace of stories, particularly in the mystery and thriller genres. This technique allows you to let readers know what the villain is doing—planting a bomb, kidnapping a baby, murdering a colleague—while the protagonist remains in the dark. This knowledge builds anticipation and anxiety for the protagonist. In *The Silence of the Lambs*, Thomas Harris shifts between the points of view of FBI agent Clarice Starling, serial killer Jame Gumb (a.k.a. Buffalo Bill), and abductee Catherine Martin, following the classic mystery/thriller POV pattern of hero, victim, and villain.

  That said, using multiple POVs is a technique that can work for any story, regardless of genre. In *A Game of Thrones,* the multiple points of view allow George R.R. Martin to keep the reader engaged and on track as he paints a complex and complicated epic story with a large cast of characters. In stories with an ensemble cast, such as Ann Brashares's *The Sisterhood of the Traveling Pants* or Karen Joy Fowler's *The Jane Austen Book Club,* multiple points of view not only help readers appreciate the perspectives of each main character, but they also help readers appreciate the connections—and disconnects—between the characters.

POV may be a tool you can use to best advantage in your pacing as well, depending on how and through whom you are telling your story.

2. INCREASE THE PRESSURE ON YOUR PROTAGONIST

"Chase 'em up a tree and throw rocks at 'em."

—Mark Twain

As we discussed previously, your protagonist needs to be a proactive character in your story whose traits, idiosyncrasies, and good and bad decisions help drive the plot. But you also need to keep the pressure on your protagonist. The following are some ways to turn up the heat as the story reaches its climax.

Increase the Romantic or Sexual Tension

You don't have to be writing a love story to use romantic or sexual tension to build suspense in your story. Whether it's the main plot or a subplot, sex and romance come with built-in story questions that you can use to amp up the drama.

- Does she like him? Does he like her?
- Will he be good for her? Will she be good for him?
- Will they sleep together? How will that go?
- What can tear them apart?
- What can bring them back together?
- Does she have a secret that could destroy them—or vice versa?
- Are they both free to love each other? Or is there a third party (or more) in the picture?
- Will Character X come between them?
- What physical, emotional, or spiritual danger can befall them?
- Will she die before he can save her—or vice versa?
- Would she sacrifice herself for him—or vice versa?
- Will their relationship survive the story?
- Will they get married and live happily ever after?

Brainstorm the ways in which you could pose—and answer—these story questions to increase the romantic or sexual pressure on your characters.

> "In fiction a sexual connection that goes awry or has cataclysmic consequences is often more interesting than one that leaves the characters sated and deliriously happy."
>
> —Elizabeth Benedict

Increase the Emotional Pressure

When readers love your characters, they empathize with them; they feel their joy, their pain, their fear. Anything you can do to keep your characters emotionally off balance can perk up the pacing of your story. Make them laugh, make them cry, scare the crap out of them—preferably in rapid succession. Make them face their worst fears, and put their biggest dreams just out of reach. Force them to make the hardest decisions, to choose between the lesser of two evils, and to face no-win situations.

Lock your claustrophobic hero in a closet; open your tender-hearted heroine to the risk of capture when she stops to help an injured child; force your military hero to decide whether to risk his entire team to save one man. Have your single heroine sleep with the wrong guy and live to regret it; let your hero's favorite uncle reveal a terrible family secret on his deathbed; surprise your unhappily married heroine with an encounter with a long-lost love.

And in between these tough emotions, sprinkle lighter, happier moments—sex and love and laughter—that provide a stark contrast to the darker side of your heroine's life.

Give your characters an emotional roller coaster ride of a lifetime—and endear yourself to readers, who'll happily go along for the ride.

Give Your Hero a MacGuffin

As we've seen in other stories, MacGuffins can help put the pressure on your protagonist. Remember Dorothy and the broomstick in L. Frank Baum's *The Wonderful Wizard of Oz,* or Sam Spade and the Maltese Falcon in Dashiell Hammett's *The Maltese Falcon*? When these MacGuffins showed up in the story, the pacing picked up as the pressure on Dorothy and Sam piled on.

If you don't have a MacGuffin in your story, consider adding one. It could do wonders for your pacing.

Puzzle Your Protagonist

In many stories, the protagonist has to figure something out—and the pressure is on to do so. Think of Robert Langdon trying to solve a murder—and uncovering an ancient mystery in the process—in Dan Brown's *The Da Vinci Code*, or the heroines of Guy Burt's *The Bletchley Circle* television series solving a series of murders that seem to have a pattern in common.

Puzzles are common elements in mysteries and thrillers, but they can also help you drive your plot and quicken your pacing, no matter what your genre. In many domestic dramas, the puzzle revolves around family secrets, as in Amy Tan's *The Joy Luck Club*, in which the modern daughters of Chinese immigrants learn the terrible truths of their traditional mothers' past lives, or Whitney Otto's *How to Make an American Quilt,* in which a young woman gathers the courage to risk her heart from the surprising stories of love and commitment shared around her grandmother's quilting circle.

Does your protagonist have a puzzle to solve? If not, add one. If so, can you make it tougher for your hero to solve? Or can you make the solving of it present even more problems and puzzles?

Take Away Something Your Hero Needs

Another way to put the pressure on your hero is to take away something that he needs to get to the next stage in his journey. Maybe he drops his gun, or she loses her phone, or the car the couple is using to escape runs out of gas. Those losses provide obstacles for your characters to overcome—and they give them something to do.

You can heighten the impact even more if, by taking something from your character, it causes her to be injured physically, emotionally, or spiritually.

- **PHYSICAL INJURY:** In Roderick Thorp's thriller *Nothing Lasts Forever* (on which the film *Die Hard* was based), John McClane cuts his feet because he has no shoes.
- **EMOTIONAL INJURY:** Philomena must face the loss of the son she searched so many years to find in Martin Sixsmith's *The Lost Child of Philomena Lee.*

- **SPIRITUAL INJURY:** In George Lucas's *Star Wars*, Luke loses his spiritual mentor Obi-Wan Kenobi.

Ask yourself what you can take away from your protagonist that will amp up the pressure—physically, emotionally, and even spiritually.

Put Your Hero in More Danger

The more danger your hero is in, the more nerve-wracking his journey is for the reader. So put Friedrich Nietzsche's mantra "That which does not kill us makes us stronger," into play, and lay on the danger as thickly as possible.

And don't think that the only danger you can threaten your protagonist with is physical danger. Again, your protagonist's physical, emotional, and spiritual health should be at risk. Make it clear to the reader that your hero could lose not only his life, but also his family, his friends, his love, his mind, and even his very soul.

3. ADD MORE CONFLICT—AND MORE KINDS OF CONFLICT

Conflict is the fuel of drama and the secret to a well-paced story. Have you milked the conflict in your story? How could you milk it more?

We discussed the seven types of conflict earlier—man vs. man, man vs. nature, man vs. self, man vs. society, man vs. technology, man vs. fates/God, and man vs. paranormal. Which of these have you already woven into your plot? Which have you not yet used? Consider how you might add new types of conflict to your story.

Make Your Villain Meaner, Smarter, Richer, Fiercer, Mightier

The more worthy his adversary, the harder your hero must work to defeat him. The harder the hero works, the better the pacing. So give your villain all the best cards in this game; make your heroine earn her victory the hard way. Stack the odds against your protagonist by making your villain bigger and better in every way.

If you're thinking, "no cartoon villains for me," keep in mind that meaner, smarter, richer, fiercer, and mightier needn't mean cartoonish. The best villains are the ones who are larger than life and completely believable. Remember our discussion of antagonists in chapter three?

Remember to incorporate traits that will make your villain believable as well as frightening.

> *"My theory of characterization is basically this: Put some dirt on a hero, and put some sunshine on the villain, one brush stroke of beauty on the villain."*
>
> —Justin Cronin

Add a Loose Cannon

The characters who worry readers the most are the ones who will inevitably do something unexpected. A worried reader is an engaged reader, so bring on the loose cannons. In some stories, the loose cannon is the protagonist, like Randle McMurphy, who bucks the system and rebels against the tyrannical Nurse Ratched in Ken Kesey's *One Flew over the Cuckoo's Nest*. In buddy comedies, the loose cannon is often one of the buddies, like Martin Riggs, who suffers from depression over his wife's death and struggles with alcoholism in Shane Black's buddy comedy *Lethal Weapon*. In stories about sisters, the loose cannon is often one of the sisters, like Gillian Owens, who becomes bored with small-town life and gets involved in an abusive relationship in Alice Hoffman's *Practical Magic*.

The loose cannon can also be the antagonist of the story, as Willy Wonka is in Roald Dahl's *Charlie and the Chocolate Factory*. Even the mentor can be the loose cannon, as Dr. Emmett "Doc" Brown is in Robert Zemeckis and Bob Gale's *Back to the Future*.

Who serves as the loose cannon character in your story? If you don't have one, create one—and make sure the cannon goes off when the reader least expects it, or whenever your story could use a jolt of energy—whichever comes first.

> *"I'm all about entertaining and keeping a reader on the edge of their seat, so to me, the social issues have to be meaningful and give the book what's really at stake, but ultimately it's not about them—it's always a personal story of everyday people thrust into life-threatening situations and having to perform heroic acts."*
>
> —Andrew Gross

> *"I try to tell a story the way someone would tell you a story in a bar, with the same kind of timing and pacing."*
>
> —Chuck Palahniuk

4. EMPLOY REVERSALS

> *"A reversal is just anything that's a surprise. It's a way of keeping the audience interested."*
>
> —Tony Gilroy

Reversals are a subset of the plus and minus scenes we discussed in chapter seven. Think of reversals as plus and minus scenes where the actions are tied to one another at the hip. That is, the positive action of the first scene reverses itself and becomes the negative action of the following scene. *Raiders of the Lost Ark* is full of such reversals. You may remember the sequence in the film where Indy goes to the saloon in Tibet to obtain the headpiece of the Staff of Ra, which he needs to find the ark. His bitter ex, Marion, has it, and she taunts him with it (negative) before accepting an advance for it (positive). Indy leaves, and Nazi thugs show up to take it from Marion, one way or another (negative). Indy comes back and rescues her (positive), but the salon burns down (negative). Marion manages to retrieve the headpiece and offers it to Indy (positive).

Another variation of reversals features an alternate pattern. Rather than having the "action, reversal of action, action, reversal of action" pattern, you have two steps forward, one step back. In effect: two plus scenes, followed by one minus scene. (You can also reverse this pattern to one step forward, two steps back.)

Take a look at your scene-by-scene plot structure. Note the patterns of pluses and minuses in your structure, and identify the reversals within those pluses and minuses. Are your reversals tied at the hip? Do they appear one right after another, in an alternating pattern? Consider arranging them so they do, for best effect. Or adjust the pattern, as I've suggested above.

5. SET UP A TICKING CLOCK—STARTING NOW

One of the best ways to build suspense and quicken the pace of your story is to add a time element. This time element, known as a ticking clock, is basically a deadline by which the protagonist must accomplish a goal … or something terrible will happen.

This something terrible doesn't have to be a bomb going off or planet Earth being blown to smithereens (or both). It can be our hero missing his once-in-a-lifetime opportunity to meet his one-and-only-destined love, as in *Made in Heaven* by Bruce A. Evans and Raynold Gideon. Or it can be a little girl determined to participate in the Little Miss Sunshine beauty pageant—if her dysfunctional family can keep it together long enough to get her there in time, which is the premise for Michael Arndt's Oscar-winning *Little Miss Sunshine*.

While we see a lot of film and TV stories with ticking clocks, it's a literary device that has been with us as long as humankind has been telling stories.

- Noah has to finish building the Ark before the flood overflows the entire world (the Bible).
- When their cruise ship is flipped by a tidal wave, a small group of passengers struggles to get out before it's too late (Paul Gallico's novel *The Poseidon Adventure*, upon which the 1972 disaster film of the same name was based).
- An FBI agent must enlist the help of an imprisoned psychopath to track down a serial killer before he kills the latest of his victims (Thomas Harris's *The Silence of the Lambs*).
- A beautiful girl must meet her Prince Charming and fall in love, all by midnight (Charles Perrault's *Cinderella*).
- A playwright travels back in time to 1912 to meet his soul mate (Richard Matheson's *Bid Time Return*, on which the 1980 classic film *Somewhere in Time* was based).

Time travel stories often feature a ticking clock, as do thrillers, mysteries, and science fiction and fantasy stories. But as we've seen, virtually any plot can accommodate a ticking clock, almost always to enormous benefit. If you haven't yet built a ticking clock into your storyline, consider doing so now and give your pacing a big boost.

6. ADD A SUBPLOT ... OR TWO

By now, you should have plenty of subplots in your storyline. But if not, consider adding another or beefing up the ones you have.

You can also use the trick of cutting back and forth between individual subplots and the main plot, and between the individual subplots. This strategy works brilliantly in terms of keeping the readers engaged and turning the pages, because the story questions posed in one subplot go unanswered when you cut back to the plot or another subplot. *A caveat:* You need to do this cutting gracefully, to ensure it doesn't make for a choppy reading experience. Think of the subplots we discussed in *Pride and Prejudice*, especially the ones involving Elizabeth's sisters' love lives, and how seamlessly they intertwine with the main plot involving Elizabeth and Mr. Darcy.

> *"Minimalism seems closest to the sophisticated storytelling of movies. Movies have really educated contemporary audiences to be the most intelligent, sophisticated audiences in history. We don't any longer need to have the relationship between one scene and the next explained. We will figure it out ourselves."*
> —Chuck Palahniuk

7. WATCH YOUR TRANSITIONS

If your pacing is a bit slow, check your transitions. Many writers spend too much time getting in and out of their scenes. When it comes to storytelling, readers are very sophisticated now; thanks to film and television, they are accustomed to quick cuts between scenes, and you can use that to your advantage.

So cut from one scene to another as quickly as possible—and pare down your transitions as much as possible. What applies to partygoers applies to writers: For the best time, get in late and leave early. This way, readers don't have to wade through unnecessary setup or denouement in your scenes. Your scenes will pop, one after another—and your pacing will pick up.

> *"If a scene is longer than three pages, it better be for a good reason."*
> —Alan Ball

8. CHECK YOUR READING LEVEL

Sometimes it's the prose that bogs down the story and slows down readers. Slow them down too much and they'll stop reading all altogether. One of the best ways to make sure your prose is engaging and easy to read is to do a reading-level check on your work.

In versions of Microsoft Word from 2004 and before, you can access the reading level tool by selecting Spelling and Grammar from the Tools menu and clicking Options. Then check the "show readability statistics" box. In versions of Microsoft Word from 2007 and onward, you can access the reading level tool under the Review tab in the Spelling and Grammar tool. Check the "show readability statistics" box in the options under Spelling and Grammar. When you run the Spelling and Grammar tool, the Flesch-Kincaid reading level will now show up under readability statistics.

The Flesch-Kincaid reading level refers to the grade level of reading proficiency needed to comprehend a given work. The average newspaper in the United States is written at a sixth-grade reading level, so if yours comes in at anything above this, you need to take a hard look at your prose. Your prose may be far denser than you think. Are you using passive voice? Do your sentences run on too long? Is your language heavy on words of Latinate derivation and light on those of Anglo-Saxon derivation? (More on this in no. 9.)

Whatever your issues, you need to figure out why your prose is so dense and fix it. Aim for a reading level between sixth and eighth grade.

"It is the function of art to renew our perception. What we are familiar with we cease to see. The writer shakes up the familiar scene, and, as if by magic, we see a new meaning in it."

—Anais Nin

9. CONSIDER YOUR LANGUAGE

As your story heats up, your language should become quicker, punchier, more direct, and more concrete. This is the language of action.

The faster the pace, the shorter the sentences should be. Use more words of Anglo-Saxon derivation, which tend to be shorter, punchier, and harder.

ANGLO-SAXON	LATIN
Go	Depart
Free	Emancipate
Meet	Encounter
Lie	Prevaricate
Bless	Consecrate
Job	Position
Wish	Desire

For the sake of comparison, let's take a look at two short if admittedly extreme samples.

> Maximillian's encounter with the assassin was arranged to coincide with the noonday repast, during which time his wife would be absent from their domicile, as she deplored the practice of conjugal feasting.

> Max agreed to meet the hit man during lunch while his wife was away from home. She hated watching him eat.

You get the idea. The rhythm of your work should match the pacing of the story. Are you writing a sensual love scene? Lean on the Latinate. Or an action scene? Go for Anglo-Saxon.

COGITATE ON THIS

Here's a quick exercise that really drives home the difference language can make in regard to pacing. Choose a short scene and rewrite it in short, punchy, declarative sentences using words of Anglo-Saxon origin.

Now rewrite the scene using longer, more complex sentences and words of Latinate derivation.

How does this change the rhythm, mood, pacing, and readability of the scene? Which comes more naturally to you? What can you learn from each version?

10. WHEN IN DOUBT, DELETE

Sometimes the best thing you can do to quicken the pace of your stories is to cut scenes altogether. Go through your storyline scene by scene and ask yourself if you really need each scene. What does this scene do that no other scene does? Is it inherently dramatic? What does the reader learn in this scene? What purpose does this scene serve?

As you read, remember the editor's mantra: When in doubt, delete.

TIPS AND TRICKS TO PACING

Still struggling with a sluggish pace? Try these tricks to add fuel to the engine of your story.

The Scene-a-Chapter Trick

More and more, writers are choosing to make each scene a chapter. This can make for shorter chapters, which gives readers the feeling that the story is really moving along.

This trick is a sort of sleight-of-hand pacing. You may choose to adopt the strategy yourself, but whether you do or not, remember that chapter length does affect the pacing of your story—and to size each chapter accordingly.

Lose That Pretty Backstory, and Your Little Flashback, Too

Backstory slows down the narrative every time, because you are literally going back in time—and sending the reader back in time as well. All that transition time interrupts the flow of your narrative. As we've discussed before, you need to use as little backstory as possible.

Flashbacks are also pace killers—on steroids. With a flashback, you haven't only slowed the story down, you've literally thrown it into reverse. You're asking the reader to switch gears, and you risk losing them every time. So before you use a flashback, ask yourself if you really, really need it—or if there's a better way to deliver information from the past.

"Usually, when people get to the end of a chapter, they close the book and go to sleep. I deliberately write my books so when the reader gets to the end of a chapter, he or she must turn one more page. When people tell me I've kept them up all night, I feel like I've succeeded."

—Sidney Sheldon

The End-on-a-Story-Question Trick

Here's another simple trick that helps keep readers turning the pages late into the night: End each chapter with a story question. Many a reader promises herself that she'll close her book and go to sleep at the end of the next chapter. (You've probably made the same promise to yourself as well. We all have.)

But when each chapter ends with a story question, it's not as easy to put the story aside, no matter how late the hour. Combine the scene-a-chapter trick with the end-on-a-story-question trick and you can keep your readers flipping through the pages all night long.

You may associate this strategy with thrillers and adventure stories—think *Raiders of the Lost Ark*, whose structure was based on the serials of old. But this is a trick you can use regardless of genre. As we've seen, story questions are critical to plot and pacing. Ending every chapter, every scene, every page, and even every paragraph on a story question can't hurt.

WRITER AT WORK

What book has kept you up all night reading? What story has refused to let you put it down until you reached the end?

Read it again, and this time read it as a writer. What tips, tricks, and techniques did the author use to keep you turning the pages? Do you recognize any from the list above? On a second reading, how does the story hold up? What can you take away and apply to your story?

Now think about the films you've seen. Which ones kept your eyes riveted to the screen? (*Zero Dark Thirty, Gravity, The Piano*) Which ones left you emotionally exhausted by the end? (*Life Is Beautiful, The Way We Were, Taken*) Which ones do you find yourself viewing over and over again? (*Enchanted April, Raiders of the Lost Ark, Dan in Real Life*).

Your answers won't be the same as mine (in italics). But think about it, and choose a film in your genre to watch again. Analyze the pacing in this film as you did for the book you chose, and ask yourself what techniques are used and how you might use them in your story.

NOTE: If you don't like any movies in your own genre, then you might consider writing in another genre!

"I picture my books as movies when I get stuck, and when I'm working on a new idea, the first thing I do is hit theaters to work out pacing and mood."

—Maggie Stiefvater

In this chapter, we've explored the many tools, techniques, and tricks you can use to set a good pace for your story. Pacing is the rhythm and tempo of your plot, the beat to which your story moves. If it's moving too slowly, your readers will grow bored, disinterested, or even frustrated. But if the tempo is just right, you'll keep them flipping pages through the night.

In the next chapter, we'll explore the various organizing principles that you can use as thematic frameworks for your plot to give your story added depth and dimension.

"There are times when I'm driving home after a day's shooting, thinking to myself, 'That scene would've been so much better if I had written it out.'"

—Larry David

CHAPTER ELEVEN
PLOT VS. ORGANIZING PRINCIPLE

> *"We picked up one excellent word—a word worth traveling to New Orleans to get; a nice limber, expressive, handy word—'lagniappe.'"*
>
> —Mark Twain

Sometimes a plot can benefit from an organizing principle, which is another tool you can use to tell your story. The organizing principle should not be confused with the plot. It isn't what *happens* in your story; it's the *framework* you use to tell your story. This framework can serve many purposes, including giving your story a unique selling proposition (USP), thereby helping differentiate it from others of its ilk.

An organizing principle can also help you add layers of meaning, provide a ready image system, enhance the setting, and deepen the themes of your story—not to mention that readers love them.

For readers, an organizing principle is a form of *lagniappe*. For those of you who've never visited one of my favorite adopted cities, New Orleans, *lagniappe* is the word used to describe the local tradition of giving customers "a little extra something" for free. It's that thirteenth cookie in a baker's dozen, the extra shot of tequila in your margarita, or even the fortune cookie in your Chinese takeout. Give your readers an organizing principle on top of your plot, and you're giving them a little *lagniappe*.

Take the runaway bestseller *Eat Pray Love,* which broadcasts its organizing principle right there in the title and then employs it throughout the plot. *Eat Pray Love*'s organizing principle is inextricably connected to its plot, its settings, and its themes in a very obvious way. That doesn't always hold true for organizing principles in stories, but in this case the blatant link makes all the difference. In this chapter, you'll learn how you can use organizing principles to enhance your plots *and* your USPs—and give your readers a little *lagniappe*!

THE THREE KINDS OF ORGANIZING PRINCIPLES

As you may have learned in your literature classes in high school or college, there are three types of organizing principles: thematic, chronological, and methodological. Let's examine each principle in turn, with the understanding that in fiction we play a little loose and fast with these rules.

1. THE THEMATIC ORGANIZING PRINCIPLE

The thematic organizing principle is structured around a particular topic or issue. This is one of the most common types of organizing principles seen in stories—and one of the simplest and most fun to implement. Let's explore some of the most successful stories that boast a thematic organizing principle.

THE SECRET LIFE OF BEES BY SUE MONK KIDD

Set in South Carolina in 1964, this best-selling coming-of-age novel is about fourteen-year-old Lily Owens, whose vague memories of the day her mother died when she was four still haunt her. When her African-American "stand-in mother" Rosaleen has a run-in with local racists, Lily and Rosaleen take off for Tiburon, South Carolina—the town that holds her dead mother's secrets. There they are befriended by the independent and industrious Boatwright sisters, three fierce black women who take them in and instruct Lily in the mystical arts of beekeeping, honey, and the Black Madonna. Each chapter begins with a snippet from various texts on beekeeping, including *Man and Insects* and *The Dancing Bees*. For example, in chapter one of the novel, we meet the motherless Lily and learn about her life with her abusive father. The chapter opens with this quote.

> "The queen, for her part, is the unifying force of the community. If she is removed from the hive, the workers very quickly sense her absence. After a few hours, or even less, they show unmistakable signs of queenlessness."
>
> —*Man and Insects*

Every chapter opens with another quote about bees. You can see how the story's themes of sisterhood, the divine feminine, and the transformative power of love will be reflected in this organizing principle, right from the very first page. Sue Monk Kidd uses the thematic organizing principle to weave bees through the plot, characters, setting, and themes of her story. Even the title, *The Secret Life of Bees*, speaks to this organizing principle: bees as the central metaphor of her novel.

Many stories use similar organizing principles to great effect. Annie Proulx's *The Shipping News* boasts chapter openers from *The Ashley Book of Knots* and *The Mariner's Dictionary*, which reflect its themes of love, family, roots, sins of the fathers, and the power of the landscape to shape human nature.

If you're thinking that this thematic organizing principle is best suited for upmarket fiction, think again. In Vaughn Hardacker's debut novel *Sniper*, each chapter of the thriller begins with snatches of advice from the *US Marine Corps Scout/Sniper Training Manual*, *The Art of War*, and top military snipers. The organizing principle enriches the plot, which centers on a rogue sniper and the Boston cop who must use his former experience as a Marine sniper to track him down.

Think about the themes of your story and the metaphors you're using to represent those themes. What organizing principles might you use to reflect those themes? How can those metaphors help you in coming up with a good organizing principle?

2. THE CHRONOLOGICAL ORGANIZING PRINCIPLE

> *"A period of time is as much an organizing principle for a work of fiction as a sense of place. You can do geography, as Faulkner did, or you can dwell on a particular period. It provides the same framework."*
>
> —E.L. Doctorow

Time is a perfectly legitimate organizing principle—and its variations are as seemingly endless as time itself.

In Karen Joy Fowler's *The Jane Austen Book Club*, a group of five women and one man meet over the course of six months to discuss the works of Jane Austen—one book a month. Bookended by a prologue and an epilogue, the bulk of the novel is organized by month, from March to August. The various themes of Austen's novels serve as the themes for the plots and subplots of the six characters' interconnected lives.

In John Irving's *The World According to Garp*, the organizing principle is the arc of an entire life—from conception to death. This organizing principle reflects the themes of the novel, which explore the meaning of life and death and the hours, days, and years in between. *The Brief Wondrous Life of Oscar Wao* by Junot Díaz also uses the arc of the hero's life as its organizing principle, introducing the reader to protagonist Oscar Wao in his childhood and then following him through adolescence and into adulthood. F. Scott Fitzgerald's short story "The Curious Case of Benjamin Button," on which the film of the same name was based, gives readers an inventive twist on this life-arc organizing principle.

Many novels use the organizing principle of a specific time period. For example, think of all the young adult novels set over the course of summer: Bette Greene's classic *Summer of My German Soldier*, Ann Brashares's best-selling *The Sisterhood of the Traveling Pants*, and Jodi Lynn Anderson's *Peaches*.

Historical stories often target a given year, as with David McCullough's *1776*. Others cover the course of a conflict, such as Charles Frazier's Civil War novel *Cold Mountain*, or the course of a single operation, such as Pierre Boulle's *The Bridge over the River Kwai*.

> "Tragedy endeavors to keep as far as possible within a single circuit of the sun."
>
> —Aristotle

In *The Poetics,* Aristotle advises writers to tell their stories "within a single circuit of the sun," by which he meant that the action of the story should take place within a single day.

There are a number of stories that endeavor to do just that. Think of Virginia Woolf's *Mrs. Dalloway*, Ian McEwan's *Saturday*, and Christopher Isherwood's *A Single Man*. Not to mention one of the most inventive applications of this twenty-four-hour organizing principle, the popular television series *24*.

Sometimes the time-related organizing principle provides a unique way of looking at a story. In Scott Neustadter and Michael H. Weber's romantic comedy *(500) Days of Summer,* the story covers a couple's 500-day relationship and uses that numbering convention to jump around in the story. This allows the writers to tell a nonlinear narrative without confusing or losing their audience. Other examples of stories whose nonlinear narratives constitute organizing principles include:

- Jonathan Nolan's short story "Memento Mori," upon which his brother Christopher Nolan based his 2000 neo-noir film *Memento.* The story explores amnesia, the nature of memory, and the shifting sands of our reality.
- David Mitchell's *Cloud Atlas,* an imaginative novel that weaves six interconnected stories across time and whose ambitious structure embodies its basic themes of (1) what it means to be human; (2) our capacity for barbarity; and (3) history repeating itself, thanks to (1) and (2). *Note:* This novel is a tour de force of structure in more ways than one; each of the six stories is written in a different genre. Check it out.
- In Craig Johnson's Walt Longmire novel *The Dark Horse,* the sheriff narrator tells the story in two time lines, one beginning on October 27 and the other beginning on October 17. The narrative goes back, forth, and forward in time until every thread of the mystery is wrapped up on October 31 (with a short epilogue on November 7). It's an engaging and entertaining approach for a first-person story, written with Johnson's trademark literate cowboy charm.
- Kurt Vonnegut's classic *Slaughterhouse Five,* which I won't say much about except that you should read it if you haven't and reread it if you have, not only for its random collage-style structure that plays with time, but also for the hilariously dire description of how the writer narrator plots his stories with crayons. It had been a long time since I'd read this antiwar novel, but in researching this book I picked it up again, and lost several hours of solid writing time in the rereading of *Slaughterhouse Five* from start to finish, even as my deadline approached. I'm now devoted to reading Vonnegut's entire oeuvre, compli-

ments of my son Mikey's bookshelf, where all of Vonnegut's books reside (because the only assigned reading Mikey ever actually completed in high school was Vonnegut).

Time Travel

Some of the most inventive plots use time travel as an organizing principle. Thanks to such classics as H.G. Wells's *The Time Machine*, Madeleine L'Engle's *A Wrinkle in Time*, and Isaac Asimov's *The End of Eternity*, we tend to think of this as a tool used primarily in the science fiction genre, but time travel is found in all kinds of stories, from romance and mystery to historical and literary fiction. What makes it an organizing principle—as opposed to simply a plot device—is that the time travel element is not just part of what happens in the story (plot), but also helps shape the manner in which the story is told or informs the themes of the story. Stephen King's novel *11/22/63* explores loss and love, memory and free will, and the nature of evil as it lays out the tale of an ordinary guy who travels back in time to prevent the assassination of John F. Kennedy. Audrey Niffenegger's *The Time Traveler's Wife* deals with the themes of sex, love, and loss in its offbeat look at the relationship between a time-traveling husband and the wife who waits in the present, past, and future for him to come home.

> *"Time, in general, has always been a central obsession of mine—what it does to people, how it can constitute a plot all on its own. So naturally, I am interested in old age."*
>
> —Anne Tyler

Common Chronological Devices

Many writers use news clippings, diary entries, letters, blogs, e-mails, tweets, and more as part of their chronological organizing principles. Some stories are written completely in letters (see the following sidebar). Others are written in diary entries, a confessional form that invites the reader into the private inner world of the character; think of Helen Fielding's *Bridget Jones's Diary*, Jeff Kinney's popular Diary of a Wimpy Kid series, and Meg Cabot's successful The Princess Diaries series.

Writers throughout history have used chronological devices to help structure their works and reflect their themes.

- In *Dracula*, Bram Stoker makes use of all the media at his disposal in 1897, from letters and diary entries to dictation cylinders and newspaper stories.
- Meg Cabot writes an entire novel as a series of e-mail exchanges in *The Boy Next Door*.
- In *Defending Jacob*, William Landay uses trial transcripts as a chronological organizing principle—and a clever plot twist.
- Lauren Myracle uses the instant messaging format in her popular Internet Girls series (*ttyl*, *ttfn*, et al.), which reveals the experiences, feelings, and interactions of high school BFFs Zoe, Maddie, and Angela.
- In Jay Asher's poignant novel *Thirteen Reasons Why*, his teenage protagonist, Clay Jensen, finds a shoebox of cassette tapes recorded by Hannah, a girl who's recently committed suicide. These recordings play a pivotal role in the story, which chronicles Clay's attempt to figure out what really happened to Hannah.
- Previously anonymous blogger Steve Dublanica dramatizes the best of his popular blog, www.waiterrant.net, in his bestselling memoir *Waiter Rant*.

WRITE ME A BOOK OF LETTERS

The epistolary novel is one of the classic forms of storytelling—from *Letters of a Portuguese Nun*, the famous 1669 work written by Gabriel-Joseph de La Vergne, comte de Guilleragues (or was it Marianna Alcoforado?—you decide) and John Cleland's bawdy 1748 novel *Fanny Hill* to such modern classics as Stephen Chbosky's poignant coming-of-age novel *The Perks of Being a Wallflower* and *The Guernsey Literary and Potato Peel Pie Society* by Mary Ann Shaffer and Annie Barrows.

Many stories also incorporate letters as part of their structure, even though they are not entirely epistolary novels in the strictest sense, as in Maria Semple's *Where'd You Go, Bernadette?*

As with the diary structure, epistolary stories can lend an air of immediacy and intimacy to the work. They also can showcase a strong voice. So if either consideration applies to you and your story, consider using this form in whole or part in your narrative.

3. THE METHODOLOGICAL ORGANIZING PRINCIPLE

The traditional definition of the methodological organizing principle doesn't concern the content of the work at all. It refers to the methodology used to research and develop the project. So we may be stretching this definition when we talk about the methodological organizing principle in storytelling but, I would argue, not by much.

In many stories, the source material itself becomes the organizing principle. This is certainly true of stories like Michael Cunningham's *The Hours*. This best-selling Pulitzer Prize winner drew the inspiration for the plot from Virginia Woolf's dazzling masterwork, *Mrs. Dalloway*. Cunningham weaves the stories of three very different women—a depressed, pregnant housewife in 1949 Los Angeles; a lesbian whose friend is dying of AIDS in 2001 New York City; and Virginia Woolf herself—in a day-in-the-life plot whose theme and prose style mirror Woolf's. This elaboration of Woolf's original story is, in effect, a methodological approach.

There are other examples as well. When Julie Powell cooked up the idea to create all 524 recipes in Julia Child's celebrated *Mastering the Art of French Cooking* and then blog about it, she did it with the hope that it might win her a book deal—which it did. Enter the best-selling memoir, *Julie and Julia: My Year of Cooking Dangerously*.

When master plotter Agatha Christie conceived her best-selling mystery, *And Then There Were None* (also published under the name *Ten Little Indians*), she also used a methodology of sorts. The premise of the novel: Put ten people on a private island off the coast of Devon—and then make them disappear, one by one. This series of disappearances constitutes the organizing principle of the work—and of its many imitators since.

Thanks to his methodological approach, author A.J. Jacobs has made his reputation as well as his fortune as a writer of best-selling memoirs that center on his adventures completing various ambitious tasks : *The Know-It-All: One Man's Humble Quest to Become the Smartest Person* in the World; *The Year of Living Biblically: One Man's Humble Quest to Follow the Bible as Literally as Possible*; *My Life as an Experiment: One Man's Humble Quest to Improve Himself by Living as a Woman, Becoming George Washington, Telling No Lies, and Other Radical Tests*; and *Drop Dead Healthy: One Man's Humble Quest for Bodily Perfection*.

The Know-It-All, arguably the best and most moving of Jacobs's works, is the memoir of a man who sets out to read the entire Encyclopaedia Britannica—all 44 million words of it. Jacobs starts at the beginning, with the *A*s, and the word *a-ak* (ancient East Asian music, for the vocabulary slackers out there) and proceeds forthwith through some 33,000 pages. As he goes, he dispenses odd facts and weaves the story of his personal life—most notably his family and friends' growing frustration with his obsession and his and his wife's struggle with infertility—throughout this alphabetical journey to knowledge (if not wisdom). It's a hilarious, fascinating, and poignant story whose organizing principle is critical to its format, plot, themes, humor, and voice.

> *"Style and Structure are the essence of a book; great ideas are hogwash."*
>
> —Vladimir Nabokov

As we've seen, some organizing principles draw their inspiration from the structures of other media or stories. Steven Spielberg directed his wildly successful *Raiders of the Lost Ark* (screenplay by Lawrence Kasdan, story by George Lucas and Philip Kaufman), on the serials he watched as a kid at the movies. Serials were long, episodic films broken into many chapters, always ending with cliff-hangers. They were shown one chapter at a time, typically at Saturday matinees—and they were designed to keep theatergoers coming back every week. Spielberg ended each scene in *Raiders of the Lost Ark* with a cliff-hanger (read: big story question), just as filmmakers did in *The Perils of Pauline* and *Flash Gordon*.

> *"I stick closely to the structure of the myths. I may have some fun with the mythology by changing the environment to modern-day, but the structure of the myths, the monsters, the relationships of the gods—none of that is made up."*
>
> —Rick Riordan

We've also looked at how the hero's journey inspired George Lucas's *Star Wars,* among other stories, driving its plot as well as serving as an organizing principle. Myths are often the inspiration for stories, and many serve as organizing principles as well. Rick Riordan has built entire series around myth as an organizing principle, including his best-selling Percy Jackson & the Olympians series.

In his acclaimed international mystery novel *All Cry Chaos*, author Len Rosen's methodology is chaos theory, as represented by his protagonist, Interpol agent Henri Poincaré; his plot, which centers on the death of a mathematician; and his themes. Fractals, mathematics, and science compete with morality and theology in a story that asks big questions about the universe and our place in it.

Best-selling mystery writer Tony Hillerman drew the organizing principles for his novels from the Native American traditions in his beloved West. His atmospheric stories embody the Native Americans' philosophy of life and love of landscape, as well as their morality and mythology. This is evident even in his choice of titles, which are invariably related to these traditions—from his first Leaphorn and Chee novel, *The Blessing Way,* to the last, *The Shape Shifter.*

> "I always have one or two, sometimes more, Navajo or other tribes' cultural elements in mind when I start a plot. In A Thief of Time, I wanted to make readers aware of Navajo attitude toward the dead, respect for burial sites."
>
> —Tony Hillerman

Choosing a specific point of view is another methodological approach to organizing principles. In some stories, POV becomes an organizing principle. As we've seen, stories with multiple POVs provide a built-in organizing principle, such as his-and-her points of view or the alternating points of view in stories featuring an ensemble cast of characters.

An unreliable narrator can also serve as an organizing principle—and give the writer a leg up on surprising the reader. Think of such stories as Agatha Christie's *The Murder of Roger Ackroyd*, Gillian Flynn's *Gone Girl*, Vladimir Nabokov's *Lolita*, Anthony Burgess's *A Clockwork Orange*, Tana French's *In the Woods*, and William Faulkner's *The Sound and the Fury.*

If you are looking for a title, you may have to look no further than your organizing principle. Organizing principles make great titles, as illustrated by the following.

- *How to Make an American Quilt* by Whitney Otto
- *Shiloh* by Shelby Foote
- *The March* by E.L. Doctorow
- *P.S. I Love You* by Cecelia Ahern
- *The Road* by Cormac McCarthy
- *The Absolutely True Diary of a Part-Time Indian* by Sherman Alexie
- *The Knitting Circle* by Ann Hood
- *The Five People You Meet in Heaven* by Mitch Albom
- *Labor Day* by Joyce Maynard
- *Captain Corelli's Mandolin* by Louis de Bernières
- *The Women of Brewster Place* by Gloria Naylor
- *On the Road* by Jack Kerouac
- *Lunch in Paris: A Love Story with Recipes* by Elizabeth Bard

Think about your organizing principle and how it might suggest a title for your story. Come up with a list of possibilities.

"I enjoy it too much—even if I knew I'd never get a book published, I would still write. I enjoy the experience of getting thoughts and ideas and plots and characters organized into this narrative framework."

—Iain Banks

FUN WITH INDEX CARDS, PART III

Not all stories have organizing principles. But if one of the organizing principles we've discussed seems a natural fit for your story, then you'll want to weave it through your narrative as you plan your plot. The following steps can help you.

1. Make the most of your organizing principle.
2. Weave it though your plot in a consistent and believable way.
3. Realize its potential as a USP for your work.

To do this, get out your index cards once more. Consider your scenes in light of your organizing principle. How might that affect the order of those scenes? The story questions? The USP?

Once you've done this, you'll want to organize your scenes according to your organizing principle and gather whatever source material you may need: information, data, quotes, recipes, news clippings, diary entries, e-mails, tweets, and so on. Now create a chapter-by-chapter outline and place your chapter openers accordingly. List the scenes that will appear in each chapter under the chapter openers. Work through the entire plot in this manner.

Once you've completed the outline, you'll have a document that will not only help you write your story, but can help you sell it as well. If you're writing memoir, this can be particularly helpful, as you may be able to use this document as part of the book proposal you use to sell the project (before you finish writing it, which is possible in nonfiction, as opposed to fiction).

You can also use this document to sell the second book in a series; it can serve as your synopsis if you are looking for a two- or three-book deal.

What follows is the document I put together when my agent shopped my memoir *Fixing Freddie* (published in 2010). As you now know, *Fixing Freddie* is a story about a dog, a boy, and a single mom struggling to heal after a difficult divorce. So the thematic organizing principle is the story of this dog-training process, which represents the single mom's efforts to gain control over not only the obstinate beagle, but also her teenage son—and her own messy life. It's a chapter-by-chapter outline that highlights the organizing principle. You can use it as a sample when preparing your own outline.

CHAPTER ONE

"Meaning what you say is just as important as saying what you mean."
—Jennifer Bridwell, *The Everything Dog Obedience Book*

After years of financial struggle, a single mom scrapes together enough money to buy a 900-square-foot cottage. She moves in with the dog, the cat, and the kid—and is promptly reminded that "you promised we could get a puppy if we ever got a house of our own." Paula doesn't need another dog, but after two failed marriages she figures better another dog than another husband.

NOTE: Paula realizes that she needs to mean what she says, with her son as well as the dog. She said she'd get him a puppy, so she gets him the puppy.

CHAPTER TWO

"The most serious problems in owning a dog arise because the initial selection was made thoughtlessly or in haste."
—Roger A. Caras, *Harper's Illustrated Handbook of Dogs*

Paula and Mikey begin their search for a puppy, a roundabout adventure that ultimately brings them to the Puppy Patch and the world's worst beagle. *Hint:* He is on sale for half price, her ex is months behind on child support, and she has just taken on a mortgage.

NOTE: Paula learns the hard way not to choose a puppy "in haste," even if he's on sale.

CHAPTER THREE

[Dogs] lie beside us in the darkness, companions of the night, eager to greet us at the coming of dawn."
—Theresa Mancuso, *Who Moved My Bone?*

Paula and Mikey take the puppy home, name him, and try to integrate him into the family and the household. *How hard can this be?* thinks the experienced mom who's mothered three babies. What Paula learns: (1) Babies have nothing on beagles, and (2) twelve-year-old boys make lousy moms.

NOTE: Cute as they are, puppies are a 24-7 proposition, and Paula finds herself on baby duty all over again.

CHAPTER FOUR

"Your goal is to have your new puppy meet 100 people in his first 100 days."
> —Jennifer Bridwell, *The Everything Dog Obedience Book*

Paula and Mikey revel in showing off Freddie, the cutest puppy in the world. After a miserable summer with his father's "new family" and the current ignominy of being the new kid at school, Mikey finally seems happy, so Paula is happy. And everyone's happy at the housewarming party they have to celebrate their new house—and Freddie is the star of the show. Paula's boyfriend, who planned to host the party with her, doesn't show up. Paula's heartbreak is offset by Mikey's happiness. The moral of the story: A beagle beats a man any day.

NOTE: Paula and Mikey try to socialize Freddie by throwing a party—and Paula feels more alone than ever when her boyfriend doesn't show up.

CHAPTER FIVE

"A Beagle will accept as much attention as you can offer, and then demand more."
> —Roger A. Caras, *Harper's Illustrated Handbook of Dogs*

Or how one bad beagle can spoil the bunch. Freddie and Shakespeare, the elder statesdog, face off over food, territory, and affection. Mikey misses his friends back home in Salem and seems unable to make new friends at his new school. Freddie is his only consolation, so he spoils him, and Paula lets him. She swears off men and decides to devote herself solely to Mikey and her new job.

NOTE: In his loneliness Mikey spoils Freddie, and in her loneliness Paula spoils Mikey.

CHAPTER SIX

"Adolescent Beagles can be particularly stubborn creatures."
—Kristine Kraeuter, *Training Your Beagle*

Freddie manages to win over Shakespeare, the perfect dog, but Isis the cat will have none of it. He bothers her, and she hisses at him and scratches him. A détente is called. Mikey is very protective of Freddie, but Paula secretly sides with the cat. At school, Mikey is showing off in class, trying to impress his new classmates. He gets into trouble in French class, and the school counselor suggests that he see a therapist. Paula and Mikey go together, and all his feelings about divorce and his dad come out.

NOTE: Boys and beagles suffer rough adolescences—and their moms suffer along with them.

CHAPTER SEVEN

"Given the relative scarcity of barking in wolves, some theorize that dogs have developed a more elaborate barking language precisely in order to communicate with humans."
—Alexandra Horowitz, *Inside of a Dog*

Freddie finds his voice—and it's a howl. He barks at the cat, the neighbors, even the wind. Shakespeare chimes in, and soon the neighbors are complaining. One neighbor brings by an ad for an electric collar. Another calls the police when Freddie gets loose and heads out onto the half-frozen lake behind the house, only to get scared and start to howl when the ice begins to break up around him. Paula saves him—and then scolds, punishes, muzzles—all to no avail. She finally spends $50 on a collar that sprays water on Freddie when he barks. Freddie eats it. Her friend Charlie the hunter visits, meets Freddie, and says, "Wow, you've got a baller! They're the leaders of the pack, the ones who lead the howls for everyone. That's a very special dog!" Right.

NOTE: Freddie communicates loudly to anyone who'll listen—and Paula has to listen.

CHAPTER EIGHT

"Apparently dogs believe that if something fits into their mouths, then it is food, no matter what it tastes like."
—Stanley Cohen, *How to Speak Dog*

Freddie chews Paula's shoes; he eats the pulls off all the kitchen cabinets; he even wolfs down whole books. Paula is at her wit's end—and then her older son, Greg, moves back home. The twenty-five-year-old had been living with his troubled father, trying to save him—and now his father is back in an institution, and Greg is emotionally and physically exhausted. Paula will help get him back on his feet. She's thrilled to have him home, but with two male humans and two male dogs in the world's smallest house now, Paula and Isis are outnumbered.

NOTE: Paula tries to teach Freddie and Greg the meaning of true nourishment.

CHAPTER NINE

"It is very difficult to contain a beagle with the time and motivation to engineer escapes."
—Laurie Kramer, Beaglesontheweb.com

Freddie follows his nose wherever it takes him—and Shakespeare goes along for the ride. Mikey leaves the front door open, and the dogs disappear into a snowstorm late at night. Paula goes after them and finds Freddie by following his howl. Greg leaves the back door open, and the dogs disappear into the bogs. Paula's not home, so the boys take off into the woods to find them. They meet a homeless guy who tells them to go get the dogs a treat and a blanket that smells like their favorite human. So they go back home, pull half a chicken out of the fridge and Paula's quilt off her bed, and go back into the bogs and through the woods.

They run home when it gets dark, abandoning the quilt and chicken to the homeless guy—and find the dogs waiting for them on the front porch.

NOTE: While Paula's at work, the boys and the beagle run wild.

CHAPTER TEN

"Standing straight, with your shoulders squared, rather than slumped, can mean the difference between whether your dog obeys a command or ignores it."
—Malcolm Gladwell, *What the Dog Saw*

Paula brings home dog-training books and tries to train Freddie. She also tries to teach Greg to write, so he can earn some money freelancing while he tries to find a job. She has three kids and three pets, so comparisons are inevitable. If Greg were a dog, he'd be Freddie. Greg does write a book but manages to spoil Freddie even more in the process, as he is home with Freddie all day while Mikey is at school. Freddie and Greg are *tight*.

NOTE: Paula tries to teach both Greg and Freddie to do what she tells them to do—with limited success.

CHAPTER ELEVEN

"Dogs that exhibit separation anxiety often have a history that includes a 'separation event.'"
—Kimberly Barry, Ph.D., animal behaviorist

Greg sells his book, gets a job, and moves to L.A. Everyone misses him—Freddie most of all. He's alone with Shakespeare and Isis now during the day while Mikey is at school, and he's very unhappy. All his bad behaviors worsen. Mikey is starting high school now and isn't as interested in Freddie. Paula realizes that she has relied on Greg for adult conversation and companionship, and now that he's gone she's very lonely herself. She needs to get a life.

NOTE: Greg moves to L.A., and both Freddie and Paula fall into a funk.

CHAPTER TWELVE

"The interest in roaming is eliminated in 90 percent of neutered dogs. Aggressive behavior against other male dogs is eliminated in 60 percent of neutered dogs. Urine marking is eliminated in 50 percent of neutered male dogs. Inappropriate mounting is eliminated in 70 percent of neutered dogs."

—Wendy Brooks, DVM

Freddie becomes very aggressive, lunging at other dogs as well as people—particularly men. Paula takes him to Dr. Barrow, the vet. He's a big guy, and Paula worries that Freddie will lunge at him, too. But Dr. Barrow and Freddie get along fine. Paula asks about neutering Freddie, as she's heard that may reduce his aggressive behavior. "It will help," he tells her, "but he'll still be Freddie." Mikey starts hanging out with some tough kids and gets caught joyriding bikes around the lake. Paula wonders how she'll survive raising another adolescent boy on her own. If Mikey's anything like Greg was, she's in trouble.

NOTE: The testosterone is running high in both boy and beagle, and so Paula gets Freddie fixed. But there's no such easy fix for Mikey.

CHAPTER THIRTEEN

"If there is a common problem among dogs, it is pulling on the leash to get where they want to go."

—Gerilyn J. Bielakiewicz, *The Everything Dog Training and Tricks Book*

Paula beefs up Freddie's exercise routine at Dr. Barrow's suggestion. She takes five-mile walks with Shakespeare and Freddie though the bogs. Shakespeare can go off leash, but Freddie follows scents instead of Paula, barks and lunges at other dogs on the path, and chews on the leash when she's not looking. He eats three leashes in three weeks. She finally invests in a Gentle Leader collar—and Freddie eats that, too. She comes across a guy with three beagles in the bogs, and asks him, over Freddie's bellowing, what she could do about his behavior. He just shrugs and says, "He's a beagle." Five minutes later Freddie trips Paula, and she lands face down in the dirt.

NOTE: Paula tries to leash-train Freddie, who will not be tamed.

CHAPTER FOURTEEN

"You cannot stop a beagle from howling. You can only redirect him."
—Cesar Millan, *Dog Whisperer with Cesar Millan*

Mikey goes to spend the summer with his father and step-mother in California, and Paula is alone with Freddie. He cries all night, because he's used to sleeping with Mikey in his bed—and Paula makes him sleep at the foot of her bed with Shakespeare. He barks all day, tears up the house, and snaps at her next-door neighbor. She starts putting Freddie and Shakespeare in the garage during the day, as she can no longer trust him in her house. Isis dies, poisoned by bad cat food. Desperate for a break, Paula puts the dogs in a kennel and goes to Connecticut for a conference—and promptly falls in love for the first time in years.

NOTE: Paula needs redirecting as much as Freddie does—and love at first sight seems to do the trick.

CHAPTER FIFTEEN

"The dog who learns that all he need do to get his way is growl will soon figure out that if a little aggression is good, a lot is better, at least from his point of view."
—Gina Spadafori, *Dogs for Dummies*

Freddie starts giving the guys in Paula's writers group a hard time. They come every Monday night, and every Monday night, Freddie harasses them. Andy, the only lawyer Paula's ever met *without* a killer instinct, tries to befriend Freddie, and in return Freddie pulls on Andy's pant leg, ripping his jeans. Andy responds by bringing Freddie treats every week, and eventually Freddie warms up to him. Mikey spends less and less time with Freddie; ever since he's come home after the summer he's been increasingly uncooperative—not doing his homework, not doing his chores, not taking care of Freddie. Paula falls into a funk after she learns that her new boyfriend has been engaged to another woman all along.

NOTE: All the males in Paula's life—Mikey, Freddie, her boyfriend—behave in increasingly beastly ways.

CHAPTER SIXTEEN

"The animal behaviorist can prescribe medication for dogs with problems that are too intense or severe to change with training alone."

—Gerilyn J. Bielakiewicz, co-founder of Canine University

After Freddie snags Andy's pants, everyone tells Paula to get rid of him. Mikey begs her not to. Paula calls Dr. Barrow, who recommends a consult with an animal behaviorist. Dr. Annie is a woman—and Freddie likes women. "Are you single?" she asks Paula. "In homes headed by single moms, male dogs often take on the role of man of the house." She prescribes an anti-anxiety drug for Freddie. Paula, who's still nursing a broken heart and torturing herself over her disastrous history with men, tells Dr. Annie, "If this doesn't work, you can just prescribe some of that puppy Prozac for me."

NOTE: The animal behaviorist gives Freddie meds, but a stressed-out Paula suspects that she needs them more.

CHAPTER SEVENTEEN

"What the dog clearly knows is to anticipate punishment when the owner appears wearing a look of displeasure. What the dog does not know is that he is guilty. He just knows to look out for you."

—Alexandra Horowitz, *Inside of a Dog*

Freddie is calmer now that he's on medication. But he's still aggressive, especially around the guys in the writers group, even though he knows them well by now. He whines for attention all during their meeting, and lunges unexpectedly at Vaughn, a former Marine, when he gets up to go to the bathroom. This prompts a conversation among the men about whether or not Paula should get rid of him. Vaughn insists that she never will, because she's formed a "negative attachment" to the dog. Paula suspects that she's formed such negative attachments to her men as well.

NOTE: Paula realizes that she is guilty of forming negative attachments to the males in her life—dogs and men.

CHAPTER EIGHTEEN

"From the dog's perspective, you're both members of the same pack, and there can only be one leader. ... Ambiguity about lead dog status would never occur in the wild; when it happens at home, your dog learns he can exhibit beastly behavior and get away with it."

—Sue Owens Wright, *150 Activities for Bored Dogs*

A new neighbor comes over to the house and makes an inappropriate move on Paula. Paula asks the guy to leave. He hesitates—and Freddie bites him. A full-fledged teenager now at fifteen, Mikey is flunking English and French, and doesn't seem to care. He has a party at the house while Paula's out of town on business, a bunch of older teens show up, and things get out of control. The cops show up—but not before someone makes off with Paula's jewelry. It's tough-love time for a boy and his dog. Paula's never been too good at tough love, but she knows it's time she learned.

NOTE: Paula realizes that it's her fault that her boy and her beagle are running wild.

CHAPTER NINETEEN

"First you learn a new language, profanity; and second you learn not to discipline your dogs when you're mad, and that's most of the time when you're training dogs."
—Lou Schultz, renowned trainer of Alaskan Huskies

Mikey is grounded. Freddie is in obedience training. Paula is learning how to be firm with them both. The same calm-assertive energy she learns to use with Freddie, she uses with Mikey. She takes up boxing and starts standing up for herself in all aspects of her life. She finally begins the novel she's always wanted to write but has put off to help other people write their books. And she starts dating again.

NOTE: Boxing teaches Paula how to stay cool, stand up for herself, and fight back.

CHAPTER TWENTY

"Dogs live in the moment. They don't reminisce about the past or worry about the future; therefore, they can move on from unstable behavior very quickly—if we let them."
—Cesar Millan, *Be the Pack Leader*

Freddie and Mikey both begin to grow up, little by little. Mikey works harder at school and starts planning for college. Freddie behaves better—even without the puppy Prozac. Paula meets a great guy who grew up with beagles and loves them. He even loves Freddie—and Freddie loves him. By the time Mikey graduates from high school, Paula's "negative attachment" to bad dogs and bad men has disappeared, replaced by a positive affection for good dogs and good men. And yes, Freddie is a good dog now. Paula's the pack leader, and Freddie's the pack follower. Unless, of course, there's a sweeter scent to follow. …

NOTE: Paula puts her penchant for bad dogs and bad boys behind her—and moves on.

THE ORGANIZING PRINCIPLE TO WRITE BY

You have a main plot and several subplots, as well as a main theme and several variations on theme. You have a well-rounded protagonist, a worthy antagonist, and a colorful cast of secondary characters who mirror your themes and variations on theme.

And now you have an organizing principle, as well as a scene-by-scene breakdown of your story. All you have to do is write it—and then polish it. In the next chapter, we'll take a look at how you can fix the common problems that might sabotage your final draft, address the conventions of your particular genre, and polish your work so it shines—and sells.

> "Humanity's legacy of stories and storytelling is the most precious we have. All wisdom is in our stories and songs. A story is how we construct our experiences. At the very simplest, it can be: 'He/she was born, lived, died.' Probably that is the template of our stories—a beginning, middle, and end. This structure is in our minds."
>
> —Doris Lessing

CHAPTER TWELVE
YOUR PLOT PERFECT CHECKLIST

"If you start with a bang, you won't end with a whimper."
—T.S. Eliot

Building a story is like building a house. Create a good plot, and you've created the foundation for your story—and framed it. But you still need to put in the plumbing, the electrical, the drywall, and more. And then you have to decorate it. These are the refinements and revisions that make a house a home. Similarly refinements and revisions are what make the difference in a story that's good—and a story that you can sell.

In an understandable if misguided eagerness to get published, many writers forgo this most critical part of the process. In this chapter, we'll explore the finer points of refinement and revision. Think of this final section of the book as a blueprint for layering, refining, and polishing your storyline. It includes a checklist for each major genre and a guide to self-editing.

Many writers often balk at the thought of refinement and revision. Don't be one of them. Polishing your work—from premise and plot to style and substance—is what will separate you from your unpublished peers. You have made all this effort to create a fine piece of work; failing to polish it now is as foolhardy as a fine cabinetmaker failing to wax his newly built mahogany highboy to a fine sheen.

Let's get started. The hard work of creation is finished—and now the fun begins!

WRITING TOWARD READER EXPECTATIONS

When the mystery lover opens a book and begins to read, she does so with the expectation that she's reading a mystery. If the plot does not meet that expectation, she buys another book, one that *does* meet that expectation. Every genre has plot conventions that are particular to that kind of story. Knowing these conventions—and how and when to play with them—is critical to the plotting of any successful work. As you refine and revise your work, you can ensure that your plots meet and even exceed the expectations of your readers, no matter what your genre. What follows is a checklist for each of the main genres, which will serve as a refinement and revision primer, reminding you of the conventions, expectations, and finer points of your given category.

THE MYSTERY GENRE

TITLE: What is your working title? For mysteries and thrillers, common titling conventions include:

- **SHORT ACTION WORDS:** *Get Shorty* by Elmore Leonard; *Never Go Back* by Lee Child; *Read It and Weep* by Jenn McKinlay; *Fear Nothing* by Lisa Gardner
- **SHORT CHARACTER DESCRIPTIONS:** *Gone Girl* by Gillian Flynn; *The Other Woman* by Hank Phillippi Ryan; *Killer* by Jonathan Kellerman; *The Racketeer* by John Grisham; *The Laughing Policeman* by Maj Sjöwall and Per Wahlöö

- **MENTION OF THE MACGUFFIN OR OBJECT OF DESIRE:** *Lethal Treasure* by Jane Cleland; *The Maltese Falcon* by Dashiell Hammett; *The Purloined Letter* by Edgar Allan Poe; *The Hot Rock* by Donald Westlake
- **SPOOKY SETTINGS:** *Mystic River* by Dennis Lehane; *The Bones of Paris* by Laurie R. King; *Dance Hall of the Dead* by Tony Hillerman; *Death on the Nile* by Agatha Christie
- **THEME:** *The Gods of Guilt* by Michael Connelly; *Kindness Goes Unpunished* by Craig Johnson; *How the Light Gets In* by Louise Penny; *All Cry Chaos* by Leonard Rosen; *A Suitable Vengeance* by Elizabeth George
- **SAYING, QUOTE, OR CLICHÉ TWIST:** *There Was an Old Woman* by Hallie Ephron; *The Hen of the Baskervilles* by Donna Andrews; *In Plain Sight* by C.J. Box; *In the Bleak Midwinter* by Julia Spencer-Fleming; *Pale Kings and Princes* by Robert B. Parker
- **PUZZLE OR CLUE:** *The Da Vinci Code* by Dan Brown; *The Jefferson Key* by Steve Berry; *The Five Red Herrings* by Dorothy Sayers; *The Twelve Clues of Christmas* by Rhys Bowen

> "At least half the mystery novels published violate the law that the solution, once revealed, must seem to be inevitable."
>
> —Raymond Chandler

USP: This is one of the most competitive categories, so make sure you have a strong USP: a one-of-a-kind villain, (Hannibal Lecter in *The Silence of the Lambs*), a unique POV (the dead girl in *The Lovely Bones*), an unlikely heroine (Lisbeth Salander in *The Girl with the Dragon Tattoo*), a dubious hero (Dexter in *Darkly Dreaming Dexter*), an unusual setting (Pemberley in *Death Comes to Pemberley*), or a clever crime (the heist in *Ocean's Eleven*).

PLOT: When plotting a successful mystery, remember that there are two main storylines: the one you show the reader and the one you don't.

SUBPLOTS: The more subplots you have, the easier it is to weave in red herrings, clues, suspects, and so on. Aim for at least two to four subplots.

THEMES: In this genre, there's no getting around life and death, justice and injustice, man's inhumanity to man, and the eternal battle between good and evil.

VARIATIONS ON THEME: The more variations on theme, the richer the story. The level of craft is high in this category, so the richer your story, the better. Think of the skillful weaving of the many themes and variations on theme we discussed in regard to *The Maltese Falcon.* They make it a classic that has survived nearly one hundred years. Be sure to hit at least some of the big themes described above, as readers of this genre expect an exploration of these themes.

PROTAGONIST: If you can create a great protagonist in a genre crowded with swell sleuths—from the überbrilliant Sherlock Holmes to the dynamic duo Rizzoli and Isles—then you can enjoy a great career. The trick is to create a character that can stand apart from all the rest, one readers can admire if not adore altogether. Once you do, make sure that your protagonist is driving the action, solving the crime, and saving the day. If she doesn't, editors will notice—and pass on your work.

ANTAGONIST: Too many villains are cartoonish; make yours admirable, deplorable, charming, and creepy—a walking contradiction. Hannibal Lecter is a good model.

SETTING: The right setting can help establish mood, which is critical in this category. Whether you choose a convent or a circus, Chicago or Chihuahua, the inner city or the outer Hebrides, be sure to show the underbelly of your setting, however it may glitter on the outside. That's where the darkness is.

PACING: Thrillers in particular demand a fast pace, as does most crime fiction. Keep the pressure on your protagonist, and remember to "bring in a man with a gun" when things slow down. *Note:* Most thrillers run around 90,000 words. Any longer and your pacing could suffer as a result. (See chapter ten.)

SERIES CONSIDERATIONS: If you're planning a series, make sure that you don't paint yourself into a corner with the first story. When Gregory

Mcdonald wrote *Fletch*, he wrote it as a stand-alone title with an ending that did not lend itself to sequels. When *Fletch* became a huge bestseller and Mcdonald was called upon to write many more novels featuring his eponymous main character, plotting the sequel was a bigger challenge for him than it needed to be.

Also, choose a title with a naming convention that will lend itself to a series. Think of *A Is for Alibi*, the first in Sue Grafton's alphabet-themed series. Or J.K. Rowling's *Harry Potter and the Sorcerer's Stone* and Stieg Larsson's *The Girl with the Dragon Tattoo*, both of which are the first novels in series whose titles feature the main character.

> *"The English tradition offers the great tapestry novel, where you have the emotional aspect of a detective's personal life, the circumstances of the crime and, most important, the atmosphere of the English countryside that functions as another character."*
>
> —Elizabeth George

TITLES COUNT

The right title can sell your book. It is, in effect, your story's headline. So invest some effort and imagination into titling your work *before* you try to sell it. That said, when you do sell it, odds are your publisher will make you change it. No matter. Your title served its purpose; let it go. Resistance is futile.

NOTE: Is your title already taken? Check www.amazon.com or www.bn.com to make sure. And reserve the domain name, just in case.

> *"The greatest compliment a writer can be given is that a story and character hold a reader spellbound. I'm caught up in the story writing, and I miss a good deal of sleep thinking about it and working out the plot points."*
>
> —Iris Johansen

THE LOVE STORY GENRE

TITLE: What is your working title? For love stories, common titling conventions include:

- **THE WORD *LOVE*:** *Endless Love* by Scott Spencer; *Love Story* by Erich Segal; *Love Walked In* by Marisa de los Santos; *Love Is a Mix Tape* by Rob Sheffield; *Love Me Forever* by Johanna Lindsey; *First Love* by James Patterson, Emily Raymond, and Sasha Illingworth
- **SHORT ACTION WORDS:** *Bite Me* by Shelly Laurenston; *The Bride Says Maybe* by Cathy Maxwell; *Release Me* by J. Kenner; *Never Love a Highlander* by Maya Banks
- **RELATIONSHIP WORDS:** *This Matter of Marriage* by Debbie Macomber; *The Wedding* by Nicholas Sparks; *Le Divorce* by Diane Johnson; *Romancing the Duke* by Tessa Dare
- **SHORT CHARACTER DESCRIPTIONS:** *The Forever Girl* by Alexander McCall Smith; *A Knight in Shining Armor* by Jude Deveraux; *The Little Mermaid* by Hans Christian Andersen; *The Spymaster's Lady* by Joanna Bourne
- **SETTING:** *Wuthering Heights* by Emily Brontë; *The Bridges of Madison County* by Robert James Waller; *Home to Seaview Key* by Sherryl Woods; *Tara Road* by Maeve Binchy; "Brokeback Mountain" by Annie Proulx
- **THEME:** *Pride and Prejudice* by Jane Austen; *Possession* by A.S. Byatt; *Sense and Sensibility* by Jane Austen; *Power Play* by Danielle Steel
- **SONGS:** *Sea of Love* by Melissa Foster; *P.S. I Love You* by Cecelia Ahern; *Wild About Harry* by Linda Lael Miller; *The Very Thought of You* by Lynn Kurland; *Blue Bayou* by JoAnn Ross
- **SAYING, QUOTE, OR CLICHÉ TWIST:** *Something Borrowed* by Emily Giffin; *Vampire Most Wanted* by Lynsay Sands; *Once in a Lifetime* by Jill Shalvis; *Practice Makes Perfect* by Julie James
- **CHARACTER NAME:** *Dr. Zhivago* by Boris Pasternak; *Rebecca* by Daphne du Maurier; *Jane Eyre* by Charlotte Brontë; *Emma* by Jane Austen; *Scarlett* by Alexandra Ripley; *Bridget Jones's Diary* by Helen Fielding; *Lucia, Lucia* by Adriana Trigiani

- **COUPLE:** *Romeo and Juliet* by William Shakespeare; *Beauty and the Beast* by Madame Gabrielle-Suzanne Barbot de Villeneuve; *Julie and Romeo* by Jeanne Ray

> "In my books and in romance as a genre, there is a positive, uplifting feeling that leaves the reader with a sense of encouragement and hope for a brighter future—or a brighter present."
>
> —Debbie Macomber

USP: You need to find a way to convince readers that these two people belong together—and if that can't happen, it's a tragedy. For a strong USP, give us odd couples, new settings, unique obstacles, and more.

PLOT: Generally speaking, your heroine can have another lover (whom she will realize in due time is all wrong for her), but the hero shouldn't. He should be free to love her only, with few exceptions. (He has a crazy wife in the attic, or a wonderful wife who's terminally ill, or a rich-bitch fiancé he must break up with so he can marry your heroine.) Basically if he sleeps with someone else while he's courting your heroine, readers may consider him unworthy of her.

SUBPLOTS: Your heroine and your hero need friends and frenemies, family and co-workers, and obstacles to overcome on all fronts. *Note:* In love stories, the second act is usually where a secret comes out which imperils the relationship. This secret often comes with its own subplot. Here's where we meet the crazy wife in the attic, the past mistake that our hero or heroine may not be able to forgive, or the true identity of the hero or heroine.

THEME: Love, love, love! Looking for it, mistaking it, finding it, refusing it, revisiting it, luxuriating in it, losing it, sacrificing for it, making it .... .

VARIATIONS ON THEME: Your subplots and secondary characters can mirror your theme and variations on theme—that's what best friends (and parents and siblings and colleagues and rivals) are for.

HEROINE: In this genre, (perhaps) above all others, you need a likable heroine. Kindness, strength, intelligence, attractiveness, and feistiness are all good attributes to give her.

HERO: In this genre, (perhaps) above all others, you need a hero worth loving. He should be handsome, smart, strong, and sexy, and tamable wouldn't hurt, either.

MEN IN WHITE, MEN IN CHAPS, MEN IN ARMOR

According to a study by neuroscientists Ogi Ogas and Sai Gaddam, who analyzed some fifteen thousand Harlequin novels, the top ten most popular heroes in love stories have the following professions.

1. Doctor
2. Cowboy
3. Boss
4. Prince
5. Rancher
6. Knight
7. Surgeon
8. King
9. Bodyguard
10. Sheriff

SETTING: The more romantic the setting, the better. Romance can bloom anywhere, but this genre in particular celebrates castles, moors, coastal communities, big-sky country, Ireland and Scotland and England, Paris and Manhattan and San Francisco, and small towns everywhere.

PACING: The relationship must drive the story. Whether your hero and heroine are busy fighting demons or rounding up cattle or surviving the apocalypse, you need to keep their relationship front and center. *Note:* Word-count requirements for this genre can vary from 30,000 words for novellas to sagas running as long as 120,000 words. Most romance publishers have very strict word-length requirements, depending on the kind of love story, so check your competition and adjust your pacing and length accordingly.

SERIES CONSIDERATIONS: If you're considering creating a series for this genre, it's important to build out the subplots, secondary characters, and setting so you have room to grow in the coming books. The narrower the focus on the hero and heroine in your first book, the harder it could be to write sequels.

> "Action, reaction, motivation, emotion, all have to come from the characters. Writing a love scene requires the same elements from the writer as any other."
>
> —Nora Roberts

THE MAINSTREAM/UPMARKET FICTION GENRE

TITLE: What is your working title? For mainstream/upmarket fiction, common titling conventions include:

- **SHORT ACTION WORDS:** *Never Let Me Go* by Kazuo Ishiguro; *Rabbit, Run* by John Updike; *Drive, He Said* by Jeremy Larner
- **SHORT CHARACTER DESCRIPTION:** *The Alchemist* by Paulo Coelho; *The Stranger* by Albert Camus; *The Kite Runner* by Khaled Hosseini; *The Prince of Tides* by Pat Conroy
- **SETTING:** *Gilead* by Marilynne Robinson; *Middlemarch* by George Eliot; *Empire Falls* by Richard Russo; *The House on Mango Street* by Sandra Cisneros
- **THEME:** *War and Peace* by Leo Tolstoy; *Middlesex* by Jeffrey Eugenides; *Catch-22* by Joseph Heller; *Heart of Darkness* by Joseph Conrad; *The Art of Fielding* by Chad Harbach; *The Art of Racing in the Rain* by Garth Stein
- **LINE FROM THE BOOK:** *The Color Purple* by Alice Walker; *To Kill a Mockingbird* by Harper Lee; *The World According to Garp* by John Irving; *The Unbearable Lightness of Being* by Milan Kundera
- **LINE FROM LITERATURE:** *The Sound and the Fury* by William Faulkner; *A Fanatic Heart* by Edna O'Brien; *The Wings of the Dove* by Henry James; *No Country for Old Men* by Cormac McCarthy
- **CHARACTER NAME:** *The Great Gatsby* by F. Scott Fitzgerald; *Lolita* by Vladimir Nabokov; *Sula* by Toni Morrison; *The*

Brothers Karamazov by Fyodor Dostoyevsky; *Olive Kitteridge* by Elizabeth Strout

USP: In literary fiction, the USP is often an authentic and original voice, a unique style, or a special character we haven't seen before. Craft is paramount here; you need to master the art of weaving theme, plot, character, setting, dialogue, image system, and all of the elements we've discussed into a seamless, layered, and lyrical narrative. The competition in this category is brutal; getting published in literary journals and racking up some awards can set you and your work apart.

PLOT: The conventional wisdom is that plot is not as important in this category as it is in genre fiction, but don't bet your career on it. The trend for upmarket fiction is beautifully written and fully realized stories in which memorable characters actually *do* something. So make something happen.

SUBPLOTS: Literary fiction is all about layering, and subplots are a critical part of that layering. So be sure to weave your subplots and secondary characters gracefully through your story.

THEME: Literature with a capital *L* means theme with a capital *T*. So go for the big themes: the meaning of life, the human condition, or the nature of the universe.

VARIATIONS ON THEME: Again, layering is critical in literary fiction—and given the importance of theme, it follows that variations on theme are equally important. The key here is subtlety.

PROTAGONIST: Your protagonist has a lot riding on his or her shoulders in upmarket fiction. So give us an unforgettable character. Give us a Madame Bovary, a Garp, a Holly Golightly, a Gatsby, a Holden Caulfield, a Mrs. Dalloway, a Hamlet, a Huck Finn, a Celie, an Atticus Finch. Atticus Finch, of *To Kill a Mockingbird,* was named the most popular hero ever by the American Film Institute, thanks to his courage, integrity, and heart. He's a praiseworthy protagonist in every way.

ANTAGONIST: You'll also need an unforgettable antagonist. Give us a Fagan, an Iago, a Mrs. Danvers, a Scrooge, or a Moby-Dick—which proves that even a fish can prove a formidable opponent when it's a great albino sperm whale that stalks the seas.

SETTING: Setting is inextricably tied to theme in literary fiction. Think the deserted island in William Golding's *Lord of the Flies,* New York City in Tom Wolfe's *The Bonfire of the Vanities,* or southern Alabama's "Maycomb County" in Harper Lee's *To Kill a Mockingbird.*

PACING: While you don't necessarily need the tight, action-driven pacing of a thriller, you still need to make sure that your literary story captures your reader's attention and keeps it. Remember, it's all in the story questions. *Note:* Literary fiction runs the gamut in terms of length. But do know that many agents—myself included—won't shop any debut novel over 120,000 words, no matter what the genre (given the resistance of publishers to buy longer works by unknowns). So adjust your length and pacing accordingly.

SERIES CONSIDERATIONS: In literary fiction, writing a series is not often the goal of the writer. But there are some "series," such as John Updike's Rabbit books and Philip Roth's Nathan Zuckerman books, whose linked novels constitute remarkable bodies of work. And of course, there are masterworks such as Marcel Proust's seven-volume *Remembrance of Things Past.* Ultimately your own literary ambitions and any commercial success you may achieve could determine whether you produce a series.

> *"I am sick of secure and smugly conventional people telling me that my work is bizarre simply because they've found a safe little place to live out the chaos of the world—and who then deny that this chaos happens to other, less fortunate people."*
>
> —John Irving

THE SCIENCE FICTION AND FANTASY GENRES

TITLE: What is your working title? For science fiction and fantasy fiction, common titling conventions include:

- **SHORT ACTION WORDS:** *Snow Crash* by Neal Stephenson; *Contact* by Carl Sagan; *The Demon Awakens* by R.A. Salvatore

- **SHORT CHARACTER DESCRIPTION:** *The Martian* by Andy Weir; *The Handmaid's Tale* by Margaret Atwood; *The Last Unicorn* by Peter S. Beagle; *The Hobbit* by J.R.R. Tolkien; *The Golem and the Jinni* by Helene Wecker
- **FUTURE/PAST:** *Nineteen Eighty-Four* by George Orwell; *2001: A Space Odyssey* by Arthur C. Clarke; *Liberty: 1784* by Robert Conroy
- **SETTING:** *The Mists of Avalon* by Marion Zimmer Bradley; *Pines* by Blake Crouch
- **WORLD BUILDING:** *Ender's Game* by Orson Scott Card; *The Hunger Games* by Suzanne Collins; *A Game of Thrones* by George R.R. Martin; *Neverwhere* by Neil Gaiman
- **OBJECT/TALISMAN:** *The Sword of Shannara* by Terry Brooks; *The Fiery Cross* by Diana Gabaldon; *The Blade Itself* by Joe Abercrombie; *The Sword of Truth* by Terry Goodkind; *The Blinding Knife* by Brent Weeks
- **TECHNOLOGY:** *I, Robot* by Isaac Asimov; *Cryptonomicon* by Neal Stephenson; *Do Androids Dream of Electric Sheep?* by Philip K. Dick; *The Time Machine* by H.G. Wells
- **THEME:** *The Left Hand of Darkness* by Ursula K. Le Guin; *Wicked* by Gregory Maguire; *American Gods* by Neil Gaiman; *Doctor Sleep* by Stephen King; *Words of Radiance* by Brandon Sanderson
- **LINE FROM LITERATURE:** *Dying of the Light* by George R.R. Martin; *I Sing the Body Electric* by Ray Bradbury; *To Say Nothing of the Dog* by Connie Willis
- **SAYING OR CLICHÉ TWIST:** *World War Z* by Max Brooks; *Going Postal* by Terry Pratchett; *A Discovery of Witches* by Deborah Harkness
- **CHARACTER NAME:** *Jonathan Strange & Mr Norrell* by Susanna Clarke; *Conan the Barbarian* by Robert E. Howard; *Odd Thomas* by Dean Koontz

> *"I love it when real science finds a home in a fictional setting, where you take some real core idea of science and weave it through a fictional narrative in order to bring it to life, the way stories can. That's my favorite thing."*
>
> —Brian Greene

USP: These are the most crowded genres of all; the bulk of my in-box is made up of queries from science fiction and fantasy writers. Which means you need a very strong USP to stand out among the competition. The key here is originality; this genre is rife with tired tropes and clichés, so if you can come up with something new and fresh, your story will stand out.

PLOT: The success of this genre, along with category killers such as *The Lord of the Rings*, The Hunger Games trilogy, and the Game of Thrones series, puts the pressure on writers to develop plots that (1) are unique in premise and (2) capture the reader's attention on page 1 and keep it through hundreds and even thousands of pages. Again, the trick is to avoid overused conventions and to come up with a more creative approach to your storytelling. You need to be very familiar with this genre to make this happen, so be sure to do your due diligence.

SUBPLOTS: Many science fiction and fantasy novels run longer than those in other genres—up to 120,000 words or more. Subplots are the key to plotting a longer work successfully—not to mention plotting an entire series.

THEME: In science fiction and fantasy, themes tend to be grand ones: the meaning of life, the human condition, what it means to be human, the effect of technology on our lives, the nature of the universe, the relativity of time, astrophysics, the possibility of other worlds, the use and abuse of power, good and evil, and more.

VARIATIONS ON THEME: Again, you need to milk the theme and variations on theme in this genre, just as you do the plot and subplots. Think of Tolkien's *The Lord of the Rings* and George R.R. Martin's *A Game of Thrones,* both masterfully crafted weavings of grand themes and variations on theme, bold plots and subplots. Ask yourself how you can incorporate these classic science fiction/fantasy themes and variations on theme in your story—and how you can put your own stamp on them.

PROTAGONIST: Science fiction may be known as "the fiction of ideas," but the most successful stories in this genre have characters as rich and well developed as the ideas upon which the stories are based. Give us a protagonist we can fall in love with and follow through this story as well as any others you may have planned. Here, too, you must beware the stock characters of the genre: the knight, the starfighter, the princess, the warrior, the robot, the elf, and so on. Give us new players; make your characters unique people—and aliens—we haven't seen before.

ANTAGONIST: In science fiction and fantasy, antagonists come in all shapes and sizes, from wizards and witches to demons and dragons—not to mention supercomputers, androids, drones, and every possible kind of (killing) machine. So let your imagination be your guide—because to create characters unique enough to transcend the tropes that have become commonplace in these genres, you're going to need it!

> "Science fiction is an amazing literature: plot elements that you would think would be completely worn out by now keep changing into surprising new forms."
>
> —Connie Willis

SETTING: In this genre, you often need to do more than establish a cool setting; you need to create an entire new world. For many writers, world building is the pleasure—and the pitfall—of these genres. You need to create a world we've not seen before—and make it compelling and believable. Again, avoid imitation; it's your originality that will win readers here.

PACING: The trick in science fiction and fantasy is to ground your story in the world you've created while introducing action in a steady stream. In effect, you're building the train as it runs down the track. Study the first chapters of such titles as *The Hunger Games*, and you'll see how to weave world building into your scenes without slowing down the action. (Also, review chapter nine of this book.)

SERIES CONSIDERATIONS: Many science fiction and fantasy stories are conceived as series. That said, you need to make sure that each story in the series stands alone. You should also come up with a series title that can accommodate the entire storyline.

"The fantasy that appeals most to people is the kind that's rooted thoroughly in somebody looking around a corner and thinking, What if I wandered into this writer's people here? *If you've done your job and made your people and your settings well enough, that adds an extra dimension that you can't buy."*

—Tamora Pierce

THE HISTORICAL FICTION GENRE

TITLE: What is your working title? For historical fiction, common titling conventions include:

- **SHORT ACTION WORDS:** *The Auschwitz Escape* by Joel C. Rosenberg; *Kidnapped* by Robert Louis Stevenson; *Falls the Shadow* by Sharon Kay Penman
- **SHORT CHARACTER DESCRIPTIONS:** *The Alienist* by Caleb Carr; *The Dovekeepers* by Alice Hoffman; *The Other Boleyn Girl* by Philippa Gregory; *The House Girl* by Tara Conklin
- **HISTORICAL FRAMEWORK:** *Memoirs of a Geisha* by Arthur Golden; *The Secret Diary of Anne Boleyn* by Robin Maxwell; *Letters from Rifka* by Karen Hesse
- **TIME:** *The Clan of the Cave Bear* by Jean M. Auel; *Ragtime* by E.L. Doctorow; *Winston's War* by Michael Dobbs

- **SETTING**: *World's Fair* by E.L. Doctorow; *The Pillars of the Earth* by Ken Follett; *Lonesome Dove* by Larry McMurtry; *London* by Edward Rutherfurd; *The Kitchen House* by Kathleen Grissom; *The Valley of Amazement* by Amy Tan
- **THEME**: *The Invention of Wings* by Sue Monk Kidd; *The Thorn Birds* by Colleen McCullough; *Gone with the Wind* by Margaret Mitchell; *The Agony and the Ecstasy* by Irving Stone; *The Age of Innocence* by Edith Wharton
- **SAYING, QUOTE, OR CLICHÉ TWIST**: *War Brides* by Helen Bryan; *A King's Ransom* by Sharon Kay Penman; *No Time for Sergeants* by Mac Hyman
- **CHARACTER NAME**: *March* by Geraldine Brooks; *Sarah, Plain and Tall* by Patricia MacLachlan; *Pope Joan* by Donna Woolfolk Cross

> "The thing that most attracts me to historical fiction is taking the factual record as far as it is known, using that as scaffolding, and then letting imagination build the structure that fills in those things we can never find out for sure."
> —Geraldine Brooks

USP: In historical fiction, the USP often centers on a famous person, place, or event. You just have to find a way to make it unique. Caleb Carr used Teddy Roosevelt's stint as the police commissioner of New York City to create the historical crime story *The Alienist*. Philippa Gregory told us the terrible true story of Mary Boleyn, who lost a king to her younger sister Anne in *The Other Boleyn Girl*. And Jennifer Chiaverini told the story of freedwoman Elizabeth Hobbs Keckley's unique friendship with Mary Todd Lincoln through the former slave's POV in *Mrs. Lincoln's Dressmaker*. Ask yourself how you can tweak your premise, POV, or protagonist to make your story stand out.

PLOT: Readers love historical fiction because it brings history to life. History class was boring in high school because it presented facts and events without any drama. It's up to you to dramatize the events of your story—and plot it for best dramatic effect.

SUBPLOTS: History is full of subplots, and your research alone should generate lots of subplot ideas. Do your homework and your biggest problem will be choosing what to leave out.

RESEARCH: If you don't do enough research, you'll likely get key facts wrong—and your readers will abandon you in disgust. But if you do too much research, you'll get lost in it—and never finish your story. Should you finish, you still risk boring readers with extraneous data if you don't pick and choose the choicest cuts of information.

THEME: It's been said that there are three sides to every story (mine, yours, and the truth), and that history is told by the victors. But through the glory of theme you get to decide whose side you are telling, whether on behalf of Mary Boleyn or her sister and rival Anne's, or both, as with South Carolinian Orry Main and Pennsylvanian George Hazard, friends who become enemies in John Jakes's classic Civil War trilogy, North and South. Common themes in historical fiction include power and the abuse of power, the price of freedom, the sins of the father, good vs. evil, the cost of progress, and the disruption of life as we know it at any given time.

> *"I like to do the research of history and the creativity of writing fiction. I am creating this thing which I think is twice as difficult as writing either history or fiction."*
>
> —Philippa Gregory

VARIATIONS ON THEME: Given the aforementioned adages about history, your variations on theme speak to those other sides of the story—win, lose, or draw. Milk those variations for all they're worth and you'll impress your readers, who know that there are two (or more) sides to every story.

PROTAGONIST: You need a proactive protagonist who makes history rather than submits to it. Even in stories written from the POV of the victims of history, we prefer heroes and heroines who fight back, sacrifice, stand their ground, and survive (or not), no matter what the cost.

ANTAGONIST: History is full of villains so heinous no elaboration is required. So if you take your cues from history, your antagonist should ring true. Just be sure to show the human side of your bad guys as well as the beast within.

SETTING: As a sense of place is more critical in this genre than perhaps any other, one of your key tasks is to create an authentic setting. Make sure that you get the details right—down to the bed knobs and the broomsticks—as well as the broad strokes. If you don't, your readers will rejoice in pointing out where you went wrong.

PACING: Just as with writing science fiction and fantasy, writing historical fiction means grounding your reader in another time and place without slowing down the action. Your research should not be apparent to the naked eye; you need to weave it through the tapestry of your story. While word counts vary, you should aim for between 75,000 and 120,000 words, especially if you are a debut author.

SERIES CONSIDERATIONS: The good news about writing historical fiction is that history does, inevitably, repeat itself. There's always another war, another frontier, and another generation to write about. So whether you envision a series or a stand-alone title, you should be able to plot a sequel if your first story proves successful. Even if you kill off your protagonist in the first book, you can still write about her friends, family, allies, or enemies. You might also consider choosing an important personage from the past (or the public domain) and building a series around him or her, as the writers of the many Jane Austen "sequels" and mystery series have done.

THE WOMEN'S FICTION GENRE

> *"I'm more interested in interpersonal relationships—between lovers, families, siblings. That's why I write about how we treat each other."*
>
> —Terry McMillan

TITLE: What is your working title? For women's fiction, (a.k.a. book club fiction), common titling conventions include:

- **SHORT ACTION WORDS:** *What Alice Forgot* by Liane Moriarty; *Reconstructing Amelia* by Kimberly McCreight; *Never Change* by Elizabeth Berg; *How Stella Got Her Groove Back* by Terry McMillan

- **SHORT CHARACTER DESCRIPTIONS:** *The Paris Wife* by Paula McLain; *Girl with a Pearl Earring* by Tracy Chevalier; *The Good Husband* by Gail Godwin
- **GROUPS OF WOMEN:** *The Jane Austen Book Club* by Karen Joy Fowler; *The Knitting Circle* by Ann Hood; *How to Make an American Quilt* by Whitney Otto; *The Joy Luck Club* by Amy Tan; *Divine Secrets of the Ya-Ya Sisterhood* by Rebecca Wells
- **SISTERS/MOTHERS/DAUGHTERS/GRANDDAUGHTERS:** *The Weird Sisters* by Eleanor Brown; *Shanghai Girls* by Lisa See; *How the Garcia Girls Lost Their Accents* by Julia Alvarez; *Secret Daughter* by Shilpi Somaya Gowda
- **TIME:** *Three Junes* by Julia Glass; *Summerland* by Elin Hilderbrand; *The Edge of Winter* by Luanne Rice; *A Wedding in December* by Anita Shreve
- **SETTING:** *Firefly Lane* by Kristin Hannah; *Fried Green Tomatoes at the Whistle Stop Café* by Fannie Flagg; *Beautiful Ruins* by Jess Walter
- **THEME:** *Practical Magic* by Alice Hoffman; *The House of Spirits* by Isabel Allende; *Like Water for Chocolate* by Laura Esquivel
- **SAYING, QUOTE, OR CLICHÉ TWIST:** *My Sister's Keeper* by Jodi Picoult; *In Her Shoes* by Jennifer Weiner; *Just Breathe* by Susan Wiggs; *Wallflower in Bloom* by Claire Cook
- **CHARACTER NAME:** *The Book of Ruth* by Jane Hamilton; *Little Bee* by Chris Cleave; *Sarah's Key* by Tatiana de Rosnay

> "If you read a book that's fiction and you get caught in the characters and the plot, and swept away, really, by the fiction of it—by the nonreality—you sometimes wind up changing your reality as well. Often, when the last page is turned, it will haunt you."
>
> —Jodi Picoult

USP: What matters most in these stories is that you give us a protagonist—usually a heroine—that readers can fall in love with. An organizing principle can also provide a great USP in these types of stories.

PLOT: These stories are for the most part domestic dramas. What separates them from love stories is that the heroine's relationships with her friends and family are as important to the storyline as her love relationship. Make sure that you build out your heroine's world; show us her friends, kids, siblings, parents, colleagues, and so on—and the effect each person has on her. Your main plot will be the most significant of these relationships—and then you can use those of lesser significance as your subplots.

SUBPLOTS: Subplots can focus on the protagonist's relationships—with each other, with men and children, with the world, and with *herself*. When it comes to your subplots, all of these secondary players—the people she has relationships with—are ripe for the picking.

THEME: Women's fiction possesses such themes as love, family, friendship, sisterhood, motherhood, self-actualization, and what it means to be a woman in the world, past, present, and future.

VARIATIONS ON THEME: Look no further than the themes listed above—and their positive and negative aspects.

PROTAGONIST: Again, it's most important that your readers, primarily female, fall in love with your heroine. She needs to be someone that women can relate to—and admire.

ANTAGONIST: The antagonists in this genre range from critical mothers and straying spouses to squabbling siblings and jealous co-workers. Your heroine may also find herself at the mercy of the society in which she lives—or her own doubts, insecurities, and past mistakes.

SETTING: Virtually any setting can work in women's fiction, but certainly there are settings that lend themselves to the genre and serve as criteria for the subgenres in this category: the South, New England towns, beach communities, islands, the suburbs, and major cities of the world, from New York to London. And Paris. Paris almost always works. *Note:* Be careful not to rely solely on kitchens, houses, bedrooms, apartments, restaurants, schools offices, and the like for setting your scenes. Try to surprise your reader; mix it up and take them—and your characters—somewhere new.

PACING: As these are often domestic dramas, you need to build in your story questions throughout your scenes. Be sure to keep your story moving on the page with action and dialogue; don't weigh down your story with too much backstory or the inner life of your characters. While word counts in this genre can vary, aim for between 75,000 and 120,000 words.

SERIES CONSIDERATIONS: Many authors writing successful women's fiction do not write series so much as they write stand-alone novels featuring the same kind of story. That is, stories revolving around women; women's roles as mothers, daughters, grandmothers, granddaughters, caregivers, friends, community leaders, and so on; and a woman's place at home, at work, and in society at large.

THE CHILDREN AND YOUNG ADULT CATEGORIES

"When you're writing a book, with people in it as opposed to animals, it is no good having people who are ordinary, because they are not going to interest your readers at all. Every writer in the world has to use the characters that have something interesting about them, and this is even more true in children's books."

—Roald Dahl

"I think kids want the same thing from a book that adults want—a fast-paced story, characters worth caring about, humor, surprises, and mystery. A good book always keeps you asking questions and makes you keep turning pages so you can find out the answers."

—Rick Riordan

TITLE: What is your working title? Children's and young adult stories are written in many of the same genres as adult stories, notably science fiction, fantasy, and mystery, so many of the same titling conventions will apply. That said, children and teenagers have virtually *no* tolerance for anything boring, which makes creating titles—and the stories that follow them—more challenging. Let's take a look at some sample successful titles in this genre.

- **SHORT ACTION WORDS:** *Chomp* by Carl Hiaasen; *Finding Hannah* by John R. Kess; *Goodnight Moon* by Margaret Wise Brown; *Crash Into You* by Katie McGarry; *Love You Forever* by Robert Munsch; *Escape from Mr. Lemoncello's Library* by Chris Grabenstein
- **OBJECT/TALISMAN:** *The Phantom Tollbooth* by Norton Juster; *Doll Bones* by Holly Black; *The Blue Sword* by Robin McKinley
- **SHORT CHARACTER DESCRIPTIONS:** *The Maze Runner* by James Dashner; *The Book Thief* by Markus Zusak; *The Boy in the Striped Pajamas* by John Boyne
- **SCHOOL:** *Vampire Academy* by Richelle Mead; James Patterson's Middle School series; *The School for Good and Evil* by Soman Chainani
- **SETTING:** *The House of Hades* by Rick Riordan; *Little House on the Prairie* by Laura Ingalls Wilder; *The Secret Garden* by Frances Hodgson Burnett; *Miss Peregrine's Home for Peculiar Children* by Ransom Riggs
- **THEME:** *Durable Goods* by Elizabeth Berg; *Holes* by Louis Sachar; *Divergent* by Veronica Roth; *The Outsiders* by S.E. Hinton
- **SAYING, QUOTE, OR CLICHÉ TWIST:** *The Perks of Being a Wallflower* by Stephen Chbosky; *Crooked Letter, Crooked Letter* by Tom Franklin; *Wild Cards* by Simone Elkeles
- **CHARACTER NAME:** *Ellen Foster* by Kaye Gibbons; *Eleanor & Park* by Rainbow Rowell; *Mr. Wuffles* by David Wiesner; *Big Nate* by Lincoln Peirce; *Flora & Ulysses* by Kate DiCamillo

> "I don't really think about what's 'age appropriate' for my audience because I think they can handle quite a bit, but I do try to think about what's honest and true to my characters … ."
> —Veronica Roth

USP: Writing for kids and teens is arguably harder than writing for adults because they don't care about anything but story. They don't care about literary criticism or awards or what they should or shouldn't be reading; they only care about the words on the page. Bore them and you lose them. More than any other generation, kids today live in a 140-character world. So having a strong USP is critical in this competitive category. You need to do your homework by reading lots of books in this category. Know your competition, and come up with something unique that rocks your readers' world.

PLOT: Kids won't stand for stories in which nothing happens. Period. So plot your story accordingly. The good news is that young people have fabulous imaginations, so stories that might be too "out there" for adults often find a home with younger readers.

SUBPLOTS: Children live in a world governed by their elders, populated by their peers, and transcended by the imaginings of their rich inner lives. Draw your subplots from these elements.

THEME: Young people are drawn to the themes that rule their lives: power (or lack thereof), institutions, family, friendship, coming of age, and more.

VARIATIONS ON THEME: Children also have a dark side, so don't neglect the negative aspects of the aforementioned themes. That said, children are naturally funny and have a fine sense of irony; you can win them over with both.

PROTAGONIST: If your readers can't identify with your protagonist, it's game over. Make sure your young hero or heroine walks, talks, thinks, and dreams like a real kid. This is tougher than you think, but if you can pull it off, you can earn a devoted readership.

ANTAGONIST: Kids live in a world in which they are small and at the mercy of bigger, more powerful people. (I once heard a therapist attribute the appeal of the Incredible Hulk to a child's perception that all adults look like incredible hulks when they are angry, and it's a relief to know that adults are really good at heart, the way the Incredible Hulk is.) So they will appreciate and fear well-drawn villains who seemingly have all the power—and applaud the protagonists who outwit them.

SETTING: Children have an affinity for settings: natural, supernatural, and otherwise. They can readily imagine the secret unseen worlds that surround us, so you neglect setting at your peril.

PACING: As we've seen, pacing is paramount in this genre. Kids simply will not read a snail-paced story—at least not for long. Each subgenre— picture books, middle-grade, young adult, new adult—has different word-count requirements, depending on the kind of story and the publisher, so do check comparable titles as well as submission guidelines to make sure you are within the proper range.

AGE APPROPRIATE: Books for kids are classified according to age level—picture books, middle-grade, young adult, and new adult. Each has different requirements in terms of length, age of characters, and reading level. Be sure you know yours—and follow them.

SERIES CONSIDERATIONS: The wonderful—and profitable—thing about writing for kids is that if you can create a story with characters and action they love, they will keep on coming back for more, which is why series are so popular in this category. (And if you're lucky, your books will backlist forever, generation after generation.) The trick is to come up with (1) an idea big enough to sustain a series; and/or (2) a character unique enough that readers will want to follow him or her through a series of adventures, even if that adventure is "only" adolescence.

THE MEMOIR GENRE

> "A memoir forces me to stop and remember carefully. It is an exercise in truth. In a memoir, I look at myself, my life, and the people I love the most in the mirror of the blank screen. In a memoir, feelings are more important than facts, and to write honestly, I have to confront my demons."
>
> —Isabel Allende

TITLE: What is your working title? For memoir, common titling conventions include:

- **SHORT ACTION WORDS**: *One Bullet Away* by Nathaniel C. Fick; *Call the Midwife* by Jennifer Worth; *Brain on Fire* by Susannah Cahalan

- **SHORT CHARACTER DESCRIPTIONS:** *Little Failure* by Gary Shteyngart; *Black Boy* by Richard Wright; *Bossypants* by Tina Fey; *Lone Survivor* by Marcus Luttrell and Patrick Robinson
- **ORGANIZING PRINCIPLE:** *My Horizontal Life* by Chelsea Handler; *The Diary of a Young Girl* by Anne Frank; *A Year of Living Biblically* by A.J. Jacobs; *Tuesdays with Morrie* by Mitch Albom; *Notes of a Native Son* by James Baldwin; *Journal of a Solitude* by May Sarton; *Eat Pray Love* by Elizabeth Gilbert
- **LINE FROM LITERATURE:** *I Know Why the Caged Bird Sings* by Maya Angelou; *Surprised by Joy* by C.S. Lewis; *Without Feathers* by Woody Allen
- **THEME:** *A Three Dog Life* by Abigail Thomas; *Night* by Elie Wiesel; *Wild* by Cheryl Strayed; *Man's Search for Meaning* by Viktor E. Frankl; *The Things They Carried* by Tim O'Brien; *The Glass Castle* by Jeannette Walls
- **SETTING:** *My Beloved World* by Sonia Sotomayor; *My Life in Middlemarch* by Rebecca Mead; *The Prince of Frogtown* by Rick Bragg
- **SAYING, QUOTE, OR CLICHÉ TWIST:** *My Age of Anxiety* by Scott Stossel; *I Can See Clearly Now* by Dr. Wayne W. Dyer; *Running with Scissors* by Augusten Burroughs; *Plan B* by Anne Lamott; *My Stroke of Insight* by Jill Bolte
- **CHARACTER NAME:** *Paula* by Isabel Allende; *I Am Malala* by Malala Yousafzai and Christina Lamb; *Angela's Ashes* by Frank McCourt; *Marley & Me* by John Grogan; *The Diary of Anais Nin* by Anais Nin

USP: A number of things can give you a strong USP for a memoir. Having lived through a unique experience—be it climbing a mountain or suffering an illness or surviving a Dickensian childhood or fighting a war or even finding God—gives you a strong USP. So does a unique voice, especially if you are funny. Also, as we've already seen, an organizing principle can provide a strong USP.

PLOT: The challenge with a memoir is to shape your true-life material into a dramatic narrative. Failure to dramatize is the most common mistake aspiring memoirists make. Be sure to structure your story dramatically. Here, again, an organizing principle can help you do this.

SUBPLOTS: Identifying the subplots of our lives requires plumbing the depths of our connections to people, places, and things. Look to these elements for your subplots.

THEME: Theme is critical to the memoir. Readers want to know what you have learned from your experience—and what they can learn in turn. Your life lessons are your themes.

VARIATIONS ON THEME: Any life well lived is a veritable feast of theme and variations on theme. If you are paying attention, you will see the negative and positive aspects of your theme and variations on theme all around you.

> "I think many people need, even require, a narrative version of their life. I seem to be one of them. Writing memoir is, in some ways, a work of wholeness."
>
> —Sue Monk Kidd

PROTAGONIST: You are your own protagonist in a memoir, which means you need to be likable, proactive, and above all, forthcoming in regard to your strengths and weaknesses. Like younger siblings, readers hope to avoid your mistakes. That's where honesty comes in, as well as a certain amount of humility. If you aren't as hard on yourself as you are on others in your memoir, your readers will sense it—and dislike you for it.

ANTAGONIST: The villains in a memoir are monsters both visible and invisible. You need to acknowledge your antagonists—be they bad bosses or neglectful parents, abusive spouses or murderous warlords—without whining. Self-pity alienates readers.

SETTING: Be sure to ground your action in setting. Revisit the places in your story if you can, if only in your memory. Show us where the defining moments of your life happened.

PACING: In a memoir, the temptation is to pile on the backstory and the asides, telling us what happened to you rather than showing us.

But to capture and hold your readers' attention, you need to pace your memoir as if it were a novel, writing fully realized scenes that weave a tapestry of memory. Word counts may vary in this category, but do aim for 75,000 to 120,000 words.

SERIES CONSIDERATIONS: The best memoirists are alchemists who transform their own lives into literature. Those who succeed in helping us understand what it means to be human by revealing themselves are often asked to repeat the gesture. Life goes on, and you can keep mining your life for material. Many memoirs settle on a given period of time—childhood, adolescence, college, wartime, an illness—and there is often room to write "sequels" if needed. Think about this if you're writing a memoir—and hope to write more.

WRITER AT WORK

Perform a genre check on your plot from beginning to end, starting with your title. Now, do the same for what you consider your toughest competition in the marketplace. That is, the category killers, the 800-pound gorillas that will be in the room when you try to sell your work.

How does your story stack up against the competition in terms of genre? How can you tweak your story to better its odds in the marketplace?

READING FOR WRITERS

Here are some of the best guides to writing in particular genres.

Science Fiction and Fantasy
- *Writing Fantasy & Science Fiction* by Orson Scott Card
- *Cosmic Critiques* by Martin Greenberg and Isaac Asimov

Love Stories
- *The Joy of Writing Sex* by Elizabeth Benedict
- *Writing a Romance Novel for Dummies* by Leslie Wainger

Historical Fiction
- *Writing Historical Fiction* by Celia Brayfield and Duncan Sprott
- *How to Write Historical Fiction* by Persia Woolley

Mystery and Thriller
- *Writing and Selling the Mystery Novel* by Hallie Ephron
- *The Elements of Mystery Fiction: Writing the Modern Whodunit* by William G. Tapply

Children and Young Adult
- *The Writer's Guide to Crafting Stories for Children* by Nancy Lamb
- *Wild Ink: Success Secrets to Writing and Publishing for the Young Adult Market* by Victoria Hanley

Memoir
- *Thinking about Memoir* by Abigail Thomas
- *Old Friend from Far Away: The Practice of Writing Memoir* by Natalie Goldberg

A MISCELLANY ON REVISION

"I probably spend 90 percent of my time revising what I've written."
—Joyce Carol Oates

"Overwriting is irritating to read because oftentimes it's a way a writer has of showing off, and of making herself too much present in her own material. Most readers want a kind of intimacy only between themselves and what's being written about, whether it's fiction or nonfiction."

—Elizabeth Berg

"There is difficulty involved in going from the basic sentence that's headed in the right direction to making a fine sentence. But it's a joyous task."

—Annie Proulx

"The road to hell is paved with adverbs."

—Stephen King

"For any writer, the ability to look at a sentence and see what's superfluous, what can be altered, revised, expanded, and, especially, cut, is essential. It's satisfying to see that sentence shrink, snap into place, and ultimately emerge in a more polished form: clear, economical, sharp."

—Francine Prose

"I want the reader to hear with his eyes."

—Gregory Mcdonald

"I like to edit my sentences as I write them. I rearrange a sentence many times before moving on to the next one. For me, that editing process feels like a form of play, like a puzzle that needs solving, and it's one of the most satisfying parts of writing."

—Karen Thompson Walker

"If it sounds like writing, I rewrite it. Or, if proper usage gets in the way, it may have to go. I can't allow what we learned in English composition to disrupt the sound and rhythm of the narrative."

—Elmore Leonard

"In writing, you must kill all your darlings."

—William Faulkner

"I always rewrite the very beginning of a novel. I rewrite the beginning as I write the ending, so I may spend part of the morning writing the ending—the last hundred pages approximately—and then part of the morning revising the beginning. So the style of the novel has a consistency."

—Joyce Carol Oates

YOUR PREFLIGHT CHECKLIST

Once you've figured out your plot and written your story, the impulse to send it out immediately can be overwhelming. Don't.

Print it out and put it in a drawer for at least two weeks, preferably a month. Then take it out and read it with fresh eyes. Fix any structural flaws (you know what they are by now). Then go through the text itself as scrupulously as possible. Use the following preflight checklist to put the finishing touches on your manuscript.

EVOKE THE FIVE SENSES

Good writing is sensual writing: It evokes all the senses. Can readers see, hear, touch, smell, and taste the world in which your story takes place? While you go through your manuscript, make sure that you are arming your prose with all of the senses. Channel your inner D.H. Lawrence, Alice Hoffman, or Anne Rice.

WHAT? OVERWRITING? MOI?

Murder your darlings, as William Faulkner once said. Whenever you find yourself congratulating yourself on your effusive or intricate prose, get rid of it. Nobody likes a show-off, least of all readers. How can you identify your darlings? To paraphrase the great Elmore Leonard: *If it sounds like writing, rewrite it.*

SPEAKING OF INTERIOR MONOLOGUE

Achieving that perfect balance of outer life (action) and inner life (interior monologue) in your story can be tricky. If you pride yourself on your voice, this advice is meant for you. (Vanity, thy name is first person.) Here's a trick that may help: Read the inner monologue in your story aloud and listen to yourself. That's the fastest way to tell if it goes on too long.

CHECK YOUR DIALOGUE TAGS

Don't use dialogue tags like *queried, proclaimed, pondered,* and so on—it drives editors crazy. Stick to *said.* Or use action instead.

BAD: "Stop!" he proclaimed.

BETTER: "Stop!" he said.

BEST: "Stop!" He pointed his gun straight at me.

WATCH FOR INADVERTENT POV CHANGES

Editors are very sensitive to POV slips; many consider it the mark of an amateur. So be careful to maintain your point of view; don't head-hop from character to character.

This is head-hopping.

> Julie stared at John, whom she'd hated ever since he dumped her last year for her little sister Jeannie. She was thrilled to see his hairline receding. **[Julie's head]**
>
> "Don't look at me that way," said John. He couldn't believe he'd ever found her attractive. He was so much better off with Jeannie. She was without a doubt the prettier and more pleasant sister. **[John's head]**
>
> "Play nice, you two." Jeannie slipped between her two favorite people and pulled them into a group hug. How she loved them both—and how she wished they'd try harder to get along, if only to make her happy. **[Jeannie's head]**

While you're reading for POV, identify any places where you might slip into the omniscient POV, which many editors hate.

This is the author playing God, otherwise known as omniscient POV.

> There was a darkness on the horizon that Lauren failed to see. Her neighbors couldn't see it either; they walked around as if in a dream, working and playing and eating and sleeping without even noticing the evil that was about to slide in under their doors and slip into their beds and strangle the life right out of them. But Lauren could survive it, if only she would look to the sky.

A quick primer regarding third-person POV:

- Stick to third-person limited POV.
- Use only one POV per scene.
- Use only six POVs per book.

When you're using first-person POV:

- Make sure you don't slip into telling rather than showing—always a temptation when writing in first-person POV.
- Don't use multiple first-person POVs. (I know, Gillian Flynn does it in *Gone Girl*, but for debut authors it's a risky choice.)
- Don't mix first-person POV with third-person POV. (I know, you see other writers do this all the time, but it's really a cheat—and tough to pull off. Again, it's a risky choice, especially for a debut author.)

LANGUAGE CLEANUP, PARTS I AND II

PART I: Lose all the clichés, weak verbs, and adverbs.

Clichés are those tired turns of phrase we hear all the time: "blue as the sky," "brave as a bull," "bored to tears."

Weak verbs include all forms of *to be*, as well as the overused verbs heard most often in daily speech. Why use *walk* when you can use *stomp, trudge, skip, tiptoe, clomp, dance, trot, hike, saunter, stroll,* or *march*?

Adverbs are those words that describe verbs—and if you're using strong verbs, you don't need adverbs. That is, why say *walk quickly* or *slowly* or *heavily* when you can say *stride* or *amble* or *galumph*? Lose all those *-ly* words, and swap out those weak verbs for stronger ones.

PART II: Go through your manuscript and eliminate all redundancies and repetitions. Run a final reading level test on Microsoft Word.

Note: If you find the revision and editing process painful, tedious, or beyond your ken, then hire a well-reviewed copyeditor and line editor if necessary. There's no shame in it, and you may learn a lot from their edits.

PLOTTING YOUR NEXT MOVE, ER, MANUSCRIPT

Congratulations! We've reached the end of the road on our epic journey to a great plot together. You are now armed with a compelling structure that works and a story that sings. Plotting isn't easy, and for many writers it's the toughest part of the writing process. But now you have the tools and techniques you need to create story after story that keeps readers turning the pages.

Most important, well-plotted stories are the ones most likely to engage agents, editors, publishers, and ultimately, your readers. With a little practice, you'll find that plotting is as fun as it is functional. It gives you the blueprint you need to relax and enjoy the writing, allowing you to focus on making your stories the best they can be, from page 1 to the end.

With this blueprint in hand, you can write the stories you were born to write, one plot at a time. Happy plotting!

> "A beginning is that which does not itself follow anything by causal necessity, but after which something naturally is or comes to be. An end, on the contrary, is that which itself naturally follows some other thing, either by necessity, or as a rule, but has nothing following it. A middle is that which follows something as some other thing follows it. A well-constructed plot, therefore, must neither begin nor end at haphazard, but conform to these principles."
>
> —Aristotle

SELECTED INDEX

Plot Perfect

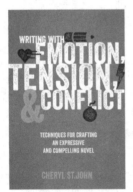